More Raves for

The Breakthrough Company by Keith McFarland

"Disdainful of too-easily-accepted 'common wisdom,' zealous at getting to the real facts of what makes some companies stall out and others thrive, Keith McFarland's *The Breakthrough Company* **offers a gold mine of insight to anyone who's ever dreamed that the business they lead can become a 'player.'** "

—The Honorable Jack Kemp, former cabinet secretary,
vice-presidential candidate, and U.S. congressman

"I loved *The Breakthrough Company*. . . . It's **a cornerstone business book and a must-read for any senior executive.** McFarland, backed by considerable research, describes the characteristics that allow a small- to medium-size company to grow into a breakthrough company—one that's significant, lasting, and influences the market."

—Caroline Little, CEO and publisher,
Washingtonpost.Newsweek Interactive (WPNI)

"In *The Breakthrough Company*, Keith McFarland gives us the clever metaphor of the Business Bermuda Triangle. The book provides insightful observations and advice that will help guide a business leader through pivotal times in a company's growth. McFarland's focus on the realities of managing costs, listening to customers, and responding with agility to external factors makes this book **a compelling how-to on thriving in today's business world.**"

—Shantanu Narayen, CEO, Adobe Systems

"In an increasingly entrepreneurial economy, fast-growing, innovative firms will be absolutely central to future economic success. With **keen insight and extensive analysis,** McFarland helps to fill a gap in our understanding of how and why some companies achieve 'breakthrough' status."

—Carl J. Schramm, president and CEO, Kauffman Foundation,
and author of *The Entrepreneurial Imperative*

"**Greatly needed!** Features marvelous analysis of the principles that enable entrepreneurial enterprises to survive and thrive. It will inspire those in charge to become true leaders by rejecting 'small' goals rooted in ego and embracing visionary values that impart moral authority up and down the organizational ladder. **I urge you to read this book: It's impressively researched, beautifully illustrated, and clearly written.**"

—Stephen R. Covey, author of the #1 *New York Times* bestseller
The 7 Habits of Highly Effective People

"*The Breakthrough Company* is a book that refreshingly and persuasively backs up—with a wealth of hard evidence—its contrarian claims regarding how to elevate a growing business to undreamt-of levels. . . . **Think *Good to Great* for those still small enough to think big.**"

—Bob Eckert, chairman and CEO, Mattel, Inc.

"**A seriously great book.** . . . Drawing from an unusually detailed and careful study of both excellent and average performers, McFarland offers a set of powerful insights into building a breakthrough organization. Managers and employees alike will find his conclusions at once provocative and useful, since they focus on the ways that ordinary people combine to do extraordinary things."

—William Barnett, Thomas M. Siebel Professor in Business,
Leadership, Strategy & Organizations, Stanford University
Graduate Business School

"*The Breakthrough Company* rocks! Start this book and you'll find yourself looking forward to evenings, weekends, and plane flights so you can read more! More than even the iconic books in this category, this look at the key issues for growing companies **provides a deep dive in terms of substance and real-world examples.** The margins of my own copy are quite literally covered with notes on ideas inspired by what McFarland has to say."

—Brad Duea, president, Napster

"**This book is unique. Every paragraph has tucked within it one jewel of insight—and sometimes more.** Fair warning to anyone who immerses himself in this analysis: You'll find yourself underlining every page!"

—Bob Galvin, former CEO, Motorola

"*The Breakthrough Company* is in-your-gut persuasive. The best books, like this one, change your mind about something important—and with each rereading prove freshly inspirational. McFarland's insightful drill-down doesn't just answer the questions that keep growth-company leaders up at night, it's **an invaluable compass pointing the way to best-in-class performance.**"

—Bob Geiman, partner, Polaris Venture Partners

"**Combining exhaustive research and compelling examples, this book passes the 'Monday Morning Test'**—you'll finish it with a list of things you'll do differently on Monday morning."

—Scott Olivet, CEO, Oakley Inc.

THE BREAKTHROUGH COMPANY

THE BREAKTHROUGH COMPANY

HOW EVERYDAY COMPANIES BECOME

EXTRAORDINARY PERFORMERS

Keith R. McFarland

CROWN
BUSINESS
NEW YORK

Library of Congress Cataloging-in-Publication Data

McFarland, Keith R.
The Breakthrough company : how everyday companies become
extraordinary performers / Keith R. McFarland.—1st ed.
p.   cm.
Includes bibliographical references and index.
1. Organizational effectiveness.   2. Industrial management.
3. Organizational change.   4. Leadership.   I. Title.
HD58.9.M426 2007
658.4'01—dc22   2007024066
ISBN 978-0-307-35218-7

Printed in U.S.A.

Illustrations by Brendan Nicholson

Design by Leonard Henderson

7 9 10 8

First Edition

To my parents,

who taught me to seek the things most worthwhile,

And to Kelli, Will, and Cole,

who remind me every day what those things are

CONTENTS

ACKNOWLEDGMENTS

THE TALMUD SAYS that learning is achieved only in company, so it only makes sense to first mention the people whose company made this intellectual journey possible.

It was Peter Drucker who first launched my search for answers on how companies break through the entrepreneurial stage of development, and it is to him that I owe the greatest debt of gratitude. Nearly a decade later, at a chance dinner meeting, Jim Collins provided the encouragement and the template of a research model that helped me to turn my quest for answers into a book.

I could not have asked for a better collaborator on this project than Darren Dahl, who helped me make the results of our five-year study come alive on the page. He was by my side on every visit I made to the nine breakthrough companies. His skill as a reporter and writer was indispensable in telling the stories of these remarkable firms.

Thanks to Michael Fife of Dun & Bradstreet for his tireless support of this project for more than a year. His tenacity and creativity enabled us to accumulate an enormous amount of information about the more than 7,000 growth companies that made up our population. Thanks also to Noyan Garemani for his help in analyzing the public companies in our study.

I am deeply indebted to my colleagues at McFarland Strategy Partners, whose indulgence allowed me to spend so much time working on this book, and who actively participated in its creation. I owe a special debt of gratitude to Brett Pinegar, who helped create the research analysis model and who managed all facets of our empirical study, while at the same time continuing to provide exceedingly important and imaginative advice to our clients. Brett's work with clients demonstrates every day how the ideas contained in this book can be used to help companies map their own trajectory to breakthrough. Another key contributor was Luther Nussbaum, our executive-in-residence, who upon retiring as CEO of First Consulting Group, the nation's premier healthcare consulting group, threw himself into the task of supporting the book project with all his energy. He served as the intellectual *consigliere* of the project these past two years.

My literary agent Esmond Harmsworth, of Zachary, Schuster, Harmsworth, is truly one in a million (I know this because when I tell my author friends what he has done to make this book a success, their jaws drop and they reach for a pen to write down his number). Rick Horgan at Crown saw the potential of this project early on and pushed our team to produce a book that was not only interesting, but that would really help people transform their companies.

The research team we assembled was wonderfully committed and resourceful, and without each of them, this book would not have been possible. I owe a special thanks to Mark Campbell, who took the job of project research leader five years ago and whose belief in what we were trying to accomplish never flagged. Thanks also to Rachel Strate, Brian Waterhouse, and Dan Creer, whose tireless energy and great questions pushed us to create and implement a rigorous research model.

A group of CEOs we came to call the Breakfast Club met with me often to help make sense of the early results and to refine my thinking on the themes that grew into chapters. Thanks to David Garrison, David Haynes, Rob White, and Brett Pinegar for their terrific input during those early-morning sessions. A number of other CEOs also read early drafts of the book and provided invaluable feedback and support. Especially important were Rob Cohen, Jose Collazo, Kevin K. Cushing, Terry Hansen, Matt Harris, Bob Hogan, Mark Holland, Eric Jacobsen, Blake Kirby, Chuck Maggelet, Bob Marquardt, Greg Martin, Kent McClelland, Davis Mullholand, Taz Murray, Oyvind Ragnhildstveit, Greg Suess, Doug Turnquist, Mark Webber, and Jim Wilburn. My discussions with Taylor Randall, Greg Warnock, and Jeff Jani were also invaluable, as was the help I got crafting the book proposal from best-selling author David Magee.

To recognize everyone from the breakthrough companies and comparison companies who assisted us in our data collection, structured interviews, and historical market analysis would require a listing of several hundred people. We want each of these people to know how much we appreciated their time and instrumental help, and regret we cannot mention each by name here. A few who were particularly important were Beverly Brown, Allison Green, Linda Haneborg, Betty Johnson, Marlys Knutsen, Charlene Little, Laura Saxby Lynch, Molly Nelder, and Sherry Terzian.

We also owe a special debt of gratitude to the nearly 1,500 managers we met with during our fieldwork with fifty-two companies over a period of six years. Our experience working side by side with you made the results of our analytical work come alive.

Jim Wilburn has been a friend and mentor for twenty-five years, and it was he, more than anyone else, who set me on the path of writing. Joel Kotkin, Ichak Adizes, Paul Albrecht, Ruth Atteberry, Dick Ellsworth, Bob Fraley, Don Griesinger, Larry Hall, Dick Kaehler, Alan and Peggy Ludington, Chuck Morrisey, John Nicks, Doug Plank, Gabriella Soroldoni, and James Thomas all encouraged me to see myself as a writer, and their encouragement has finally borne fruit—though probably not in the same decade that any of them might have anticipated. Tom Turney, Steve Carpenter, Don Clark, Jose Collazo, Steve Hauck, and Steve Olson were all instrumental people in my early years as a technology CEO, and their influence in these pages will be obvious to them.

Finally, a special thanks to Jennifer McMichael, whose fingerprints are all over this book—from assisting in the data analysis, manuscript review and revision, and supporting me in the myriad of other ways she supports me each day.

If you want to build a ship, don't drum up the men
to gather wood, divide the work and give orders.
Instead, teach them to yearn for the vast and endless sea.

ANTOINE DE SAINT-EXUPÉRY

1

INTRODUCTION

The beginning of knowledge is the discovery of something
we do not understand.
FRANK HERBERT

BUMPED INTO *Überguru* Peter Drucker one afternoon in 1994, on
a tree-lined sidewalk at Claremont University. Over a Diet Coke,
we had a short conversation that would change the course of
my life, and would result—almost fifteen years later—in the writing of
this book.

I was in my mid-thirties at the time, and had just been named
chairman of Collectech Systems—a two-time *Inc.* 500 technology
company based in Los Angeles. I believed Collectech had the potential
for exponential growth—perhaps even to revolutionize the industry—
but I also sensed that we were at a crucial transition point that would
require wrenching changes if we were going to reach our full potential. Making those changes, I feared, might also run the company
aground. At the time I ran into Drucker that fateful afternoon, I was
making the three-hour, round-trip drive to Claremont University's
Drucker Center three times a week to take PhD classes from Drucker
and his colleagues, hoping they could help me make sense of the
difficult issues we faced as a company. My frustration, however, was

growing and I decided to ask the master for some help. "Why can't I find the book that helps people like me solve the real problems of moving beyond the entrepreneurial stage of development?" I asked Drucker. After a moment of thought, he looked up and flashed his famous toothy, Zen master grin. "Because," he grunted in his thick Austrian accent, "you haven't written it yet."

Shortly after our conversation, the wheels came off of our business, and I didn't have time to think about books, neither reading nor writing them. I dropped out of the doctoral program with only my dissertation left to complete and spent the next several years fighting for our firm's survival. Collectech emerged from the crisis stronger than ever, with a new business model that propelled the company from revenues of $10 million to $100 million in just over three years. As the company transitioned out of that difficult time, my mind returned again to that conversation with Drucker. Where, I wondered, was the book that could help a leader steer a firm through the difficult terrain my firm had just navigated, the terrain that lies just beyond the entrepreneurial stage of development? Drucker's words echoed in my mind: ". . . you haven't written it yet."

Then, in 2002, I agreed to be a keynote speaker at a CEO conference in Detroit. At dinner the night before the event, I found myself seated next to the event's other keynote, *Good to Great* author Jim Collins. We discussed his book over dinner and I shared with him my frustration about the lack of books on how to help companies break through the entrepreneurial stage. I pointed out that all the *Good to Great* companies were big companies (in his book the average company has sales of $32 billion),[1] years or even decades away from their entrepreneurial roots. I wondered aloud whether we would learn different things if we studied companies closer to the time of their entrepreneurial breakthrough. "What a great research question," he replied, and then went on to encourage me to do my own study using research methods similar to those he used in *Good to Great*.

SOMEONE NEEDED TO WRITE THIS BOOK

On the plane ride home from Detroit, I decided that if the universe delivers signs, mine could not be any clearer. Two of the world's most respected observers of the business world had told me that I needed to write this book. I reached into the seat pocket and pulled out an air-sickness bag and wrote out a list of three questions that would become the basis for *The Breakthrough Company:*

1. Why do most companies start small and stay that way?
2. What is special about the handful of companies that successfully "break through" the entrepreneurial stage of development?
3. What can a leader do to ensure that his company maximizes its chances for breakthrough?

You might think that there would be hundreds of books on the subject, but a quick review of the bookshelves of any bookstore proves otherwise. Business books tend to fall into two broad categories: (1) How-to books for the small business owner on subjects like basic management, sales, et cetera; and (2) books on leadership and management that focus primarily on the very largest businesses.

> Only about a tenth of 1 percent (0.10%) of U.S. firms ever achieve revenues of more than $250 million in sales. A tiny 0.036 percent will grow to reach $1 billion in sales.

In fact, 99 percent of the business advice churned out by the publishing and consulting industries is written for people working at giant firms. Think I am exaggerating? Consider this: In America, only about 0.10 percent of businesses ever achieve annual sales of $250 million[2]—a tiny size relative to the companies in *Good to Great*. And yet the majority of business books written clearly focus on that top tenth of a percent. Does it seem like every magazine article or book you pick up mentions the same companies? That is because they do. We went to the Harvard Business Review Web site (*HBR*) and typed in the names of five companies that seem to pop up most often in magazine articles and business books. Here's what we found:

- 502 articles mentioned IBM
- 438 articles mentioned General Electric
- 122 articles mentioned Dell Computer
- 169 articles mentioned Wal-Mart
- 73 articles mentioned Southwest Airlines

The five big companies produced a total of 1,304 search hits from the roughly 2,000 articles that have been published since the *HBR* was founded in 1922. Even after adjusting for the fact that many articles refer to more than one of the "big five" in the same article, nearly 50 percent of all of the articles ever published by the *HBR* mention at least one of the five companies (nearly 25 percent of the articles mention IBM alone). These are all truly great companies, and I am sure they have much to teach us about running a business. Does it stand to reason, however, that just five firms account for 50 percent of the business knowledge created over the past eighty-five years? And what really can the leader of a small or mid-sized firm learn by studying the ways of IBM? Wouldn't it be better if a person studied the success factors of firms more like his or her own?

If you are like most businesspeople, you live a very different life from the ones lived by business celebrities described in the headlines of *BusinessWeek* and *The Wall Street Journal*. You don't relax in company-owned New York apartments, travel about in teak-paneled private jets, or enjoy severance packages that guarantee you riches whether or not you succeed at your job. Instead, chances are you live your life on the ground, shoulder to shoulder with your troops, fighting for beachheads in tough markets. And you are probably also genuinely and deeply interested in what your company makes or creates—whether it be equipping the world's largest telecommunications companies with the latest technology or distributing construction materials. To you, a business is far more than boxes on an organization chart or a collection of assets to be exploited. Your company is probably a place where people band together to do what humans have been doing since they left the caves: working together to build something important—something bigger than themselves.

> A search of the Harvard Business Review Web site revealed that nearly 50 percent of the articles published by the *Harvard Business Review* mention at least one of the following companies: IBM, GE, Dell, Wal-Mart, and Southwest Airlines.

Most of us will never run an IBM or a GE, but millions of us around the world run mid-sized entrepreneurial companies, some of which have the potential to become significant, lasting, and difference-making organizations. But which ones? What are the characteristics that will separate those that break through from those that don't? And what can we do as leaders to help our organizations maximize their potential for breakthrough?

My research team and I, along with a panel of thought leaders, have spent the past five years searching for answers to these questions. We set out to discover what enables little firms to become big. Our search led us to create and analyze what we believe is the most comprehensive database of more than 7,000 of America's fastest growing private and public companies. In addition, we have talked to more than 1,500 key executives, and reviewed and cataloged more than 5,600 articles. And to make sure we understood the issues from the inside out, we conducted intensive ninety-day studies with fifty-two firms ranging in size from $9 million to $3 billion in annual sales.

> We studied more than 7,000 companies, talked to more than 1,500 key executives, and reviewed and cataloged more than 5,600 articles, annual reports, and studies.

My goal was to conduct the most exhaustive research ever undertaken on the subject, and to write the book that I had always wanted to read—the one that fills in some of the details of the territory that lies just beyond the entrepreneurial stage of development. I wanted to identify the secrets of breakthrough.

THIS IS NOT INTENDED TO BE A RECIPE BOOK

We do not suggest that our reflections here on the dynamics of breakthrough are the be-all and end-all on the subject. As Boris Pasternak once said, "What is laid down, ordered, and factual is never enough to embrace the whole truth: Life always spills over the rim of every cup." Our hope is that the ideas contained within this book make some small contribution to the conceptual blueprint of how businesses grow and that what is laid down in these pages spills into other "cups" of inquiry in the future.

As hard as it is to grow a company, wouldn't it be nice if there was a "recipe" for creating a company with sustained high performance? It is tempting to dream that if we could just find the right combination of ingredients—a cup of customer loyalty, two tablespoons of *Blue Ocean Strategy,* a dash of reengineering, and a pinch of Six Sigma—we could unlock the secrets of building the breakthrough company. But believing in that dream would be like believing that one could, after a lifetime of "painting by numbers," suddenly produce a masterpiece. That just doesn't happen. However, if someone with a stroke of talent studies the work of great masters and comes to understand the interplay of light, color, structure, and composition, and then spends hours and hours playing with these aspects on his own canvas, he might create a great painting one day. In cooking, the goal of a person looking for a recipe is to cook an edible meal. The goal of aspiring chefs is to gain such a deep and visceral understanding of tastes and textures that they can create something wholly new and distinct—a breakthrough, so to speak. Breakthrough performance, whether in cooking, painting, and/or growing a business, is hard. In our study we were struck by how the people at all levels of the breakthrough companies seemed to get that. We are honored that they allowed us into their kitchens and studios—they reminded us of chefs in their aprons, drizzling on the olive oil, and painters bent over colorful canvases. We hope we do their stories justice in these pages.

2

THROWING THE DYNO

The important thing is this: to be able at any moment to sacrifice what we are for what we could become.

CHARLES DUBOIS

A SHORT HIKE from my home stands a 1,000-foot face of sheer granite that the locals call the Thumb. I recently found myself balanced well up that precipitous wall on a too-small foothold looking across at a too-distant handhold leading up to the next pitch. As I mentally planned my retreat back down the face, my climbing partner let me know she wasn't having it: "Keith, time to throw the dyno!" she shouted from below.

In climbing parlance, a "dyno" (short for dynamic) is a quick, gymnastic leap to a distant hold. If you miss, you can get pretty banged up. I pressed my face against the warm rock face, drew a deep breath, and closed my eyes—then opened them and lunged upward for the hold. Leaving the safety of my position, I stretched for what I hoped was the safety of another, higher position—just beyond my grasp.

Growing a business can be a lot like rock climbing. Most businesses start out carving small but secure footholds at the lower elevations of some industry—usually by spotting some overlooked niche in the market they can defend. Some are satisfied to stay in the lower elevations and eke out a living. But for many, as time passes their aspirations rise, and their eyes turn upward toward footholds and handholds just out of reach. These are the breakthrough companies, the ones always focused on the next challenge up ahead, the ones ready to "risk what they are for what they can become." Breakthrough companies are distinguished by their willingness to throw the dyno.

What does it take to build a breakthrough company, to move from chasing markets to actually influencing them? Five years ago we launched what we believe is the most exhaustive research effort in history to answer this question. We created a database of 7,000-plus companies—every company that was listed on *Inc.* magazine's annual list of the 500 fastest growing since it first published the list in 1982. Using a broad range of public and private resources, we gathered information on each company's growth rate, profitability, and size, and rank ordered them according to their long-term financial performance (for a detailed description of our research, see Research Note B, The Breakthrough Study).

The tables that follow show the revenue and profit performance of the nine breakthrough companies identified by our study.[1] In the fifteen years following their appearance on *Inc.*'s list of the 500 fastest growing companies, the median revenue of these nine companies grew from $14.4 million to more than $700 million.[2] Cumulative revenues of the nine companies grew from $298 million to $6.6 billion over fifteen years, and at the end of 2006 these nine companies had combined revenues of $7.5 billion. And these companies are distinguished not just by their revenue growth—they are profit machines. They outperformed their competitors on profit by a factor of 3 to 1. A person looking for a blueprint for long-term profitable growth would be hard pressed to find nine better examples.

Six of the nine companies we studied went public during the period 1993–2004. A dollar invested in each of these companies at their initial public offerings (a $6 total investment) would have been worth $250 if each stock were held for thirteen years following its IPO. That same $6 invested in the S&P 500 over that same time period would have yielded just $25—meaning that an investment in six public breakthrough companies at the time of IPO grew ten times faster than

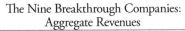

The Nine Breakthrough Companies:
Aggregate Revenues

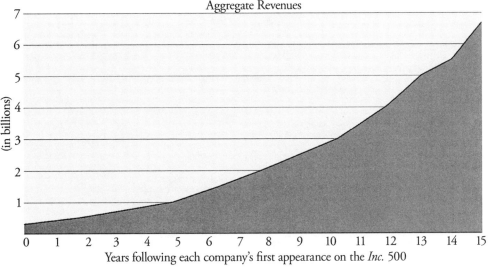

Combined Revenues
(in billions)

Years following each company's first appearance on the *Inc.* 500

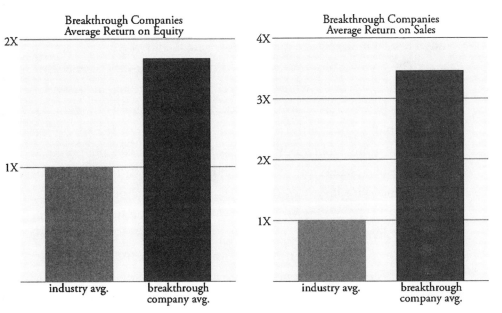

Breakthrough Companies
Average Return on Equity

industry avg.   breakthrough
company avg.

Breakthrough Companies
Average Return on Sales

industry avg.   breakthrough
company avg.

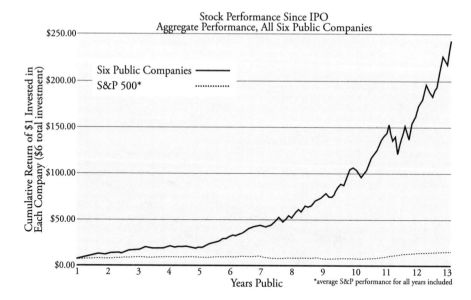

Stock Performance Since IPO
Aggregate Performance, All Six Public Companies

the S&P.[3] If an investor held those same six stocks until December 31, 2006, the value of the initial $6.00 investment would be $482.36, generating a staggering 7,939 percent return.

What impressed us most about these nine breakthrough companies was not their similarities, but their differences. They were founded in places as diverse as the "American Siberia" of northern Minnesota, sunny Florida, innovation-centric Silicon Valley, and glass-skyscrapered Dallas. The breakthrough companies come in a wide variety of shapes and styles: high-tech, low-tech, no-tech, and everything in between. ADTRAN, which manufactures networking equipment in Huntsville, Alabama, employs some of the most sophisticated microprocessor design and manufacturing technology in the world and generates phenomenal financial results. When the world's major banks began tracking financial transactions for links to terrorist activity, they didn't turn to the U.S. government for help; they visited the SAS Institute, the business intelligence and analytical software and services company in Cary, North Carolina. Chico's FAS in Fort Myers, Florida, shook up the fashion industry by becoming the anti–runway-model company by designing

The Breakthrough Companies

Company	First Year on the Inc. 500	Revenues That Year	Current Status	Location
ADTRAN	1992	$42.6 million	Public	Huntsville, AL
Chico's FAS	1989	$6.2 million	Public	Fort Myers, FL
Express Personnel	1988	$50.0 million	Private	Oklahoma City, OK
Fastenal	1982	$3.7 million	Public	Winona, MN
Intuit	1990	$18.7 million	Public	Mountainview, CA
Paychex	1982	$14.4 million	Public	Rochester, NY
Polaris	1986	$90 million	Public	Medina, MN
SAS	1982	$10.1 million	Private	Cary, NC
The Staubach Company	1985	$2.8 million	Private	Addison, TX

flattering apparel for middle-aged women, while Express Personnel in Oklahoma City created a network of staffing franchises with profit levels that would make any fast-food franchisee drool.

Our study makes one thing clear: Building a breakthrough company is less about choosing the right industry and more about acting on the opportunities already available in your existing business. All nine companies evolved from humble beginnings. Chico's didn't start as a fashion house; its founders, Marvin and Helene Gralnick, began by buying folk art items in Mexico and selling them to tourists back in Florida. Then, they started experimenting with sweaters and clothing. Today, more than twenty-four years later, Chico's boasts the *highest profit per square selling foot of any clothing retailer.* At about $780 sales per foot, Chico's easily trumps the figures posted by the Gap ($409), Ann Taylor ($482), and even the Limited ($543).[4]

When Tom Golisano started Paychex, the payroll processing company in Rochester, New York, he spent his mornings drumming up new business selling door-to-door, and then used his afternoons and evenings to input payroll information by hand for his small business clients. Paychex, which was founded in 1971, went on to achieve ten straight years of more than 30 percent profit growth and, at the time of this writing, its stock was trading at ten-times revenue. That's ten-times *revenue,* not profit.[5]

GROWTH MATTERS

"What if I don't want to build a big company?" you might ask. There are thousands of profitable small and medium-sized businesses out there that support comfortable lifestyles for thousands of entrepreneurs and business owners, right? True enough, but the harsh reality is that over the long term, companies either grow or die.[6] Getting your business to grow profitably frees up resources that you can invest in new products or in expanding the value you provide to customers. One thing you can count on: If you are not investing in making life better for your customers, your competitors will be. Growth is also important if you hope to attract and keep the best employees. For employees, growth means opportunity for advancement and new and more exciting challenges. If employees can't get those expanded opportunities at your firm, they are likely to move to another firm where they can.

And growth isn't just important for the company itself, it is important to the nation. One study suggests that just 4 percent of companies generate 60 percent of all new jobs in the U.S. economy.[7] Figuring out how to turn everyday companies into breakthrough performers should be a national priority.

But growth by itself isn't the answer. Our study of twenty-five years of *Inc.* 500 data suggests that just as many *Inc.* 500 firms fail to reach their true potential because they grew *too fast* as because they grew too slow. In rock climbing, "throwing the dyno" is a quick, momentary move; in business it is a state of mind. Breakthrough is less a matter of bold strategic leaps than it is one of willful and diligent ascent from one foothold to the next. The difficult task of leadership is to make sure the organization raises its ability to handle growth as rapidly as it does its revenue line. Only then will it be able to achieve sustained profitable growth.

LETTING THE NUMBERS DECIDE

So where is the best place to discover the characteristics that enable breakthrough? We immediately ruled out just cherry-picking from the same lists of big-name companies most people write about. We wanted to be more scientific, to let hard analysis of performance numbers guide us.

We also ruled out the sort of ivory-tower research that is disconnected from the real issues faced by real business. We spent five years in intensive fieldwork with fifty-two different U.S. firms ranging in size from $6 million to $3 billion. Each field study lasted a minimum of ninety days. We spoke with from twenty to sixty people per company (1,441 in all) to learn their individual perspectives regarding where their firm stood, including the firm's potential for growth, its most promising products or services, its most difficult competitors, its relationships with customers, and its most important internal and external problems. Then for periods ranging from ninety days to three years, we worked with those companies as they created initiatives to boost their performance. The field studies, more than any other aspect of our research, gave us real-world insights into how breakthrough capabilities are actually built. (For a detailed description of our fieldwork, see Research Note A: Exploratory Fieldwork.)

We finished our third year of field studies armed with a list of questions that would drive our broader empirical research. We settled on *Inc.*'s list of the 500 fastest growing U.S. firms as a data source because it is the most widely recognized list of U.S. growth companies available (see Research Note C, *Inc.* 500). We built a database containing performance information on every *Inc.* 500 company listed between 1982 and 2004 (more than 7,000 companies in all). We then combined this information with data from public and proprietary data sources like Hoover's and Dun & Bradstreet to see what had become of these companies in the years since their *Inc.* 500 appearance.

While many of the companies were still in business either as private or public entities, a high percentage had been acquired by larger companies or had gone out of business altogether. Our research team went to work on the survivors, matching up their revenue and profit growth numbers with industry figures to identify nine companies that posted the top performance. To narrow our focus, we set a filter to exclude any companies with annual revenues of less than $250 million and more than $2 billion. We eliminated those with revenues of less than $250 million to make sure that the companies were big enough to have faced the full range of obstacles on the path to breakthrough. We eliminated those above $2 billion because we believed that former *Inc.* companies with revenues in excess of $2 billion (like Microsoft and Oracle) may now be so large that the characteristics of breakthrough may be too hard to locate and isolate in them.

We then added additional information on historical financial performance and conducted intensive research on these remaining companies using sources such as Reuters on-Demand, LexisNexus, and Thompson. We divided our list between public and private companies and rank ordered each list based on cumulative revenue growth rate, profitability, and size as compared with the industry average. We then reviewed annual reports going back as far as twenty-four years and gained access to industry reports from third-party analytical firms such as Gartner and IDC, as well as industry reports from the investment community. We tapped every news and data source we could find for background—more than 5,600 reports, white papers, and articles from the national, local, business, and specialized trade press in all. We also conducted longitudinal analysis of the financial performance of each breakthrough company and compared that performance with the general stock market and industry segment benchmarks. Since all of the breakthrough companies and their comparison companies were private for some portion of the 1982–2004 comparison period, we sought, and in most cases received, access to private historical information that aided us significantly in our research. This information included: company histories, copies of presentations at company events, annual strategic plans and budgets, project summaries, videotaped interviews, and, in many cases, unpublished and detailed product, market, competitive, and financial information.

But only so much research can be done from a computer screen or in a library. In our most important phase, my research team and I bought plane tickets, made car reservations, and set out to do some old-fashioned shoe-leather reporting—logging hundreds of hours of interviews with people at all levels at the nine breakthrough companies.

COMPARISON COMPANIES

We wanted not only to study companies that most successfully navigated the route to breakthrough, we wanted to compare them with similar companies that failed to achieve the same sustained levels of performance.

Our comparison studies were able to shed considerable light on the key factors that enable breakthrough performance. Consider for example Fastenal, an industrial distributor in Winona, Minnesota, and one of its key early competitors, Endries International, located in Brillion, Wisconsin. Not only were both companies founded around the same time (Fastenal in 1967, Endries in 1970), there was only a four-hour drive between them. Despite competition from the likes of established veterans like W.W. Grainger in nearby Lake Forest, Illinois, both companies had early success selling nuts and bolts to area manufacturers, and by 1983, when Fastenal earned its spot on the *Inc.* 500, both companies had revenues of several million dollars a year. But something changed soon afterward. While Endries continued to grow modestly over the next twenty years, even topping $150 million in revenue in 2004, Fastenal hitched a ride on a rocket ship. By 1993, Fastenal earned $100 million in annual revenues and by 2004, it crossed the billion-dollar threshold, outpacing its would-be rival tenfold. In 2006, just two years later, as Fastenal opened its two-thousandth store and cracked the top-10 of trade magazine *Industrial Distribution*'s list of the country's largest distributors, Endries quietly sold its 30 locations to another rival, Ferguson in Newport News, Virginia.[8]

Comparison Companies

Breakthrough Company	Comparison Company	Comparison Company Current Status
ADTRAN	PairGain	Acquired
Chico's FAS	J. Jill Group	Acquired
Express Personnel	Westaff	Public
Fastenal	Endries International	Acquired
Intuit	Meca Software	Acquired
Paychex	InterPay	Acquired
Polaris	Arctic Cat	Public
SAS	SPSS	Public
The Staubach Company	Studley Inc.	Private

Why were Fastenal and the other eight companies able to break through while Endries and the other comparison companies were not? Were they really that different? Was there something more than just luck at play? You bet.

A FEW SQUIRTS FROM THE GRAPEFRUIT

Anyone who has ever made a study of anything knows one thing for certain: The best part is when you come face-to-face with the unexpected. Surprising findings are, as star detective Charlie Chan once said, "like squirt from aggressive grapefruit." Our study produced "grapefruit squirts" at every turn, so many that we concluded that much of what is believed about what it takes to build a breakthrough company is just plain wrong. Here are just a few of the surprises we uncovered:

(1) The most interesting companies may not operate in the markets that Wall Street and the business press consider interesting or "cool."

When we launched our study, we worried that perhaps the best-performing companies would all come from a single sector of the economy like tech, leaving us with findings that wouldn't be applicable to the broader market. But our concerns were unfounded. Many of the breakthrough companies began in market segments experts considered unattractive at the time. We weren't surprised to identify several high-tech firms like Intuit, SAS, and ADTRAN among the breakthrough companies—but we certainly didn't expect to find a nuts-and-bolts distributor, a snowmobile maker, a payroll processor, or even a niche real estate business. At its start, Tom Golisano's strategy to process payroll for companies with an average of seventeen employees seemed downright quaint,[9] as did Roger Staubach's idea for a commercial real estate business that primarily represented tenants. When W. Hall Wendell Jr. led a managed buyout of Polaris in 1981, the snowmobile business was on its back.[10] As the research opened our minds, we learned that breakthrough companies actually fall into three categories: (1) those in hot markets that figure out how to dominate those hot markets; (2) those in dud markets that figure out a way to ignite the excitement in their sector; and (3) those in stalled or dead markets that figure out a way to transition into more attractive markets.

(2) Sticking to the knitting won't always get you there.

Just as the breakthrough companies ignored the so-called experts when it came to the prospects for their industry, they also kept redefining their businesses. While the textbooks—and the consultants—might have suggested that Polaris should remain focused on its core snowmobile business, the company hopped the fence into the far more competitive and profitable ATV market, facing off against some of Japan's most powerful *keiretsu* at a time when most believed Japanese industry would take over the world.[11] ADTRAN recently left the relative safety of its telecom niche to do battle over corporate clients with Cisco, the multibillion-dollar tech company in San Jose, California.[12] When Intuit squared off against Microsoft in the small-business accounting market, after having just bested Bill Gates to gain control of the market for personal financial management software, there were many who questioned Scott Cook's sanity. Cook's decision, however, like the ones made by the other breakthrough company leaders, was critical to creating the kind of performance that put these companies on our distinctive list.

(3) Don't look for extraordinary people; build a place where ordinary people can do extraordinary things.

While they certainly obsessed about each individual hiring decision, breakthrough companies also focused on creating systems that helped their people grow along with the business. "We built this company hiring who we could afford to hire," said Lee Hein, a regional vice president at Fastenal. "What we found was that the average company today doesn't have a clue what people are capable of if you believe in them."[13] Consider also Express Personnel, a company that earns its way by helping people find jobs: more than 350,000 billed hours' worth in 2006 through its 588 franchise locations in the United States and Canada.[14] While the staff at headquarters in Oklahoma City is involved in the awarding of franchises, do you think they are involved in each of the decisions made on the front line at Express? Think again.

(4) It's not about where (or whether) you went to school.

The diversity of the people who established and/or are running the nine breakthrough companies is simply astounding. The group includes: a former college professor and PhD in mathematics (Jim Goodnight at SAS); two Harvard MBAs (Intuit's Scott Cook, who is also a Bain Consulting alum, and Tom Tiller, once one of General Electric's rising stars); a guy who finished his associate degree (Tom Golisano at Paychex); and Scott Edmonds, who hit the bricks right out of high school in Virginia and rose to become CEO of Wall Street darling, Chico's. Not only is Bob Funk, the CEO of Express, an ordained minister and cattle rancher, he's also the elected chairman of the Federal Reserve's Conference of Chairmen, which advises the Board of Governors of the Federal Reserve System.[15] The success of these individual leaders, however, seems less related to their background, training, and expertise than how they see the world, and what they do with those insights. More on this in chapter 5, Building Company Character.

(5) You don't always need other people's money.

We've all heard the professional investor's elevator pitch, "Sure, you can grow your business, but you can grow it faster with our money." We were shocked by the fact that not one of nine breakthrough companies was funded by venture capital in their start-up years. Scott Cook tried to raise venture money for Intuit and was turned down by more than twenty firms (he accepted a small amount of private money just before Intuit went public in 1993, mainly to tap the genius of Silicon Valley legendary VCs John Doerr and Burt McMurtry).[16] Of course, bringing in outside money at the right time can be a good thing. We saw considerable evidence in our fieldwork, in fact, that the right financial partner at the right time can greatly increase a company's prospects for sustained growth (for more on the potential benefits of outside money, see our discussion in chapter 7, Erecting Scaffolding).

(6) How employees feel about working in a place is a significant driver of success.

The first company we visited on our tour of the breakthrough companies was Intuit. As we waited in the lobby before our meeting with cofounder Scott Cook, we noticed an award from *Fortune* magazine, naming Intuit one of *Fortune* magazine's best places to work, hanging prominently on the wall.[17] As we moved around the country visiting the other breakthrough companies, we experienced déjà vu as that same award kept popping up. When we returned home from our travels, we weren't really surprised to learn that the three companies that applied for *Fortune*'s Best Places to Work award made the list a combined twenty years.[18] A key discovery, driven home in our visits to one breakthrough company after another, was that the task of building a great place to work wasn't delegated to the human resources department alone. The top people in the company thought about it every day.

UNRAVELING THE BREAKTHROUGH DILEMMA

One key point we noted from our field studies was how different the average $2 million firm is from the average $250 million firm, and how different it still is from the average $2 billion firm. As a firm grows, it undergoes subtle changes in how it makes decisions and sets priorities; it often even develops a different language for identifying and communicating what is important. This realization highlighted a key challenge involved in achieving long-term growth: the need for a company to learn to operate differently as it grows larger, while at the same time retaining all the best qualities that allowed it to thrive as a smaller business. Breakthrough companies seek to integrate new tools, processes, and ideas to help them better manage the growing complexity of their worlds without, at the same time, losing the firm's unique aspects that inspire people to give their best efforts.

Writers often lump companies into two general categories, "entrepreneurial firms" and "professionally managed firms,"[19] a categorization that both oversimplifies and distorts how firms really work. We spent time in nearly seventy firms, many that clearly fit the classic definition of "entrepreneurial firm," and yet it would be unfair and inaccurate to characterize all of them as "unprofessionally managed" as some experts would. Many of these companies were, in fact, managed in a very professional way—though perhaps not in the way a manager in a large bureaucratic organization would recognize. Conversely, we spent time in several large organizations in which the "professional management" tail had clearly begun to wag the company dog. What these firms needed most, it seemed to us, was a healthy dose of entrepreneurship.

We began to see the story of the breakthrough company not as a journey from an entrepreneurial firm to a professionally managed firm, but from small or mid-sized entrepreneurial firm to *entrepreneurial enterprise*.

The next six chapters of the book describe the path to building an entrepreneurial enterprise. Chapter 9, Graduating from Tough Times

Small to Mid-Size Entrepreneurial Firm		Entrepreneurial Enterprise
Leader is sovereign	*Chapter 3:* Crowning the Company	Organization is sovereign
Strategy as adaptation	*Chapter 4:* Upping the Ante	Focus resources in a few big bets
Character reflects the tribal clan	*Chapter 5:* Building Company Character	Systematic character-building

BREAKTHROUGH

Win because we're small	*Chapter 6:* Navigating the Business Bermuda Triangle	Win through structural advantages
Rely on our own ideas	*Chapter 7:* Erecting Scaffolding	Incorporate the best outside ideas
Build commitment for the vision	*Chapter 8:* Enlisting Insultants	Question fundamental assumptions

U, considers how firms react differently to setbacks and crises and looks at how breakthrough companies turn lessons learned during periods of hardship to their long-term advantage. Chapter 10 gives some of the highlights of what we learned in the more than five years we spent actually working with companies, how firms at all stages of development can build breakthrough capabilities. This was perhaps the most important insight our study produced: There is really no such thing as a breakthrough company, rather there are principles of breakthrough that any firm can adopt to create breakthrough performance. Provided below is a summary of those breakthrough principles, which make up the remaining chapters of this book:

CHAPTER 3: CROWNING THE COMPANY

Is an organization built to meet the needs of its leader or founding family, or does it strive to be something that is bigger than any one of its members? Breakthrough companies, our research found, go to great lengths to create organizations built around the belief that the good of the organization, and not the whims of leadership, should drive the firm.

CHAPTER 4: UPPING THE ANTE

Think entrepreneurial leaders are, by definition, big risk takers? Think again. Often when they get ahead in the game, they tend to begin to play tight, at the very time their firms are positioned to rake in the big pots. Intuit and Polaris would not be the household names they are today if it were not for their willingness to place increasingly bigger bets as the stakes of the game grew bigger.

CHAPTER 5: BUILDING COMPANY CHARACTER

It turns out that how the people in a company treat each other and their customers is vital to breakthrough. But we discovered that most breakthrough companies don't spend a lot of time drafting values statements and fretting about corporate culture. They focus instead on aligning what they say with what they actually do. Anyone can write a values statement. It is quite another thing to imbue an organization with character.

CHAPTER 6: NAVIGATING THE BUSINESS BERMUDA TRIANGLE

When small firms succeed, it's usually because they get good at leveraging the advantages of smallness: giving customers what they want, reacting quickly, and keeping costs low. But it's hard to continue to act small as you get bigger. If companies learn this lesson too late, they risk being lost in the Business Bermuda Triangle.

CHAPTER 7: ERECTING SCAFFOLDING

Scaffolding is a temporary structure built outside a building to enable construction workers to work on increasingly higher levels of a building. In the same way, we found that breakthrough firms build "scaffolding" for their organizations: outside resources and ideas that enable them to take their businesses to the next level.

CHAPTER 8: ENLISTING INSULTANTS

Walter Lippmann once said, "The best servants of the people, like the best valets, must whisper unpleasant truths in the master's ear. It is the court fool, not the foolish courtier, whom the king can least afford to lose."[20] Breakthrough company leaders realize that what is true for a business today might not be true tomorrow—and that it is vital that they build an atmosphere in which people are encouraged to question the fundamental assumptions of the business.

CHAPTER 9: GRADUATING FROM TOUGH TIMES U

Nothing tests an organization like a crisis and, without exception, each of our breakthrough companies faced a pivotal moment that could have radically altered the firm's future. Breakthrough leaders, as compared to most CEOs, see difficult times as opportunities for the organization to develop a crystal-clear focus on its most important initiatives and even to tap into energies in people that tend to go dormant during the good times.

CHAPTER 10: BUILDING BREAKTHROUGH CAPABILITIES

Parallel with our empirical and field studies, we worked with a number of firms to help them develop the capabilities that would help them become successful entrepreneurial enterprises. This chapter describes some of the most important things we have learned about moving companies toward breakthrough performance and beyond.

AFTERWORD: POST-BREAKTHROUGH—AVOIDING BREAKDOWN

Does a company need one set of characteristics to reach break-through and another to continue a trajectory of growth as a big company? In this chapter, we reflect on the future fate of the breakthrough companies.

CASE STUDY IN THROWING THE DYNO
The Olson Company

Through our fieldwork with companies, we had the opportunity to watch first-hand companies successfully throwing the dyno. I had been tracking the Olson Company since Steve Olson founded it in 1988 in a small office he shared with Mark Buckland and an administrative assistant. Today Olson has grown into one of the nation's leading providers of in-town affordable living—winning the titles of Fastest Growing Builder in America and U.S. Homebuilder of the Year.

Steve contacted us in 2002, when his company's revenues were about $200 million. "Our challenge," Olson told us at the time, "is to get people at all levels of the organization involved in building the strategy for the future of the company." We worked with him and a group of twenty key managers for several years to develop and implement a dynamic approach to strategy that gave the company the ability to rapidly adapt on the fly and to tap the knowledge of people working in the regions to effect change.

Since then, revenues at the Olson Company have more than doubled to $500 million and the company has a several-billion-dollar construction backlog. More important, the Olson Company has grown from a mid-sized business to an *entrepreneurial enterprise,* capable of focusing its resources on a few big bets, building tangible structural advantages in its market space, incorporating the best ideas from outside the company while still staying true to its own unique company character.

3

CROWNING THE COMPANY

The bottleneck is always at the top of the bottle.
PETER DRUCKER

SCHOOLCHILDREN AROUND THE world learn that George Washington was the founding president of the United States, but not everyone knows that he nearly became the founding *king*. This turning point at the dawn of America's democracy, one that could have given Washington the honor he so craved as a young man, also helps illustrate the primary reason why so many entrepreneurial companies fail to crack the breakthrough barrier: Their founders fail to "crown the company."

At the end of the American Revolution, the fledgling nation was deeply troubled; bankrupt, exhausted by eight years of war, and torn with internal dissention. Some in the military believed that unless they crowned a king, the nation's chances of achieving unity—and survival— were slim. General George Washington was their natural choice. The nation's other founding fathers were a brilliant bunch—Thomas Jefferson, Alexander Hamilton, John Adams, and James Madison—but as a leader, Washington towered above them all. And as the Revolutionary War came to an end, his status was at its apex. As commander-in-chief, he had single-handedly held the revolution together and led a ragtag militia to triumph over the world's greatest military power. But when

Washington learned of the plan to crown him king, he flatly refused the offer. Rather than accepting the crown for himself, Washington insisted on crowning the country. Americans were building a nation that would be far bigger than any one person, he believed, and in large part because of his decision, the world's greatest democracy took root.[1]

Is your company building something that is far bigger than its leader? Without Washington's crucial decision to crown the country, it is unlikely that America would have come to occupy its current position on the world stage. And similarly, our research suggests that in order to achieve breakthrough, a company's leaders must be willing to "crown the company." In other words, they must put the interests of the firm above their own, harnessing the power of people at all levels in building the firm's future. Too many leaders, after they achieve some level of success, tend to make their organizations all about them. The investment community and business press share the blame; all too often, they are the ones bestowing the royal treatment on these individuals when perhaps, if they dug a bit deeper, they would discover that an organization's success is always the result of the efforts of many people.

If anyone in business today would have the right to make a business all about himself, it would be Roger Staubach, founder of The Staubach Company. After winning the Heisman Trophy as a junior at the Naval Academy in 1963, he delayed his NFL debut to complete a tour in Vietnam. He was considered past his prime in 1969 when, at the age of twenty-seven, he signed on as a tenth-round draft pick of the Dallas Cowboys. It was at the ripe old age of twenty-nine, after sitting on Coach Tom Landry's bench for two years, that Staubach burst into the sports world's consciousness, earning Most Valuable Player honors in the 1971 Super Bowl on his way to becoming one of the most famous and respected quarterbacks in football history.[2]

But if you walk into Staubach's office just outside of Dallas, you'll notice there's something missing: just about anything related to football. And if you ask him why his Heisman Trophy, his two Super Bowl rings, or even a photo commemorating his induction into the NFL's Hall of Fame aren't proudly on display, he'll tell you, "It's because we're building something here that is bigger than Roger Staubach."[3] Like Washington, Staubach sees himself as serving something larger than himself. He has crowned The Staubach Company.

> Visit Roger Staubach in his office and you'll notice that something is missing—practically anything relating to football. Ask him why and he'll tell you, "It's because we are building something here that is bigger than Roger Staubach."

Staubach started working in the Texas commercial real estate business in 1977, a couple of years before he retired from the NFL. While he knew that he could make a career in the industry, he figured he needed to carve out a niche for himself. After seeing how frustrated his commercial tenants were when they dealt with landlords, the idea hit him: He could focus on the tenant representation side of the business.[4] While it was groundbreaking enough for someone in the brokerage business to build a business around the tenants, Staubach left an indelible mark on the industry when he decided to move outside his stronghold in Dallas and make The Staubach Company a national business. To face off against established competitors like New York City–based Studley and Grubb & Ellis, Staubach tapped brokers around the country who would work under the Staubach banner, but would be free to operate their individual offices as entrepreneurial enterprises. "Even with all of Roger's star-power, he knew he wouldn't grow much past $40 million on his own," said Greg O'Brien, who has worked for the company since 1993 and who was named CEO on July 1, 2007. "He knew that in order to grow, he couldn't be the quarterback on every deal. The company needed to become bigger than him to last."[5]

To lure the best and brightest brokers to his team, Staubach granted them an equity stake in the company. At the same time, he developed the Staubach Constitution, a playbook of sorts that fosters a platform of teamwork and a common set of values for the entire company to follow and live by. For example, in an industry that Staubach says operates on a "fee-and-me" principle, Staubach's brokers commonly share information and, perhaps more extraordinarily, celebrate each other's victories. "Roger has attracted the best of the best, given us a common goal and empowered us to become part of something that is bigger than ourselves," Greg O'Brien told us.[6]

Staubach's main competition over the years has been from Julien J. Studley, who ran a tenant representative firm that bore his name up until 2002.[7] Studley, founded in 1954, was one of the forerunners in the tenant rep business in the ever-turbulent New York City real estate market while Staubach was struggling to find a toehold in Dallas. And, by most accounts, the Studley firm was run by the charismatic Julien Studley, a Holocaust survivor, known also for his presence on New York's fund-raising circuit and having a hand in just about every major real estate deal in the city. While the firm eventually expanded to twenty

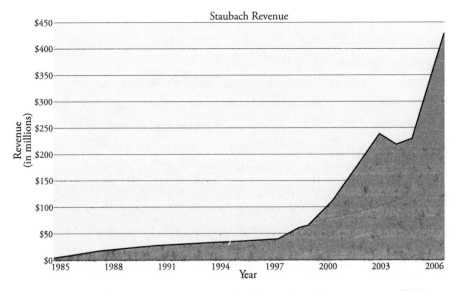

Staubach is a private company that does not publicly share information on company profitability.

offices nationwide, Studley's customer base remained in New York with its founder, who retained 100 percent ownership until 2002, when, at the age of seventy-one, he sold the company to forty-five of his brokers. Over a shorter time frame, The Staubach Company grew from a single office into more than sixty around the country, employing more than fourteen hundred people. Since making the switch to turn his brokers into owners, Staubach has seen his revenues skyrocket from $20 million in 1993 to more than $400 million in 2006, which, based on industry estimates, is about double Studley's revenues.[8]

Staubach, like George Washington, had come to understand that the success of his venture did not rest on his shoulders alone. It was only when he empowered his entire organization to operate independently did The Staubach Company really take off.

This concept of "crowning the company," where leaders serve their company rather than have the company serve them, emerged early during our five years of fieldwork. We found that companies tended to fall into two broad categories: companies that were organized around the leader, and companies that were organized around a vision that was bigger than any one person.[9] At first we thought that the act of crowning the company might relate to a leader's humility; it made sense to us that humble leaders would be less likely to make the company all about them than arrogant ones would. But George Washington wasn't known for his humility. Some historians even believe that the ferocity of his fight against the British was, in part, fueled by his thwarted attempts early in his career to achieve British rank.[10] Crowning the company appears to go much deeper than a leader's personal humility. Like Washington, the leaders we studied seem to understand something fundamental about how the world works: Most people would rather serve an institution in which they feel some ownership than serve a king. No, crowning the company is not just a reflection of some personal attribute of the leader; it is a strategy and a set of principles. Any leader and any organization can move toward greater organizational sovereignty.[11]

Of the fifty-two companies we encountered in our exploratory fieldwork, most were organizations primarily organized around the leaders or family owners. Only a handful were what we term "sovereign organizations"—companies where leaders have successfully crowned the company—as evidenced by the creation of a strong sense of shared responsibility for the success of the firm at all levels of the company. We were surprised that the size of the company did not necessarily correlate with how its leaders acted. We saw firms with billions of dollars in revenue that were clearly organized around a kingly leader, while the leaders at other, smaller firms had successfully crowned the company.

Most striking was the fact that all nine breakthrough companies had crowned the company in a powerful way. As we visited them around the country, we were amazed that the leaders echoed a nearly identical business philosophy—one that honored the organization more than the individuals in it. It also surprised us to learn how early in their histories these companies developed a commitment to crowning the company. When Bob Kierlin hatched the idea for Fastenal, which he envisioned as a place where contractors could go to buy screws, nuts, and bolts in a myriad of shapes and sizes, he was working for IBM as a cost engineer. Though he liked the work at IBM, he disliked the inertia in its decision-making process. "I learned firsthand at IBM that most big companies do a poor job of getting the best out of people," said Kierlin. "The main reason they fail is that they don't really believe in their people. Managers in those days were taught that a manager's job was to plan, organize, staff, direct, and control. And I guess if you don't believe in your people, it's right to expect that you are going to have to do a lot of organizing and directing and controlling."[12] So when Fastenal opened its doors on November 28, 1967, Kierlin and his four cofounders dethroned themselves from the very beginning. "The very first step in creating our organization was for us to realize that this wasn't about us—it was about the people in the stores," Kierlin told us.[13] Using this mantra as a guide, Kierlin and his

	Organizations That Crowned the Leaders	Organizations That Crowned the Company
Strategy	CEO/Founder makes major strategic decisions, often with the input of a handful of close advisors	Strategic issues openly and actively debated throughout the organization; all the major functional areas (product development, finance, operations, sales) contribute meaningfully to strategy formulation
Ethos	Personal loyalty to the leader and his vision	Commitment to doing the very best job possible for the organization, even if that means "bucking the system" or questioning the firm's fundamental assumptions
Management views its job as	Running the business	Creating an environment where people get better at spotting what is important, and at making and implementing decisions
Culture	Often purely a reflection of the personal characteristics of the leader or founder	Though strongly influenced by the leader, tends to more broadly reflect the people who make the organization, as expressed in their stories of shared experiences
New Ideas	Come primarily from senior management	Regularly and systematically come from throughout the firm
Interdepartmental conflict is resolved by	Kicking the issue upstairs	Affected departments sitting down and discussing the issue
People are celebrated for	Heroics (saving the customer, solving the big problem, etc.)	Bricklaying (helping to build robust and sound processes that make organizational heroics less necessary)
Biggest no-no	Act in a way that might be interpreted as disloyalty	Fail to have the best interest of the company at heart

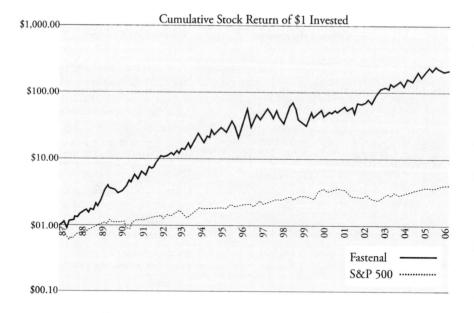

team created a company that encourages entrepreneurial thinking and decision making throughout a growing worldwide network of more than 10,000 employees and more than 2,000 stores. Store managers operate like small-business owners, entrusted to monitor their own bottom lines and are given the authority to instantly expand their inventory to satisfy a customer's need. In return, store managers receive incentive pay that typically represents 50 percent of their income. "The greatest benefit here at Fastenal is that everybody gets to make his own decisions and be a part of the business," Kierlin told us. "They all know they have an equal shot at everything."[14] And it would be hard to argue with the results: Fastenal has tripled its market capitalization over the past ten years while growing revenue by almost five times in the glamorous world of industrial fasteners and supplies.[15] Fastenal's Will Oberton, who took over from Kierlin as CEO, was selected as 2006 CEO of the Year by stock-rating firm Morningstar, beating out Cisco CEO John Chambers and American Express CEO Ken Chenault. Not bad for a small-town Minnesota guy whose company distributes nuts and bolts.[16]

THE ENTREPRENEURIAL MIND: SOMETIMES ITS OWN WORST ENEMY

With success stories like Staubach and Fastenal to point to, why is it that so many companies fail to crown the company? Part of the answer, at least, may lie in how most entrepreneurial leaders are wired. The personality characteristics that the entrepreneur relies on to begin building a company—like snap decision-making and stick-to-it stubbornness—can, if the entrepreneur fails to adapt them, become liabilities as the company grows. Also, entrepreneurs may find it difficult to adapt *because* of their success: a success won with one set of skills and mindset. It's tempting to think that success can be repeated in the future with the same game plan. When things start to slip, the temptation is to do the same old things, only more aggressively and urgently.

To get inside the mind of the entrepreneurial leader, we turned to The Attentional and Interpersonal Style inventory, known as TAIS, which has been used for more than thirty years to select and train high-performance individuals such as Olympic athletes, military commandos, and top business executives.[17] We profiled 250 *Inc.* 500 executives over a two-year period to find out what really makes entrepreneurs tick and how their strengths might actually sometimes work against them. For example, while most early stage entrepreneurs are great at multitasking—playing many different roles throughout the company as needed—at some point, the entrepreneur needs to admit that he or she can't do it all anymore. Breakthrough executives understand this. "I was tired of waking up with my head feeling tight, like I was wearing a hat," Staubach told us. "I decided to find a way to share that responsibility."[18]

CAN ENTREPRENEURIAL LEADERS' STRENGTHS WORK AGAINST THEM?

They can, if the leaders are unaware of what their strengths are and the times at which those strengths might not be called for. Here's what we learned when we administered The Attentional and Interpersonal Style (TAIS) psychological inventory to 250 of America's fastest growing companies.

They're great at figuring stuff out: Entrepreneurs, contrary to popular opinion, think as much as they act. TAIS results show that entrepreneurial leaders rank highly in strategic thinking, which means that they are adept at analyzing complex situations and quickly identifying where and when to act. Their appetite for action and intellectual stimulation, however, may cause them to spread themselves and their companies too thin. Entrepreneurs also may have the tendency to surround themselves with people who are unable to spot the company's leverage points independently, which stalls the company's ability to grow beyond its founder.

They can change directions at the drop of a hat: Entrepreneurs are masters at adapting on the fly. As their companies grow, however, they may find that their penchant for changing directions quickly becomes a problem. As an organization grows larger and more complex, a leader cannot simply shout new marching orders down the hall, expecting everyone to quickly fall into line.

They're great at juggling a lot of balls at once: Leaders of fast-growth companies often display an aptitude for information processing that allows them to act on numerous initiatives simultaneously. When this trait is combined with the ability to generate lots of new ideas, an entrepreneur may find his or her company running down too many projects on the periphery rather than focusing on the primary drivers of their business.

If there is a shot at the buzzer—they want to be the one to take it: According to our TAIS results, entrepreneurs tested extremely high on their ability to perform well under pressure—scoring 45 percent higher than CEOs of larger firms. These high scores are more often linked with military commandos and elite athletes rather than businesspeople. Entrepreneurs also scored highly on their need for control. In other words, when the game is on the line, delegation is the furthest thing from an entrepreneur's mind: He or she not only expects to take the game-winning shot, he or she *needs* to.

They're driven, driven, driven: TAIS measures something called "focus over time," a trait that identifies a person's bulldoglike persistence in pursuing goals through thick and thin. Entrepreneurs, like Olympic-caliber athletes, score highly on this ability. The entrepreneur's drive to beat the odds during the early stages of a company's growth, however, may become an obstacle as their company matures. Entrepreneurs who fail to transition from a "win-at-all-costs" to a "win-where-it-counts" approach risk burning out their critical internal resources.

They're loyal to a fault: While one might expect that entrepreneurs lead through their visionary ideas, the TAIS results show that entrepreneurs actually influence people through deep personal relationships. Entrepreneurs, in other words, are successful because they build positive personal and emotional connections with people and groups, traits more commonly associated with sales people. These connections can become a liability, however, if entrepreneurs lose their ability to make objective decisions about personnel they've become quite friendly with or with whom they've worked for a long time.

Marvin and Helene Gralnick, who founded Chico's Folk Art Specialties back in 1983, were the quintessential entrepreneurial couple, churning up a big wake wherever they went. The couple originally met in Guadalajara in 1972, where a vacationing Helene met the then hippie Marvin, who was making a living embroidering fringed leather vests that he sold back in the United States. They got married, left Mexico in 1976 following the collapse of the Mexican economy, and headed for Sanibel Island in Florida. The couple kept up their Mexican connections, however, making four trips a year to load up on arts, crafts, and clothes, which they in turn sold at a significant markup to vacationing snowbirds. When they decided to officially open a store, they called it Chico's, in honor of a friend's parrot. In those early years, the Gralnicks did everything from deciding what to buy and how to

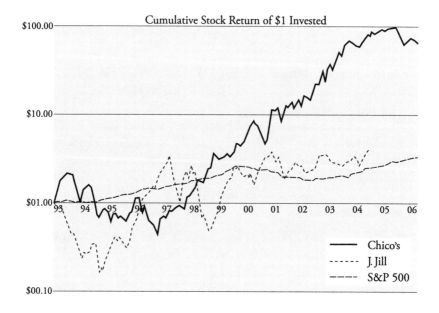

price it, eventually deciding to focus exclusively on selling clothes to baby boomer–age women. Marvin and Helene were the chief product designers; they personally chose the fabrics, patterns, and even the cut of the clothing before outsourcing the manufacturing to a plant in Turkey.[19]

But by 1988 the informal systems and processes the Gralnicks had cobbled together were stretched to the breaking point. When Charlie Kleman showed up at Chico's offices in Fort Myers, Florida, to conduct an audit to see if the company was in the condition management thought it was, he found what he called organized chaos. "On my first day, I remember all these people scurrying around these twelve-foot-high piles of clothes that stretched to the ceiling," Kleman, now Chico's CFO, recalled. "When I asked what those clothes were, I was told that they were returned items, which I quickly realized the company had not accounted for. The Chico's founders didn't have any kind of inventory or computer system and they were *proud* of it. I had to go get a card table and folding chair from my house because they didn't even have anyplace for me to work."[20]

So what's the answer? Does every company reach a point at which it needs to jettison the founding team and bring in the professionals? Some venture capitalists would have you believe so. It is a knee-jerk reaction for some VCs to, in the interest of "professionalizing management," automatically bring in new leadership whenever they make an investment. Folks like these see the world divided neatly into two categories: entrepreneurs and professional managers, and they believe that great entrepreneurs simply cannot grow into great leaders of big companies. Many fear that a company's growth may be stunted due to what they see as a founder's natural tendency to resist giving up control. We call this the "Just Let Go" myth—the idea that *by definition* entrepreneurial leaders are incapable of leading an organization once it gets to a certain size.

> Firms quickly outgrow the capabilities of their founders, right? We found no evidence to support this commonly held belief. Many entrepreneurial leaders, if they understand the ways in which they will need to adapt, can play an important role in their companies for years or decades—and their companies may perform better as a result of it.

Some interesting new research on the roles of company founders suggests that investors who arbitrarily show the founder the door do so at their own peril. Rüdiger Fahlenbrach, of Ohio State University, studied the 2,300 largest U.S. companies and discovered that founders were still running 11 percent of those firms. In analyzing the ten-year performance of these companies from 1992 to 2002, Fahlenbrach found that these founder-run companies outpaced the stock market by 8 percentage points a year.[21]

> The average tenure of the top twenty-five managers at Fastenal is an amazing 22.3 years. The average tenure of the next level down is ten years, and the average age of that group is thirty-four years old.

In eight of our nine breakthrough companies, in fact, members of the founding team or their handpicked successors continue to shape the company's current and future direction. At Fastenal, the average tenure of its top twenty-five managers is an amazing 22.3 years.[22] Will Oberton, who succeeded Bob Kierlin as CEO in 2002, has worked for the company for twenty-seven years. Organizations on the way to crowning the company are also filled with team members like Bob Strauss, who, at thirty years, has a longer tenure than Oberton but was willing to take a supporting position when the board looked elsewhere to fill the head job. Strauss even pointed out to us that he was the one who actually hired Oberton for a sales trainee job back in 1980.[23] Even at Polaris, W. Hall Wendell Jr., who led a management buyout in 1981 and served as CEO and chairman of the board for more than twenty years, has eased into retirement, but he remains a close friend and confidant of Tom Tiller, the company's current CEO.[24] It is clear after talking to the people at these nine companies that it is less a question of the founder letting go than it is of adapting his or her role as the company evolves. That means that the founder doesn't necessarily have to hold the top spot but, in most of our breakthrough companies, they remained deeply involved in some way.

There appear to be clear and significant advantages in having the founders stick around, provided the founder is committed to building a sovereign organization. One advantage is the founder's ability to recognize the subtle changes that develop in the business, the market, and in the customer's needs. All of the breakthrough founders were hands-on executives in the beginning: engineers, clothing designers, and salesmen. It was having a deep knowledge of their craft that helped these founders identify an opportunity and move on it. Another important reason to try to keep founders and long-term employees around is that they can serve as important keepers of the "company character" (see chapter 5: Building Company Character).

The first mistake many outside analysts and investors fall prey to is making the assumption that entrepreneurs lack the ability to adapt.

Company	Year Founded	Founders	Role
ADTRAN	1985	Mark Smith	Chairman of the Board*
Chico's	1983	Marvin and Helene Gralnick	Chairman of the Board†
Express Personnel Services	1983	Robert Funk Bill Stoller	Chairman and CEO Vice Chairman
Fastenal	1967	Bob Kierlin	Chairman of the Board
Intuit	1983	Scott Cook	Director and Chairman of the Executive Committee
Paychex	1971	Tom Golisano	Chairman of the Board
SAS	1976	Jim Goodnight	Chairman and CEO
Staubach	1977	Roger Staubach	Chairman‡

*Smith was serving as chairman of the board when he passed away in March of 2007.
†Gralnick resigned in Dec. 2006
‡In typical "crowning the company style," Staubach turned over the reins of the company to long-time lieutenant Greg O'Brien just as this book was going to press, and will continue to serve the company in his new role as executive chairman.

The truth is that entrepreneurs are actually some of the most adaptable people on the planet—the survival of their company in its earliest days attests to that. The issue is often less whether an entrepreneurial leader is capable of adapting and more whether an entrepreneur is aware of the need to adapt and is willing to get help in figuring out how (see chapter 7: Erecting Scaffolding and chapter 8: Enlisting Insultants).

Clearly some organizations do outgrow their founding management teams and eventually require an infusion of "new blood" with different skills and perspectives. Adapting may not always be a pleasant experience for founders or members of the founding team. Some founders may try to go along with necessary changes to an organization, but will think deep down that the new rules don't apply to them. They may still believe the company "runs on their time," and they may still cling to running the business the way they always have. Marvin and Helene Gralnick of Chico's struggled in this way. They reveled in running their business as an "anticorporation," says Charlie Kleman, and moved so fast they sometimes forgot the basics, like adopting standard processes such as managing their inventory, budgeting, or polling the cash registers in their retail stores.[25] Facing the fact that the company has outgrown you requires courage and humility. Intuit cofounder Scott Cook, for one, fired himself as CEO when he believed the company needed someone with a different perspective and skill set.[26] How many entrepreneurs, however, would have the confidence to follow Cook's example?

STEPS TOWARD GROWING THE COMPANY

The path from entrepreneurial upstart to breakthrough company is not always an easy one. Marvin Gralnick, for example, who resigned from the board of Chico's in December 2006, has hired his replacement as CEO four times. Gralnick's first three successors, who stepped in during Chico's path to breakthrough in the 1990s, failed to keep the company's vision and the design of its clothes in line with its core customers: female baby boomers. In each of these instances, the board intervened and asked Gralnick to step back in to right the ship and salvage the company's morale.[27]

For Chico's, the fourth time was the charm when CEO Scott Edmonds was tapped to replace Gralnick in 2003.[28] Unlike Gralnick's previous two replacements, Edmonds, who joined the company as an operations director in 1993, worked his way up through the organization. From its modest beginning as a tourist trap, Chico's has evolved into one of the fastest-growing retailers in the country, posting more than $1.65 billion in annual revenues on the strength of its growing retail network of more than 925 stores that sell not only Chico's clothing but also its two additional brands: White House | Black Market and Soma by Chico's.[29] And it is Chico's focus on product development— its designers personally sampling fabrics and trying on new designs to check their fit before they ever get off the cutting floor—that sets it apart from competitors like J. Jill. When Chico's got its start, J. Jill was the model it was chasing. "When I first joined Chico's in 1997, we talked a lot about J. Jill and how we wanted a catalog like theirs," Patricia Murphy Kerstein, former chief merchandising officer of Chico's, told us. "But clothes that looked good in the catalog didn't measure up when you tried them on in the store."[30] And while Chico's was indeed chasing J. Jill in 1997—J. Jill's revenues of more than $135 million for the year just about doubled Chico's results—their paths soon diverged. As J. Jill began to expand into things like furniture, lamps, and housewares, Chico's was sorting out management team issues and getting back to making the clothes that, in Murphy Kerstein's words, "delighted our customers." Just eight years later, as Chico's knocked out hit style after hit style, and cracked the billion-dollar revenue mark for the third consecutive year, J. Jill, with revenues stuck at $450 million, was acquired by rival Talbots Inc. for $517 million in May 2006.[31]

We asked Scott Edmonds of Chico's about how a leader needs to change his approach as a company grows, and he reached into a folder and slid a map of sorts across the table to us.[32]

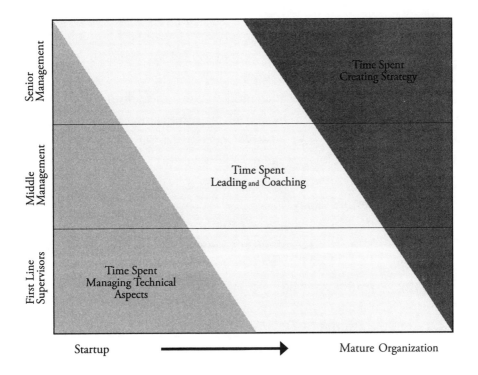

Using his map as a guide, Edmonds explained that in the early years of a company's life there is no middle management, and top executives find themselves jumping between hands-on running of the business, and leading and coaching the front-line people. As the business grows, senior managers spend less of their time actually running the business day to day and more time leading and coaching, as well as coming up with strategies to transform their opportunistic little business into a business with meaningful advantages in the marketplace. Likewise, people in middle management and on the front lines must make similar shifts as the business grows. By the time the business has become a sovereign organization, strategy is discussed and shaped at all three levels of the firm (for more on this, see chapter 10: Building Breakthrough Capabilities), and leading and coaching is seen as a key activity, top to bottom.

Driving down the decision making is a common theme among the breakthrough companies and it was one of Scott Edmonds's first big pushes when he replaced Marvin Gralnick in 2003. Under Gralnick, managers were accustomed to kicking every decision upstairs to the CEO's desk. Edmonds killed the practice on the spot. "I didn't have the time to solve every dispute and when I did get involved, I usually only had half the information," Edmonds told us. As a solution, Edmonds has pushed his department managers to solve their problems head-to-head in real time and to circle back with him only when they have come to a resolution. "I knew we needed to kill the old hub-and-spoke system," Edmonds told us. "Now conflicts are resolved every day that I don't even know about. We no longer tolerate triangulation and it has changed my life."[33]

Blair Bryan, who manages the southeast region for The Staubach Company, told us a story about how Roger Staubach killed the practice of triangulation early on in his company. "One day early on in the company, two brokers were arguing over who should get the lion's share of a commission on a recent deal, and they went to Roger to help them resolve the issue," Bryan said. "Roger listened to each broker make his case. Then he said that he was going to give the entire commission, including the percent due to the company, to charity. Next time, he told the brokers, 'Work it out between yourselves.' " Bryan went on to say, "I tell that story to each of my new hires and I haven't had a broker bring me a commission dispute in the ten years I have been running my region."[34] Bryan's story illustrates what Roger Staubach discovered early on: To build a company bigger than himself, he first had to crown his company to operate without his constant presence.

We discovered in our research that organizations that effectively "crown the company" and reach the sovereign organization stage of development have a number of advantages over their competitors. First, they tend to be better able to recruit and retain great people:

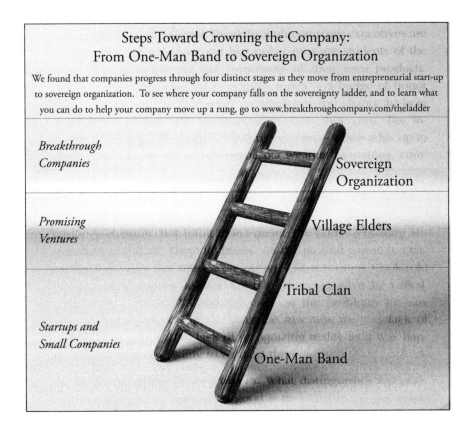

Steps Toward Crowning the Company:
From One-Man Band to Sovereign Organization

We found that companies progress through four distinct stages as they move from entrepreneurial start-up to sovereign organization. To see where your company falls on the sovereignty ladder, and to learn what you can do to help your company move up a rung, go to www.breakthroughcompany.com/theladder

Breakthrough Companies

Sovereign Organization

Promising Ventures

Village Elders

Tribal Clan

Startups and Small Companies

One-Man Band

people who want to be a part of something bigger than any one person. The average employee turnover rate in the brutally competitive software and real estate businesses is about 20 percent, while SAS and Staubach have attrition rates of less than 5 percent.[35] In addition, folks working in a sovereign organization tend to be much more highly committed to the company's vision than if they worked at a place where senior management constantly told them to "go back to work and leave the driving to us." Finally, a sovereign organization can adapt more quickly to customer needs and competitive moves. Since people throughout the organization have an understanding of where the company is going and how it plans to get there, they can make important decisions on the fly and be confident they're doing the right things to enhance the company's overall competitive position.

> The average annual employee turnover rate at Staubach and SAS is 5 percent, compared with averages of about 20 percent for their industries.

KEYS TO CROWNING THE COMPANY

But how do people like Scott Edmonds, Bob Kierlin, and Roger Staubach actually go about crowning their companies? Turns out breakthrough companies use a myriad of approaches in their quest to build a sovereign organization. Here are some we thought were most important.

CROWN THE CUSTOMER FIRST

If a company doesn't work hard every day to keep the eyes of every person in the organization fixed squarely on the customer, people are going to care more about what is going on in their own departments than what concerns the customer. On the other hand, if everyone in the organization is taught to view their own departmental activities as always secondary to the needs of the customer, then employees will consider the customer their top priority.

It was early in his real estate career that Roger Staubach recognized a need in the industry: an opportunity to play the role of tenant advocate. The incentive for traditional real estate brokers was, of course, to see how much money they could make on a commission by collecting fees from both the buyer and the seller. If the broker had to bend a rule or two, or burn a customer once in a while in the quest for a larger fee, so be it. What Staubach recognized was that his company could actually serve the customer first and still make good money. To augment this point, Staubach introduced a concept that even today seems completely out of whack with the industry: The Staubach Guarantee of Value. What Staubach guaranteed customers was that they could negotiate his broker fee down—even eliminate it—if they felt they didn't receive full value for their money.[36] As you can imagine, Staubach's guarantee didn't sit well with his competitors, but his clients absolutely loved it. And because this guarantee was built around his constitution and a culture of teamwork, as well as a good payday, his brokers love it too. "Roger has always taught us that we want our customers to control our compensation," Greg O'Brien told us. "By putting our guarantee in writing, it eliminates the bad actors and puts our focus on serving our customers. We have incentive to not only earn our full fee, but for the customers to award us a bonus as well. At year's end, our brokers always rank among the top earners in our industry."[37]

AIM HIGH

The leaders of our breakthrough companies set out from the beginning to build something great. Most of us are motivated by bold visions and challenges, and the more talented a person is, the more dramatic that vision needs to be. That vision may, at first, be even bigger than what many employees see as possible. When Lee Hein heard Bob Kierlin talking about his vision of Fastenal becoming a billion-dollar company when it was still selling about $11 million worth of nuts and bolts in places like La Crosse, Wisconsin, and Dubuque, Iowa, he thought his boss was nuts. "Matter of fact, I thought he was smoking something, if you know what I mean," he told us tongue in cheek.[38] While there are hundreds of women's clothing brands today, Scott Edmonds and Chico's strive to stand out. That means that Chico's designers are encouraged to experiment with new fabrics and designs in pursuit of the next bestseller. "We want our customers to have a powerful emotional connection with our clothes," Edmonds told us.[39]

AVOID THE TRAPPINGS OF CORPORATE ROYALTY

Lavish offices, exorbitant perks, corporate jets that whisk top executives to the Caribbean every weekend: all to be avoided. All too often, entrepreneurial leaders wind up building personal fiefdoms rather than sovereign organizations. Breakthrough executives are certainly paid market rates, but in every other respect, they tend to receive the same treatment and benefits package as any other employee. Just as George Washington toughed out the long winter in 1777 alongside his troops,[40] breakthrough leaders understand that they are paid to serve the organization, not the other way around. While he ran a billion-dollar company for almost forty years, Bob Kierlin never paid himself more than $125,000 a year and never once approved any stock options for himself. In 2000, Kierlin put aside a block of his own shares in the company to use for employee grants.[41] Kierlin, who has lived in small-town Winona and still maintains his only residence there, is famous in the company for buying secondhand suits and for making annual trips around the country hitching rides with Fastenal truckers, eating dinner at McDonald's, and sharing a room at the Days Inn. Like Washington leading his troops into battle, Kierlin made sure he led from the front lines. "Bob was always a great listener and he always tried to fit in as one of us," said Bob Wittenberg, who has been driving trucks for Fastenal for more than twenty-five years.[42]

SHIFT FROM COMMANDER TO COACH[43]

Leaders play a variety of roles and often need to shift between them, relying on their intuition to match the situation. As a company evolves, leaders will have to choose whether to change *persons* or to change *people,* a subtle and important difference. For example, a sales manager for a $10-million company may not have the best skill-set, abilities, and knowledge to run the same department when it's grown to $100 million. The leader's first option is to change persons: to terminate the sales manager and hire an outside replacement with big-company experience. Making a switch of that nature can, of course, be a gamble. While the company may gain the experience it was looking for, it will lose years of experience, tacit company knowledge, and perhaps intuition into what the clients want. That's why it is essential for leaders to adapt their skill-sets to begin coaching and developing new capabilities throughout the organization. In this way, Chico's Scott Edmonds explained, he is like a football coach trying to field the best possible team, given the type of opponent the company is facing. "I have had some hard conversations where I had to tell someone who has been here ten years that I have to bench them," Edmonds told us. "At that point, it's up to me to coach them or to find another way they can contribute to the organization."[44] (For more on this, see chapter 10: Building Breakthrough Capabilities.)

DON'T LET LOYALTY BECOME A LIABILITY

For some organization members, all the coaching in the world just won't get them to where they need to be, and despite a leader's best efforts, these folks just won't grow fast enough to keep up. Many entrepreneurial leaders, however, are slow to act when it comes to non-performing team members, especially when it comes to longtime employees. Too often, leaders make excuses for employees under the guise of loyalty. Venture capitalist John Hamm, a former CEO himself, has described this behavior as "when loyalty becomes a liability."[45] Fastenal CEO Will Oberton, on the other hand, told us how important it is to evaluate each member of the organization objectively. "We are not willing to take away responsibility from a position because of the person in it," Oberton told us. "We can't leave people in a role if they are not making the goals. That creates a ripple effect and begins to hold everyone else back."[46]

> Entrepreneurial leaders need to make sure their loyalty to the troops doesn't become a liability. Every effort should be made to grow people along with the company. But when it becomes clear that someone isn't up to the task, they need to be moved to a role where they can still make a contribution or moved out of the company.

ENCOURAGE "CHAOTIC COMMUNICATION"

One of the most common attributes that breakthrough leaders shared was an open-door policy that extended not just to senior management, but to the entire company. That's right, any employee of The Staubach Company can actually walk into Roger Staubach's office in Addison and get something off his chest.[47] Staubach, in fact, encourages it, as long as it is not on a Monday after a Dallas Cowboys loss. This is an example of what Fastenal founder Bob Kierlin calls "chaotic communication" and he thinks it is the lifeblood of a sovereign organization. He even wrote a book that discusses the concept that anyone in the organization should be encouraged to talk to anyone else at any time.[48] It was a principle Kierlin came across in 1962 when he was studying for his MBA at the University of Minnesota. After graduation, and a few unhappy years with little or no communication at IBM, Kierlin founded Fastenal and kept his door open to anyone—whether they had good news or bad—from day one. "I always knew how big a problem we had, based on the number of people that came to my door," Kierlin told us.[49]

CUT PEOPLE IN ON THE ACTION

While we know that breakthrough companies dispense with what have become common perks, they are by no means cheap when it comes to handing out growth opportunities or even some financial incentives as well. It is typical for Fastenal's store managers, for example, to earn double their annual salary as a performance bonus while machine operators who work in the company's custom-tool division can earn more than $40,000 a year with little or no college education.[50] At Polaris, since employees are strongly encouraged to use the company's products as often as possible, the company keeps a fleet of snowmobiles and ATVs available for employees to check out over the weekend at no charge.[51] Eight of the nine breakthrough companies grant either stock or stock options to their employees, while the ninth company, SAS, provides otherworldly benefits like flexible workdays; subsidized gourmet cuisine; free on-site health care; an on-site recreation and fitness center, including a full-size basketball court; and an elementary school–size day-care center where parents pay $350 per month (pre-tax) per child, a fraction of the cost of comparable care in today's market.[52]

Perhaps the most important ways to cut people in on the action don't involve money. The "action" many people care most about is the ability to be a part of something important and bigger than themselves. They want to use their minds, skills, and energy to impact where their organization goes and how it gets there.

IT TAKES A TEAM

One overarching theme we uncovered in studying the breakthrough companies is that it takes more than just the entrepreneurial leader to create a sovereign organization—it requires the organization as a whole to buy into the concept as well. While there would be no

Fastenal without founder Bob Kierlin, the company could not have evolved into a sovereign organization if not for the likes of business development head Bob Strauss, regional VP Lee Hein, and longtime truck driver Bob Wittenberg continually working to make the company better. The example continues with Scott Edmonds at Chico's and Greg O'Brien and Blair Bryan at The Staubach Company—all of whom have continued to evolve along with their companies. The trick for the leader, of course, is to not only find and recruit the best talent, but also not to be blinded by loyalty when the organization outgrows the capabilities of some of its members.

As a nation, we are indebted to George Washington who, in refusing to be crowned king of the newly formed United States, set this nation on a path to become so much more than any king could have created. Breakthrough leaders are motivated by the same sense of confidence in the potential of people to accomplish great things. But the history of the nation might have turned out very differently when you consider the story of another one of the Continental Army's best and brightest field commanders. Not only had he been born within the colonies, he had, like Washington, fought in the French and Indian War, fighting for the British against the French. After displaying cunning and bravery at victorious battles like Ticonderoga and Saratoga, the young soldier soon found himself a brigadier general and on the fast track. But the new general became jealous of the success and fame of other leaders like Washington after he was skipped over for subsequent promotions. For this officer, the war became about his own legacy and not the cause. Not long after the war turned with the victory at Saratoga, the young general, now facing corruption charges after stripping another officer of his command and facing pressure at home from his Tory wife, made plans to hand control of the Hudson Valley over to the British in return for money and a commission in the British army. The plot was soon thwarted, and with Washington's victory at Yorktown, the war was won. That traitorous general was, of course, Benedict Arnold. And who knows where the country and the world would stand today if he and not Washington had won at Yorktown.[53]

CROWNING THE COMPANY
The Key Ideas

1. Breakthrough companies tend to be created and led by people who are determined to build something bigger than themselves. Rather than treat their businesses like their own private fiefdoms, they "crown the company."

2. The strengths that help entrepreneurial leaders thrive in the early stage can become weaknesses if leaders do not adapt along with their companies.

3. The definition of leadership changes as an organization grows. In the early stages, managers focus almost exclusively on "running the business." As the business grows, leaders must develop coaching skills and strategy skills.

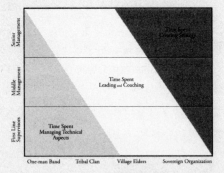

4. Breakthrough companies go through four distinct stages: One-man Band, Tribal Clan, Village Eldership, and Sovereign Organization.

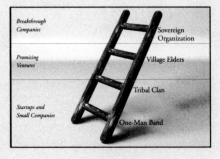

5. Breakthrough companies crown the company by: (i) crowning the customer first; (ii) aiming high; (iii) avoiding the "trappings" of corporate royalty; (iv) shifting leadership style from "commander" to "coach"; (v) making sure they don't let loyalty become a liability; and (vi) cutting people in on the action.

CROWNING THE COMPANY "SQUIRTS FROM THE GRAPEFRUIT"
(Findings That Surprised Us)

1. Eight of our nine breakthrough companies found ways to involve the founders for a great deal of the firm's life. We found no evidence that founders are, by definition, ill-prepared to run breakthrough companies. Organizations usually "outgrow" their leaders because the leader fails to understand and implement changes in his/her leadership approach. For leaders who accomplish this shift, there is evidence to suggest that it will pay off in terms of increased performance when compared to non-founder-run firms.

2. When entrepreneurial leaders fail to keep pace with their companies, it is often not due to their weaknesses, but rather an overuse of their strengths. Their intense drive and ability to juggle a lot of balls at once and quickly change directions, so important in the early stages of development, can, if not recognized, undermine them in later stages.

BREAKTHROUGH IN PRACTICE
Tips for Crowning the Company

1. Go to *www.breakthroughcompany.com/theladder,* and use our interactive tool to determine where your company is on the path to crowning the company.

2. E-mail the link to the Crowning the Company tool to others in your organization and discuss the results. Explore how your firm can leverage its strengths to move toward greater organizational sovereignty.

4

UPPING THE ANTE

*Progress always involves risk; you can't steal second base and keep
your foot on first base.*

FREDERICK WILCOX

WHEN YOU FIRST meet Intuit cofounder Scott Cook, he doesn't
come off as much of a gambler. He reminds you instead of an
energetic college professor—inquisitive, intellectually playful,
and cerebral. As we began our interview in a borrowed conference
room at Intuit's Silicon Valley world headquarters, he bounded to the
whiteboard and, like Socrates, perhaps the greatest professor of all
time, turned from interviewee to interviewer. "What exactly do you
mean by breakthrough?" he asked. "Do you really think there is some
kind of black box a company must solve before it can scale from the
start-up stage to a mature, billion-dollar firm?" After more than an hour
of verbal ping-pong, we finally regained control of the interview, but
not until Cook was satisfied that we were, in his words, "on to something really big here."[1]

Cook is so sharp and so curious about a wide range of subjects
that it would be easy for an interviewer to overlook Cook's singular
talent: the ability to size up and act on the potential of any given
strategic situation. In other words, Cook is exceptional at placing the
right bet at the right time.

In the fall of 1986, he felt his hand was being called. He and co-founder Tom Proulx had spent the previous four years scratching and clawing their way out of Cook's basement where they had designed Intuit's flagship personal finance product, Quicken. While the company had achieved some success by selling Quicken to consumers through its partnerships with several banks around the country, the product had yet to reach the kinds of sales volumes Cook and Proulx knew they needed to achieve critical mass. Though they had survived so far, and managed to sock away $100,000, Cook and Proulx understood that they needed to do more to make it through another four years.[2]

At the time, most software companies relied on wholesalers and retailers to sell their products for them. The rub, however, was that wholesalers and retailers wouldn't stock a company's product unless consumers knocked on their doors demanding it. "I started calling up the owners of these stores and interviewing them about how their business worked," Cook told us. "They kept telling me that they wouldn't buy my product until I created the demand for it. Distribution is like rope, you can pull it in but you can't push it. That's when I decided we needed to hit some kind of homerun to create the demand for Quicken."[3]

The problem was, of course, that launching a saturation media campaign to generate this kind of interest took a lot of money, far more than the $100,000 Cook had in the bank. That's when he hatched a bold plan. He had been reading about how another software company, Borland, had begun marketing directly at consumers. Cook thought that by running ads for Quicken in periodicals like *PC* magazine and *InfoWorld,* he could get consumers to buy directly from the company. If he could generate enough consumer excitement about the program, he figured, perhaps the distributors would bite.[4]

Cook decided it was time to throw his "Hail Mary" (a term coined, coincidentally, by breakthrough company CEO Roger Staubach when he was quarterback of the Dallas Cowboys).[5] Cook decided to invest all of his company's net worth, the entire $100,000, in a single direct-marketing campaign, knowing that if it didn't work, Intuit would be bankrupt. Cook says that when he presented the idea to his cofounder Proulx, he got the reaction he wanted. "Tom said let's go for it," Cook recalls. "He said let's either go out in a blaze of glory and get on with our lives, or let's grow big. I don't want to continue existing as the living dead."[6]

The campaign, which featured full-page ads in dozens of magazines touting the slogan "End Financial Hassles—$49.95" along with product information, customer testimonials, and a toll-free telephone number—was a rousing success. The company's phones rang off the hook for weeks, and the resulting sales roughly tripled the wildest expectations of the team. Stoked by this increased demand, droves of wholesalers and retailers began to stock the product, which further enhanced Quicken's position both in the market and on retailers' shelves.[7]

Cook understood early that if Intuit was going to make it, he was going to have to place some bets. More important, Cook understood that as the stakes in his business grew, so did the pile of chips his company needed to put into play. It was this understanding of when to up the ante time and time again that enabled Cook to build Intuit

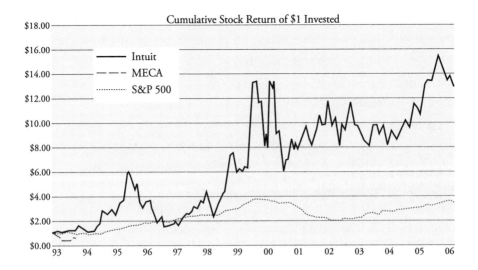

Cumulative Stock Return of $1 Invested

into one of the great software companies in history and, in turn, made him one of the most sought-after board members in America. He has since lent his advice to such household names as Amazon.com, eBay, and Procter & Gamble.[8] The story of Intuit is an object lesson that any company, regardless of size, needs to bet big in order to grow big.

THE PSYCHOLOGY OF BETTING

Pug Pearson, the 1973 World Series of Poker Champion, made this observation about human nature:

> *The real thing to know is that folks will stand to lose more than they will to win. That's the most important percentage there is. I mean, if they lose, they're willin' to lose everything. If they win, they're usually satisfied to win enough to pay for dinner and a show. The best gamblers know that.*[9]

With only a fifth-grade education, Pearson had put his finger on the concept of "loss aversion," a concept that would later be made famous by Israeli economists Daniel Kahneman and Amos Tversky.[10] The idea behind loss aversion is that people don't always behave in the rational manner that classic economic models predict that they should. For instance, when they get ahead in the game, loss aversion kicks in, and they begin to take fewer risks—playing it safe—even if the odds say a wager is likely to pay off. They are willing to settle for "dinner and a show" rather than risk their winnings.

Evidence suggests that loss aversion is at work wherever people perceive risk: at the poker table, on Wall Street, and when businesspeople place bets on markets and capital equipment. Our research suggests that one thing that separates a breakthrough company from the rest of the pack is a willingness to up the ante, to place bigger and bigger bets as the business grows—combined with the instincts to place the right bet at the right time.

Entrepreneurs are born risk takers—this plays right to their strengths, right? Wrong. We were surprised to learn that entrepreneurial leaders, in fact, are often more risk averse than is popularly believed. In our psychological analysis of the 250 *Inc.* 500 CEOs mentioned in the last chapter, we were particularly surprised by one result: There appears to be no significant correlation between risk tolerance and starting or running an entrepreneurial business. At first, we thought we must have been misinterpreting the data, but after reviewing the findings again, it occurred to us that a widely held view about entrepreneurial leaders—that they are by definition big risk takers—may be incorrect. That is because in calculating the risks involved in starting a business, many get the math wrong. To most successful entrepreneurs, starting a business isn't much of a risk at all.

On the surface, it may appear to some that Harvard MBA Scott Cook took an enormous risk when he quit his job at Bain Consulting to start the software firm that he would later call Intuit. But when we talked to him, we came to understand that his decision was based upon a completely different calculus. "I'm actually a conservative, risk-averse type," Cook told us. "After I saw the opportunity to solve a common problem, I figured that the worst thing that could happen was that I would spend a few years paying off credit card debt. To me, it looked like a risk-free decision."[11]

> The idea that entrepreneurial leaders are, by definition, big risk takers is a myth. Some are, some aren't. More important, there is evidence that entrepreneurs actually become *less risk tolerant* as they begin to achieve success—the very time when they need to be "doubling down" on their businesses.

Scott Cook didn't risk much in starting Intuit because he didn't have much to risk.[12] We found this to be a common thread among all the breakthrough company founders. Bob Kierlin, for instance, launched what would become Fastenal from the place next door to his father's auto parts supply shop in Winona, Minnesota, with barely a dollar to his name, knowing he could go back to another corporate job.[13] Marvin and Helene Gralnick founded Chico's and risked nothing by selling discounted clothes and trinkets they picked up from their travels in Mexico.[14] Likewise, roughly 73 percent of America's fastest growing companies are started with $100,000 or less, and about 86 percent are started with less than $300,000.[15] And, contrary to popular perception, most new businesses aren't started with risky "new to the world" ideas like eBay or Google, which promise to reshape an industry—only 12 percent of *Inc.* 500 founders attributed their success to "an unusual or extraordinary idea," and 88 percent reported their success was mainly due to "exceptional execution of an ordinary idea."[16] (When Scott Cook started Intuit, there were already forty-six personal finance software programs available that essentially performed the same function as the one he created, leading him and cofounder Tom Proulx to joke that Intuit had enjoyed 47th-mover advantage.)[17] Most entrepreneurial companies, especially in their early stages, also try to avoid risk when it comes to tackling their competition. Only 4 percent of high-growth firms report that they compete with Fortune 500 companies, and 91 percent say they compete only with small companies or that they have no direct competitors at all.[18]

Not only are the people who start and run early-stage businesses not necessarily big risk takers, the theory of loss aversion suggests that as their companies begin to achieve success their appetite for risk may actually *decrease*. In poker parlance, once the entrepreneur gets a small chip lead, he or she begins to play tight. As we came to understand the psychology of most entrepreneurial leaders, it was easy to figure out why. Remember Pug Pearson's evaluation of a typical poker player—someone who will accept a smaller reward when faced with a potential loss. Similarly, when most company owners, especially those whose business is there to provide a certain kind of lifestyle, are faced with decisions that could produce a loss, they are willing to settle for pots that are much smaller than we might initially think. "Three reasons companies fail to break through is because they fear losing control, losing their expertise, and losing their financial freedom," Bob Strauss, a thirty-year veteran employee of Fastenal and one of Kierlin's key lieutenants, told us. "They stop taking risks because they are afraid of losing what they already have."[19] In other words, entrepreneurial leaders often equate consolidating their winnings with safety when, in fact, the opposite is true. The only true path to safety and success for themselves and their organizations, as Fastenal, Intuit, and our other seven breakthrough companies have proven, is a willingness to increase the size of the wager as the stakes increase.

INTUIT GOES ALL-IN

Fueled in part by the success of its direct-marketing campaign in 1986, Quicken continued to gobble up market share in the personal finance space. Not only had the company survived its initial big bet, it was thriving because of it. Then, in 1991, Intuit moved into what was at the time the highest-stakes game on the planet. Bill Gates came calling, saying he was thinking about buying the company. During the due diligence process, Microsoft, which was actually about to release its own product, Microsoft Money, learned as much about Intuit and Quicken as possible, and then made an abrupt low-ball offer along with a curt ultimatum: "If you don't work with us, we are going to win. Are you going to work with us or not?"[20] Despite the long odds of taking on Microsoft, the undisputed 800-pound gorilla of the software world, the Intuit team decided to go all in.

Even before Microsoft began issuing ultimatums, Intuit had been struggling for almost a year to complete a Windows-version of Quicken. After learning about Microsoft Money, Cook and his team realized it was very unlikely they'd be able to beat Microsoft to the market with a Windows-compatible product (Intuit was already supporting Macintosh and DOS versions of Quicken). To CFO Eric Dunn, that meant it was time to lay down an even bigger bet. Dunn approached Intuit cofounder Proulx and offered a deal: In return for getting the Windows project back on track, Dunn asked for a sleek, black BMW coupe. Proulx agreed. While Proulx, Cook, and the management team huddled to discuss their marketing strategy, Dunn moved his entire development team out to a beach community near Monterey, California, where they began working around the clock to catch up with Microsoft.[21]

While Dunn coded away, Cook dramatically unveiled his "Crush Microsoft" strategy in a 1991 board meeting. He understood that, owing to important bets made in the earlier stages of the company's development, Intuit's sole advantage over Microsoft was its intimacy with its customers. While he conceded that Microsoft Money would hit the market before Dunn could finish, Cook outlined a series of bets to capitalize on what he called "second mover advantage." First, Intuit broke its tradition of not preannouncing products (a marketing tactic often referred to as vaporware) and began aggressively promoting its pending Windows-version software. The bet was that customers would wait for the new Quicken even as the boxes of Microsoft Money began lining the shelves of their favorite retailers. Next, to build loyalty among retailers, Intuit included with its product package a $15 coupon redeemable only for software bought in stores. After identifying Microsoft's price point, Cook gambled by not only cutting the wholesale price of Quicken for Windows by $4, he also hiked the suggested retail price by about $20—guaranteeing a margin that would make the new software one of the most profitable products on store shelves. The gamble paid off. Microsoft Money debuted to relative silence and never achieved a significant share of the market.[22]

No sooner had the Intuit team caught its breath, however, when word came that Microsoft was launching a small business accounting package called Microsoft Profit, which had been developed by the leading software company, Great Plains. At the time, Intuit's own small business package, QuickBooks, represented a small portion of its total revenues. As the management team huddled yet again, several naysayers argued that Intuit had already tempted fate once; better to stick to the personal finance market and cede control of the small business marketplace to this new partnership between Microsoft and Great Plains. Cook would have none of it, however, arguing that Intuit had no other choice but to double-down on its bet. So they did. Leveraging its early bets on customer-centric and user-friendly functionality, marketing prowess, and channel relationships, the Intuit team did the seemingly impossible—again: It chased Microsoft out of town. Microsoft acknowledged defeat and sold Profit back to Great Plains soon afterward.[23]

The dynamics of placing big bets is a philosophy Scott Cook personally teaches all Intuit managers even today. "We teach our managers to swing for home runs; we can't continue to grow if we settle for singles," Cook told us.[24] Intuit is unwilling to, as poker champion Pug Pearson said, "stand to lose more than they would stand to gain." They understood that, unlike bets in a poker game, their bets on the business are cumulative: Each correct bet sets them up for the next, achieving in effect a "layering" of bets. Over time, the payoffs from these wagers gave them real advantages in the marketplace, thus reducing the company's overall risk. That's right: Intuit's willingness to place bigger bets actually *decreased* its risk, making the firm's long-term prospects even safer.

LITTLE BETS AND THE ILLUSION OF SAFETY

The idea that safety comes as a result of placing larger wagers is difficult for many entrepreneurial leaders to get their heads around. Who would have blamed Cook and Proulx if they decided to play it safe and sit on their $100,000? They could have finally paid themselves salaries and continued to chip away at the market through their bank partnerships.

Having survived the trials of a start-up, many company founders believe they have earned the right to relax a bit, build some cash reserves, and even to take some of that money off the table. The best way to preserve their success, they reason, is to stop making the big bets, and begin making small, incremental bets at the margin instead. Now we'll just stick to the knitting, they say, let us put our heads down and just keep focused on doing what got us here. And that strategy is fine, for whatever time that company's competitors also stick to their knitting. Competitors, however, rarely act the way we'd like them to; if a company is not changing the field of play in their industry, they can be sure that their competitors will. There's nothing wrong, of course, with seeking a life in which you can fund the golf membership, pay the mortgage, and live a comfortable life—as long as all your competitors are similarly satisfied with the status quo. In today's intense global environment, however, where hungry competitors are literally emerging from everywhere, the status quo is a myth.

> "Sticking to the knitting" is great, until the day you discover someone in China is knitting the same things you are, but knitting them faster, more cheaply, and in colors and styles your customers prefer. Only companies that continue to adapt through a series of progressively bigger bets will successfully reach breakthrough.

In our on-site fieldwork with more than fifty companies, we found that many entrepreneurial leaders are quick to rationalize why the idea of placing bigger bets doesn't apply to them. One common argument we got from managers was that since their companies weren't all that profitable, they didn't have much to bet. We also heard managers tell us that their companies simply weren't large enough to shift the field of play in their industry. In reality, of course, most companies that successfully change the rules of engagement in their market are small when they do it. Remember, when Intuit launched Quicken, it was the *forty-seventh product on the market* and was launched from Cook's basement. Cook was also resource poor in the beginning. Twenty venture capital companies rejected him before he eventually turned to family and friends to borrow the money to get his new company started.[25]

Surprisingly, we even heard from entrepreneurs who felt that their industry lacked the kinds of opportunities that warranted placing any big bets at all on their futures. Try telling that to Bob Kierlin, a man who saw the seeds for a multibillion-dollar business in literally selling nuts and bolts, or to Roger Staubach, who had the audacity to think that he could build a global real estate brokerage business not by selling buildings but by servicing tenants instead. When thirty-seven-year-old Hall Wendell led a management buyout of Polaris Industries from Textron, its parent company, in 1981, the snowmobile industry was in a freefall. Due to skyrocketing fuel prices, exorbitant interest rates, and record-low snowfalls, the industry had consolidated from 140 companies to just four, and Polaris was bringing up the rear. It was an industry Textron wanted out of, fast. "Textron was evaluating where it wanted to go and Polaris didn't fit," Wendell recalled in a speech to commemorate Polaris's fiftieth anniversary. "Textron originally bought Polaris when the snowmobile was a growth industry. It wasn't a growth industry anymore."[26] As president and CEO, Wendell was brought in to find a buyer for Polaris. There were none to be found. Wendell figured that by running a leaner and more nimble business, Polaris had enormous opportunities before it. So he organized a team of investors, which included most of the existing management team, as well as his father, and hashed out a leveraged buyout deal with Textron president Bev Dolan to buy Polaris for about $350,000. "We outlined the deal on the back of a bar napkin in about fifteen minutes," Wendell recalled.[27] By 1987, just six years later, Polaris had not only regained a dominant position in the snowmobile industry, it had launched a bold and successful bid to enter the burgeoning all-terrain-vehicle market, and netted more than $98 million in a lucrative initial public offering.[28]

The most common argument we heard during our fieldwork, however, was that many CEOs simply did not see themselves as big risk takers. What these men and women didn't realize at the time was that by avoiding the risks associated with a few key smart, big bets, they may have been taking the biggest risk of all.

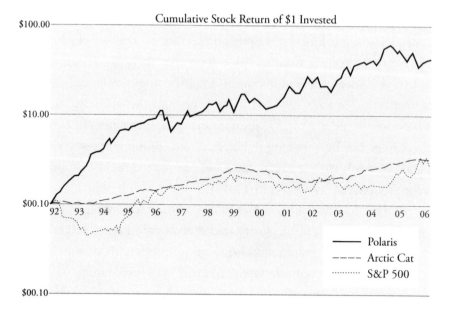

Cumulative Stock Return of $1 Invested

Polaris
Arctic Cat
S&P 500

WHAT MAKES SOME ENTREPRENEURIAL LEADERS AVOID BIG BETS?

Psychology: Not all entrepreneurial leaders are big risk takers. Many entrepreneurial leaders we interviewed talked about reaching "the number"—the point at which they would earn enough money to feel secure about their own personal financial situation—and beyond which they were unwilling to take more risk. Here's where the right financial partner can really help a company, allowing owners to "take some money off the table" while allowing the company to keep increasing the size of its bets.

Low expectations: Many companies are started by people simply wishing to escape the irritations of working for a larger company. Their motivation initially is to provide themselves with a job without the annoying accessory called a boss, and once they achieve some success, they—like Pug Pearson's typical poker player—are willing to settle for "dinner and a show."

Family pressures: Most U.S. firms are family-owned firms, and because of these family connections, entrepreneurs sometimes begin to see themselves more as stewards of generational family wealth rather than as competitors in an industry. Ironically, this stance may cause them to avoid making the kinds of investments that will keep the business competitive over the long term.

Employee resistance: Interestingly, executives of breakthrough companies report that one of their biggest challenges is keeping employees in the mode of conquering new territory and placing new big bets. It turns out that many employees, especially those who lived through the drama of the start-up, harbor a hope of more stable times ahead—when the pace of change is not as fast. We found that leaders of breakthrough companies resisted the temptation to let the organization rest for long, and always focused the attention of employees on the next pitch to be climbed.

Investor interests: Entrepreneurial leaders beware. Depending upon an outside investor's time horizon, an investor's interests and the interest of the company may not align. Professional investors have to be concerned about things like exit strategies and timing returns to match the raising of their next fund. If an investor wants to set one of his portfolio companies up for immediate sale, he may discourage the company from making investments in the short term. This can also cut the other way; some professional investors have been known to push their companies to "swing for the fences" in terms of financial returns and to place bets that are inherently more risky than management would like.

Cultural setting: Although our study included only U.S. companies, we came across considerable anecdotal evidence that the home country of a company may impact the degree to which it is willing to place big bets.

GAMBLING GIVES BETTING A BAD NAME

One key difference between betting in poker and betting in business is that with poker, a bet is just a bet. Except for its ability to affect the emotional state of one's opponent, the act of wagering on a single hand of poker doesn't in any way increase a player's chance of winning the next hand. The *results* of a hand—in the form of a higher chip count—are what puts a player at an advantage or disadvantage.

> In poker, a bet is just a bet. How the cards fall in one hand doesn't impact how they fall in the next. But in business, a bet is also an investment, which can combine with past and future bets in a way that creates a real advantage. We call this kind of bet an *exponential bet*.

In business, the opposite is true: The act of wagering can dramatically shift the odds in a company's favor. An effective bet in business is more than just a bet, it is an *investment*. Companies, like poker players, have limited resources to take action with. Instead of a pile of chips, companies have employees, capital, and equipment. With every investment a company makes, either explicitly like opening a new manufacturing facility or retail location or tacitly as in reducing administrative costs to offer a lower price to customers, it is using its pile of chips to make a bet. Unlike bets at the poker table, however, investments can be highly targeted and strategically linked together in what we call *exponential bets,* which determine the difference between winning and losing. Smart bets (investments) are how companies develop knowledge about markets and capabilities that their competitors have difficulty matching. In short, good bets are how companies achieve advantages over their competitors, and how they improve their odds of success. Our research into breakthrough companies shows that, quite simply, as a company grows, so must the size of its bets.

> Too many business leaders read books on business, hoping to emulate the bets of others. This almost never works. Instead, a leader should focus on improving his own play—seeking a deeper understanding of the "game" of business, improving his ability to better calculate the odds, and learning how to better understand himself, his own company and its competitors.

What makes Intuit and Polaris breakthrough companies is not that Scott Cook quit his job and ran up significant credit card debt or that

Hall Wendell and his management team emerged from their LBO with a 20-to-1 debt-to-equity ratio.[29] Roughly 600,000 people launch new companies in similar ways in the United States every year.[30] Intuit and Polaris are breakthrough companies because they have repeatedly demonstrated a willingness to up the ante as the stakes increased throughout their companies' histories, and when necessary, to go "all in" by gambling all of their available resources.

THE PHYSICS OF BIG BETS

In thinking about how the right big bet at the right time can shift the field of play in a company's favor, we came across a model created by Amar Bhide of Columbia University, who has spent the last two decades studying entrepreneurial companies.[31] Bhide thinks that

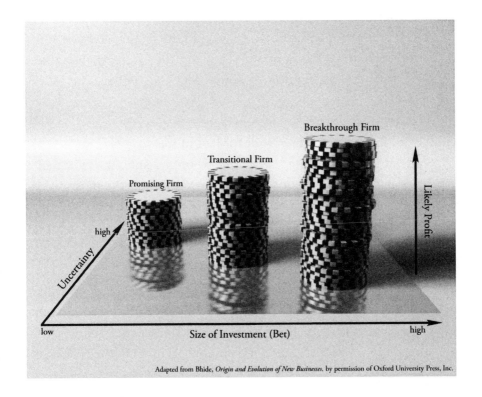

Adapted from Bhide, *Origin and Evolution of New Businesses*, by permission of Oxford University Press, Inc.

promising companies like Polaris and Intuit start out in environments with a lot of uncertainty and that require relatively low levels of initial investment to get started, but are also unlikely to produce significant profits. As the companies grow, they will be successful if they increase the size of their investments (bets) in things that will be more profitable and with lower uncertainty. Firms unwilling to place the bigger bets are likely to remain "stuck" in highly uncertain environments that are not all that profitable, and they may also see whatever market power they have garnered eroded by competitors who are willing to up the ante.

Let's apply the model to Polaris. When Hall Wendell led a "restart" of tiny Polaris in 1981, there was nothing but uncertainty as far as the eye could see. Fuel costs had spiked to historic highs, interest rates were over 20 percent and snowfall levels had been stuck at record lows for years. The once-burgeoning U.S. snowmobile industry had shrunk from more than one hundred suppliers to four, with Polaris dead last. This uncertainty, however, true to the model, allowed Wendell to get into Polaris for a song—buying the company for about $350,000 plus the assumption of some debt. But Polaris was never going to make any real money just selling snowmobiles. For one thing, it was a seasonal business, which meant Wendell's plant idled and his employees had to find other work for half of the year.[32]

Some at Polaris thought it was time to up the ante. It was actually Chuck Baxter, vice president of engineering, who was the most persistent about a prototype all-terrain vehicle he and his team had cobbled together with spare parts during their downtime in the summer of 1981. "We had recognized that the ATV was kind of similar to the snowmobile in terms of people going outdoors to play," recalled Baxter. "So we started experimenting."[33] Though the team came up with a working three-wheel model similar to the ones introduced at that time by Japanese manufacturers like Yamaha and Honda, Wendell, wary of the competition, wouldn't bite. Unless Baxter found another company willing to partner with Polaris in a private-label agreement, the project would be killed. When overtures along these lines to both John Deere and Cenex, a giant farm cooperative, failed, Wendell shelved the project.[34]

Two years later, however, due in part to the fact that Baxter wouldn't give up, Wendell made a bet to revive the ATV program, realizing he was going up against powerful Japanese companies fifty times the size of Polaris. Several months later, the new four-wheel model, complete with a two-stroke engine and an automatic belt-driven transmission like that found on the company's snowmobiles, was introduced to distributors. "Everyone laughed at us at first," recalls Mike Malone, Polaris's chief financial officer. "They were used to ATVs that worked like motorcycles, so they called ours the 'rubber-band-powered' ATV."[35] After the initial impression wore off, however, the distributors liked what they saw: The automatic transmission was easy to operate, it had a single braking system as opposed to the complicated hand-and-pedal technique required to ride the Japanese version, and it even had floorboards instead of the conventional foot pegs common to motorcycles. By the summer of 1984, Wendell was committed and increased his full-time workforce from 50 to 200, and by March 1985, the first ATVs began rolling off the line. Rather than compete with the Japanese in the three-wheeler sport and recreation market, Polaris billed its machine as "the all-purpose ATV that works as hard as it plays."[36]

By focusing its efforts on a four-wheel version, Polaris was also able to tout the safety of its machines after the Consumer Product Safety Commission declared three-wheelers unsafe, a decision that hurt the Japanese severely.[37] As a result, Polaris quickly made inroads into both the sport and utility markets while continuing to invest in new production facilities and innovations that helped fuel the company's overall growth. Though it would take ten years before its ATV sales outpaced those of its snowmobiles, Polaris now owns 30 percent of the North American market, and ATV sales now account for more than 65 percent of Polaris's total revenues while snowmobiles represent only 10 percent. Polaris's big bet not only helped put the company on the map, it helped transform a market that now sells more than 1.3 million vehicles every year.[38]

Polaris placed an even bigger bet in 1998 when it decided to build an entire new product line—a motorcycle—from scratch. It involved betting millions of dollars of shareholders' money that could have been spent on the company's core snowmobile and ATV lines, but it also required the company to do something it had never done before—build a street-legal and safe two-wheeled machine in the face of heavy competition not only in the United States, but from Japanese and European manufacturers as well.[39]

The end result, however, was that Polaris was able to mitigate its risk in two ways: (1) Polaris had watched how Harley-Davidson had risen from its own ashes and developed a cult following around its brand by tapping into a rising demographic, the baby boomers; and (2) although Polaris had never built a motorcycle before, it had the confidence it had gained from developing its now thriving ATV business while facing similar odds from international competition. Also, as an employee-owned, nonunion shop, it knew it could operate leaner and meaner than its American counterparts. "We have a habit of going up against people fifty times our size," Tom Tiller, Polaris's current CEO, told us. "First it was Honda, Yamaha, Kawasaki, and Suzuki, and today it's Harley-Davidson. We've had trouble in every business we've ever entered. We win because we are very stubborn people up here in Minnesota."[40]

The figure below maps the sequence of bets made by Polaris and Intuit as they moved from bit-players to major forces in their industries. The futures of both companies were highly uncertain in the beginning stages. In the early years, however, both companies excelled in ways that were important to customers. Intuit pioneered the

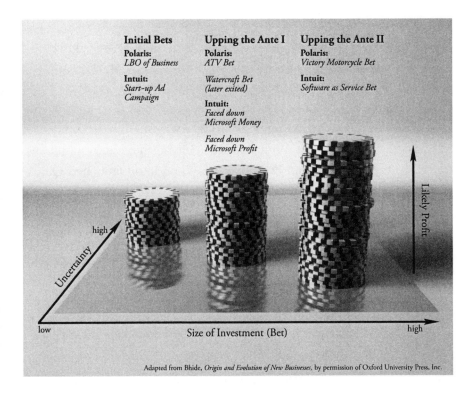

Initial Bets	Upping the Ante I	Upping the Ante II
Polaris: *LBO of Business*	**Polaris:** *ATV Bet*	**Polaris:** *Victory Motorcycle Bet*
Intuit: *Start-up Ad Campaign*	*Watercraft Bet (later exited)*	**Intuit:** *Software as Service Bet*
	Intuit: *Faced down Microsoft Money*	
	Faced down Microsoft Profit	

Adapted from Bhide, *Origin and Evolution of New Businesses,* by permission of Oxford University Press, Inc.

"checkbook-like" user interface for its Quicken product, and Polaris produced snowmobiles that were more durable and boasted higher performance. Both companies spent these early years winning the respect and trust of distributors and constantly improving the customer experience.

> One of the most important things a leader can do is learn to distinguish between a big bet and a bet that is merely risky.

Both companies, however, were likely to get stuck in the backwaters of their industries if they weren't willing to move out of their comfort zone. Both continued to place big bets, facing off against big competitors—Intuit against Microsoft and Polaris against Honda, Yamaha, Kawasaki, and Suzuki. Though big, these bets weren't irresponsible. Cook knew he had the best user interface, and he correctly calculated that if he made the right moves with consumers, they would wait for the new Windows version of Quicken rather than jump to Microsoft Money. Likewise, he knew from observing the hundreds of small businesses that were using Quicken for their business accounting system that QuickBooks could be a success. When Intuit launched Quick-Books in 1992, it earned the majority of its $84 million in annual revenue from selling Quicken. Today, while some 15 million people continue to use Quicken (to the tune of more than $200 million in 2006), Intuit now sells its QuickBooks product to more than 7 million small businesses, earning revenues of more than $750 million, which at 37 percent of the company's total revenues, makes it the largest segment of Intuit's business.[41] Though Polaris had never made an ATV before, the company realized that the snowmobile would make an excellent "platform" for a new kind of ATV. The entire worldwide snowmobile industry accounts for about 165,000 units sold each year, compared with an ATV industry that sells about 1.4 million units, at an average retail price of about $5,000 apiece.[42] And that shift paid off, as about 66 percent of Polaris's sales now come from ATVs. These bets gave Intuit and Polaris new sources of revenue, greater leverage with distribution channels, and increased profitability—making their futures far less uncertain.

TYPES OF BETS

Breakthrough companies combine different kinds of bets to help maximize long-term success.

Market bets. Bets that companies make about the kinds of markets they will enter. Polaris's bets on the ATV and their Victory motorcycle are examples of market bets.

Process bets. Companies can place bets that shift the competitive landscape, or that enable them to gain process efficiencies on their competitors. Intuit's process bet on direct-marketing capabilities allowed it to both lower its cost of entry and to influence the distribution channel's purchasing decisions.

Resource bets. Many firms make bets based upon the acquisition of resources to achieve an advantage. The types of resource bets range from proprietary technology and patents to people. Intuit made key acquisitions like QuickPay and TurboTax to jump-start their entry into the small business accounting and tax preparation markets, respectively.

Location bets. Companies also regularly make location bets about where to deploy their assets. Staubach bet that there was a national and maybe even a global market for his tenant representation strategy, which caused him to expand aggressively outside his home market of Dallas/Fort Worth.

Channel bets. Companies regularly exploit relationships with channels in ways that give them an advantage. Intuit placed a sizable channel bet when it began selling Quicken directly to consumers to help fuel interest from retailers. Channel bets are tricky, however, because they are difficult to change once they are put in place. It is important, therefore, to "peel the onion" especially carefully on any channel bets (see "Peeling the Onion," later in the chapter).

Polaris and Intuit both continue to place big bets on the future. Though the ATV market is large compared with the market for snowmobiles, the motorcycle market dwarfs both, which, unlike the other two, is a global market. Total sales of heavyweight motorcycles in 2005 were about $10 billion, with another $1 billion in overseas markets—making a fat target for Polaris's Victory line of motorcycles.[43]

Similarly, Intuit finds itself today moving into unfamiliar terrain as it expands beyond the market for packaged software into the online realm of software as a service. One of Intuit's initial forays into the Internet, Quicken.com, strangely enough, was a disaster. "We got caught up in the dot-com hype and created something that our customers weren't asking for," Scott Cook told us.[44] Now, more than six years later, Intuit is using lessons learned from the original Quicken.com debacle to offer its customers things they *have* asked for, like the ability to pay bills online or to purchase Google's AdWords for their small business.[45] As a result of bets like these, both Quicken and QuickBooks continue to gain in popularity, raking in about $1 billion combined in 2006.[46]

As Intuit was making these increasingly larger bets, what was happening to the other forty-six companies that got to the market *before* Intuit? The answer is they were mostly dying off one by one or were burrowing into small niches that were out of the line of sight of the major players.

MECA Software, once the market leader, was sold in 1996 to H&R Block, and its flagship program, Managing Your Money, was sold to a consortium of banks and eventually dropped out of existence. Why did MECA Software, which once had an enviable lead on Intuit, fail to capitalize on that lead? "We chose to sell to a much larger company in H&R Block, believing this would give us the tools to succeed. Instead, we got lost in their huge mass. H&R Block had priorities above and beyond consumer software," Eric Jacobsen, the former vice president of marketing at MECA Software, told us. "We had the premium personal finance product in the market and were getting roughly $200 for the product while others were getting $50. We had the best tax product on the market and were gaining share. But once you decide to sell, control falls out of your hands."[47]

As the example of Quicken.com above shows, not all bets pay off, however, and both Polaris and Intuit have played their own losing hands over the years. Polaris achieved a foothold in the personal watercraft market, only to abandon it later. Intuit initially opted to use banks as their distributors for their software, thinking that banks would promote the software to their customers as value-added services. While Intuit did achieve some success at convincing banks to resell the product through two years of dogged salesmanship, only the Bank of Hawaii achieved any success as a reseller.[48] More recent examples of bets that didn't pay off include Intuit's early and perhaps premature push into the electronic bill payment arena, as well as its now failed foray into online travel and expense-reporting tools. Overall, however, Cook told us that three out of every four bets Intuit has made have been successful drivers of the company's growth. "The key for us is to never stop betting and to drill that idea into our managers," Cook said.[49]

ESSENTIAL BUSINESS POKER SKILLS

Like in poker, the act of placing the right bet depends on a player's knowledge of the game, ability to calculate odds, understanding of the other players, and understanding of himself. Great business leaders use these same concepts to distinguish between a mere "two-of-a-kind" strategic opportunity and a "royal flush."

Understanding the Game. Breakthrough company executives are students of their industries just like poker pros are students of the game. Polaris employees are consumers of their own products. They proudly announce their "cylinder index"—a badge of honor based on horsepower that gives an employee the chance to brag about how many of the company's products they own. For instance, CEO Tom Tiller owns 23 Polaris vehicles—which adds up to a cylinder index of 105—and, Minnesota weather permitting, commutes to work on his Victory Vegas cruiser.[50]

Calculating the Odds. The ability to calculate the odds on the fly often determines the difference between winning and losing in a business situation. But Intuit didn't divine the odds of beating Microsoft from the air: They did heavy, on-the-ground research. During the few times that Intuit went off track, it was often, Cook told us, because company leaders failed to demand what he called, "rigor with urgency."[51] Cook reflected on the problems he saw cropping up in the company. What he saw was the ". . . lack of dealing with data . . . the lack of recognizing reality as it was happening and moving swiftly to readjust thinking."

Understanding the Other Players. What distinguishes top players from those who are merely good is their ability to "get inside the heads" of their competitors. When, in 1991, Microsoft abandoned its efforts to acquire Intuit and changed course by launching its own personal financial management software, Cook instructed a key lieutenant to read everything she could get her hands on regarding Bill Gates. Intuit even brought in a former Microsoft executive as an advisor. His whole job was to help the Intuit executive team understand how Microsoft approached things.[52]

Understanding Yourself. Another element that separates a great poker player from a good one is self-knowledge. It is the leader's willingness to get up every morning, look in the mirror, and be brutally honest with him or herself that leads to turning that mirror toward the organization as a whole. That is why Tom Tiller was so grouchy when we caught up with him in the fall of 2006. While Polaris was on track to post more than $1.7 billion in sales for the year, it wouldn't be enough to keep its remarkable streak of twenty-four consecutive years of record profit growth alive. Not only had Polaris's stock price stumbled, it had lost its overall market-share lead in the snowmobile business as well. "We lost focus on some of the key drivers of the business and we were slow to react to changes in the business," Tiller told us after emerging from a morning-long brainstorming session with his board. "We became victims of our own success. You begin to get a sense that you will always come out on top, no matter what. I think we are finally pissed off enough to go take back our position."[53]

PEELING THE ONION: MAKING YOUR BETS COUNT

The breakthrough companies we studied all combined a willingness to place bigger and bigger bets with the skill of placing the right bets. As we talked with breakthrough executives about how they decide which bets to place, they described a process we call "peeling the onion" on an investment decision. Peeling the onion, it turns out, is shorthand for a process of engaging in a spirited debate about which bets will best propel a company toward its strategic objectives. More so than at

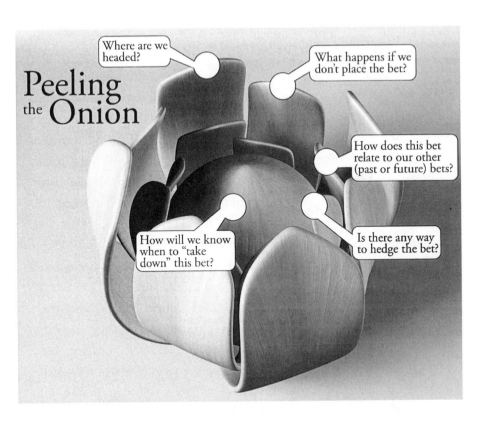

comparison companies, employees at several levels of breakthrough
companies were engaged in deep discussions about what quality of
bets the company is making (for more on this, see chapter 10: Building Breakthrough Capabilities). Though each breakthrough company
we studied has its own unique way of peeling the onion, the figure
below presents a list of questions that breakthrough companies tend
to ask themselves when preparing to place a big bet.

1. WHERE ARE WE HEADED?

No question is more important in this process of peeling the onion
than this one: When breakthrough companies are considering making
a bet, they fanatically return to the vision they have for the firm and to

their strategy for accomplishing it. One of the things that struck us as we talked with founders and early executives of breakthrough companies was the degree to which they refused to see their companies as merely bit players. As we saw in chapter 2, leaders of breakthrough companies envisioned their companies, even at their most nascent stages, of someday being important firms. A bold vision is what fuels a company's appetite for big bets. Any company that finds itself struggling to place big bets should revisit its vision. Does that vision, however, require the company to stretch or to merely state what the company does? As we spent time with breakthrough companies, we were impressed by how well people in the trenches understood where the company was headed and how it intended to get there. Sometimes that vision was recorded in a written statement, and often it was not. What was important was that a broad cross-section of company managers and employees understood and embraced it, and they regularly described the bets the company was contemplating in terms of how well the proposed bets appeared to serve the overall goal of the firm. Breakthrough managers ask themselves, "Does this bet, better than any other we can imagine, best position us to achieve our goal for this company?" If the answer is no, then the company is likely to pass on the bet.

2. WHAT HAPPENS IF WE DON'T PLACE THE BET?

If a bold vision provides the fuel for a company's willingness to place big bets, a well-thought-out strategy is its navigational system. Breakthrough companies not only link all of their bets to the company's objective; they also relate it to the company's strategy by asking, "What do we risk by *not* taking this bet?" In other words, can the company afford not to make a particular bet to either attack a new market or to defend an existing one?

As in poker, understanding how other players are likely to respond to your actions can be the critical difference between winning and losing. In poker, when one player is said to "go over the top" of another player during a hand, he has made an aggressive bet that causes the other players to fold. Consider the example of Polaris's approach to Arctic Cat, a rival based in Thief River Falls, Minnesota, just sixty miles from Polaris's home of Roseau. At one time, in the early 1980s, Arctic Cat and Polaris were roughly the same size with their fortunes tied to the seasonal snowmobile industry. When Polaris made its aggressive bid to enter the ATV market in 1985, however, Arctic Cat was slow to respond. As a result, ever since, the company has continued to struggle to establish itself as more than just a snowmobile company.[54]

Similarly, a company that aggressively defends a market, or that aggressively pursues a new market, may cause other companies to avoid attacking them. The bet a company places, therefore, can serve as an important signaling device to warn competitors about which markets or customers the company intends to defend vehemently.[55]

Companies can also "bluff" by attempting to keep their real intentions secret from competitors. One of the problems with engaging in discussions with a competitor on a potential merger is that through the due diligence process, that competitor is likely to learn a company's real capabilities and intentions. If the merger talks subsequently fall apart, the company has essentially lost its ability to "bluff." That's precisely what happened in 1991 when Microsoft approached Intuit about a potential merger. Through the due diligence process, Microsoft learned enough about Intuit to decide that it was vulnerable, at which point, it essentially scuttled the merger talks and decided to compete with Intuit head-to-head. Cook was so angered by this that when Microsoft tried again to buy Intuit in 1993, he refused to give Microsoft any proprietary information, insisting that if Microsoft wanted to buy Intuit, it could do so using only information on the company that was widely available to the public (Microsoft's second and final merger attempt was stopped by the U.S. Department of Justice because of anti-competition concerns).[56]

When thinking about the ramifications of not placing a bet, companies also ask themselves, "What are potential alternative bets, and how do they compare with the bet we might consider?" The breakthrough companies we studied tended to be ruthless prioritizers. It is not enough for them to make "good" investments. They view every dollar freed up for investment to be an important strategic opportunity, and they work hard to make sure that the bets they place represent the very best opportunity to move the business forward.

Companies all too often get into investment habits that merely extend past behaviors without stopping to think deeply about where the business is headed and how best to get there. Companies sometimes limit the range of investment possibilities they consider to what they can easily finance. Think about that for a minute: Many companies allow their strategy to be dictated by their lenders. Breakthrough companies, on the other hand, first determine the kinds of bets they need to place to get them in the right strategic position, then they figure out how to finance them. Some companies also mistakenly base investment decisions on extrapolations of investments made in years past. A clothing retailer like Chico's, for example, could have developed the bad habit of basing its investment decisions simply on the number of retail locations it planned to open each year. Similar companies might not have stopped to ask themselves how their industry might be changing and what new opportunities could be tapped. Chico's CEO Scott Edmonds, on the other hand, continues to monitor which segments of the apparel business are growing, especially as they relate to Chico's core customer: baby-boomer women. By listening to his customers complain about how Victoria's Secret failed to make intimate apparel that appealed to them, Edmonds saw an opportunity in 2004 for his company to enter a new market. He opened ten stores under a new brand called Soma, which featured a line of high-quality women's underwear and sleepwear. The line was sold in more than thirty-nine independent stores as well, and also, through boutique arrangements in many of the more than five hundred Chico's brand stores.[57]

> Breakthrough leaders guard against falling into the habit of established betting patterns by thinking deeply about where the market is going. With each bet they place, they ask themselves: Does this bet help us change the field of play in our market?

3. HOW DOES THIS BET RELATE TO OUR OTHER BETS?

Breakthrough companies understand that the power of a bet lies in its relation to other bets. When doing so, they often consider the following formula: One + One + One = Six. That's the math of the exponential bet, the art of linking bets together to build real advantages over your competitors. To the breakthrough companies we studied, a bet was never a stand-alone event—it was a step in the path of building a position of advantage. It was in discussions with breakthrough executives like Tom Tiller that we first came across the concept of an exponential bet, one that exploits a bet's relationship with previous bets to produce exponential results. Polaris, for example, has continued to leverage its early bets on building innovative features that its employees and customers recommended. But since snowmobiles are a seasonal product, Polaris dealers were slow in the summer, making it difficult for them to focus on the line. Since Polaris had focused so intensively on innovation in the snowmobile market, it was leveraging its technology and partners to construct some of the earliest, and safest, four-wheeled ATVs (Polaris's first ATV was essentially a snowmobile on wheels). The payoff from that bet was further increased when the Polaris Ranger—a utility version of an ATV—rolled out of chief engineer Chuck Baxter's skunk works garage, and became, at the time, the most profitable product in the Polaris lineup.[58]

A second and equally important issue in the linking of bets is the question of whether the firm has the resources (or the courage) necessary to pursue the opportunity after the original bet. In the words of Paychex founder Tom Golisano, "I've never made an investment in my life that only required the amount originally anticipated. These things always end up requiring lots more than you think."[59] When the Polaris board authorized the Victory Motorcycle, they authorized $20 million—despite the fact that competitors Excelsior and Indian were funded to the tune of $130 million and $70 million respectively.[60] Tom Tiller's first day as CEO at Polaris happened to be launch day. "The first Victories off the line lacked polish and detail," he told us (Polaris was in the habit of making tough, off-road vehicles), and reviewers rated the Victory as having the worst quality of any motorcycle on the road. More problematic, however, was the fact that each new bike cost Polaris about $3,000 more to produce than the company could sell it for. "We obviously had a problem," Tiller told us.[61]

Tiller and Polaris could have taken stock of their situation and decided that they didn't have the resources or the skills to invest in improving the Victory's quality, especially if their costs continued to soar. As stubborn Minnesotans, however, Polaris doubled-down on their bet and sent their engineers back to their drawing boards with the goal of not only improving the bike's style and design, but also reducing the cost to produce it. The result? The Polaris Victory Vegas was recently named by J. D. Powers as the best-quality motorcycle in the world.[62] And, perhaps more important, as competitors like Indian and Excelsior fade away, the Victory line, with expected sales of 9,000 bikes in 2006, is now consistently turning a profit for the company while offering its dealers the healthiest margins of any of the Polaris vehicles.[63]

4. HEDGING BETS

The fourth layer of the onion asks, "Is there any way to hedge this bet?" In 1990, Intuit competitor MECA Software, creator of Managing Your Money, put itself up for sale. Both Intuit and competitor ChipSoft wanted to buy MECA Software, which also sold a tax preparation package called TaxCut. The 800-pound gorilla, Microsoft, had also approached MECA Software about a deal. An intense round of negotiations quickly followed.[64] Intuit wanted to buy MECA Software for two reasons: (1) Managing Your Money was a direct competitor to Quicken, and the Intuit team feared that if Managing Your Money fell into the wrong hands, such as Microsoft, it might become a formidable competitor; (2) Intuit wanted to enter the tax preparation market and envisioned TaxCut as a short cut to get there. ChipSoft, on the other hand, was the market leader in the tax preparation market with its product TurboTax, and the Intuit team reasoned that if ChipSoft successfully purchased TaxCut and established a monopoly, Intuit would have a tougher time launching a tax preparation product of its own.

While Cook and his team were determined to win the bidding war against ChipSoft, they were wise enough to hedge their bet. Intuit knew that MECA Software didn't own the engineering rights to the TaxCut code, it merely licensed the marketing rights from the program's creator, Dan Caine. Intuit called Caine and talked to him about the pending sale of MECA Software. They learned that Caine was concerned that ChipSoft had targeted MECA Software as an acquisition simply to eliminate TaxCut as a competitor. As an engineer, Caine wanted to see things built, not shut down. Leveraging that motivation, Caine and Intuit cut a deal that would give Intuit a chance to license the TaxCut software for itself.[65] Not only was Caine now assured that his product would live on, Intuit had hedged its bet brilliantly by circumventing ChipSoft to ensure that it could move into the potentially lucrative tax preparation market even if it failed to acquire MECA Software. MECA Software eventually did agree to sell to ChipSoft, but after the deal raised the hackles of the U.S. Justice Department, H&R Block swooped in to acquire MECA Software and TaxCut instead.[66] With few options available to it, and with its engineering legs cut out from beneath it, ChipSoft reversed course and sold itself to Intuit.[67]

> Breakthrough companies often hedge their bets, but they don't hedge on their commitments to them. Once they decide to place a bet, they bring the full force of their efforts to bear on winning the bet.

Most of us understand the idea of hedging a bet: a move to minimize or protect against a loss by counterbalancing one transaction against another. We found numerous examples where breakthrough companies effectively hedged their bets, like Intuit was able to do by acquiring a license to TaxCut's engineering code. But when faced with a potential big bet, too many companies confuse this proactive process of hedging with another common definition of hedging, which is to "act in a noncommittal or ambiguous manner." This kind of hedging can have deadly results. Our study of breakthrough companies suggests that before making a bet, organizations are rife with controversy as members debate the merits of making the bet or not. The difference, however, is that once the bet is decided upon, the organization brings the full force of its commitment to bear. While these companies may place additional bets to make sure they "win, even if they lose," they don't "hedge" through indecision; they pursue victory with all their might.

5. KNOWING WHEN TO FOLD 'EM

Not all bets work out, and smart leaders, like good poker players, know when to fold a losing hand. Consider the example of Polaris's recent decision to scuttle its personal watercraft line (PWC). Launched in

1992, the Polaris PWC was a response to the rising demand for what an article in *Forbes* labeled "$3,000 to $6,000 water skis with handles and motors that shoot across the water at speeds of up to 40 miles an hour."[68] As with the ATV, Polaris saw the PWC market as another chance to use its manufacturing wherewithal to diversify beyond snowmobiles and to expand beyond its traditional markets in the colder northern climates. The Polaris product did well despite competing against well-known brands like Kawasaki's Jet Ski and Bombardier's Sea-Doo and, by 1995, PWC sales accounted for 10 percent of the company's total revenue.[69] By 2004, however, the personal watercraft trend had clearly peaked and Polaris made the decision to exit the market completely. "The industry grew at a 20 percent clip for a number of years before stabilizing around 1995," Tom Tiller told us without betraying an emotional attachment to the line. "We originally thought of the Jet-Ski as a 'snowmobile-on-water,' but the technologies weren't as transferable as we originally thought. We also recognized that the distribution channel for the Jet-Ski was more marine-oriented, which did not fit our dealer profile. So we stopped making them."[70]

Polaris's now defunct personal watercraft line is an example of how companies need to ask themselves, "How will we know when it is time to 'take down' the bet?" What is thought-provoking about this concept is not that entrepreneurial leaders would ask themselves this question, but rather that they ask themselves this question *before making the bet*. When this question is asked before making a bet, and answered with brutal honesty, it will illuminate all of the logic discussed in the previous three layers of the onion. The question asks the bettor to imagine what conditions would have to develop that would make the bet no longer meaningful. Answering this question (1) tests the company's commitment to the bet; (2) forces the team to reexamine alternative bets; and (3) causes the team to recalculate the odds that the bet no longer serves the company's best interest. The question also forces the team, at least for a moment, to divorce itself from whatever emotional momentum may have developed in favor of the bet—and to note that the bet is dependent upon a set of conditions that may, in fact, change. By thinking through beforehand how changes in conditions might change the appropriateness of the bet—the company sets itself up to adapt effectively as the environment around it changes.

WHAT ABOUT LUCK?

In presenting our preliminary findings on upping the ante to several thousand executives in Europe, Asia, Australia, and the United States, the conversation always turns inevitably to the question of luck. Is it possible, we are often asked, that the breakthrough companies we studied were simply luckier than companies that didn't break through? What we did find interesting is that in conducting more than a hundred interviews of members from all levels of our breakthrough companies, not one person attributed his success to luck. Rather, the common theme from our interviews was that each of the breakthrough companies was founded on a bet on a rising market or markets, and the company stoked its growth by continuing to place bets on its future. In other words, breakthrough companies created their own luck through hard work and timing.

We would not be so naïve as to suggest that luck did not play some role in the success of any or all of the breakthrough companies. In studying the trajectory of companies like Intuit and Polaris, we were struck by how many scenarios that could have gone against the companies worked out in the end as a result of factors often outside the company's control—like the widespread adoption of personal computers or the rise in popularity of recreational vehicles like ATVs and motorcycles. At the same time, we were struck by how often outside factors also negatively impacted the companies we studied, and yet they still found a way to prevail. We considered for some time whether it might be possible to find some meaningful measure of luck that would enable us to test whether breakthrough companies were more fortunate than their peers, but soon gave up the attempt. What appears to be bad luck in the short term often ends up being neutral, or even good luck, in the long term. The opposite is also true. It would be difficult, if not impossible, to separate true luck from the actions of companies and their competitors. We believe that, in the end, both good luck and bad luck are randomly distributed. While luck may be a factor in determining whether or not a firm breaks through, it is not a factor upon which we advise companies to depend. In the words of R. E. Shay: "Depend on the rabbit's foot if you will, but remember, it didn't work for the rabbit."[71]

UPPING THE ANTE

The Key Ideas

1. One distinguishing characteristic that breakthrough companies share is a willingness to "up the ante" as the business grows.

2. A willingness to place big bets is not, by itself, sufficient. Breakthrough companies demonstrate significantly higher levels of skill at placing bets than do comparison companies.

3. Unlike gambling bets, bets in business are investments that can, over time, tip the odds in a company's favor. What's more, business bets can be cumulative—they can build on each other to create real advantages in the marketplace.

4. There are five basic types of bets: market bets, process bets, resource bets, location bets, and channel bets.

5. As in poker, a person wishing to master the art of the effective bet will focus on (a) understanding the game; (b) calculating the odds; (c) understanding his competitors; and (d) understanding himself and his company.

6. To optimize any particular bet, a team should "peel the onion" on the decision.

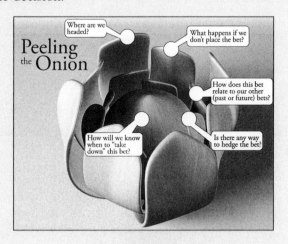

Peeling the Onion

Where are we headed?

What happens if we don't place the bet?

How does this bet relate to our other (past or future) bets?

How will we know when to "take down" this bet?

Is there any way to hedge the bet?

UPPING THE ANTE "SQUIRTS FROM THE GRAPEFRUIT"
(Findings That Surprised Us)

1. Contrary to conventional wisdom, entrepreneurial leaders are not necessarily big risk takers. Our analysis of more than 250 CEOs of America's fastest growing companies suggests that entrepreneurs are distributed across the entire risk-tolerance spectrum.

2. Only a fraction of new firms are started with a "new to the world" idea—those start-ups that usually get all the press. Seventy-one percent of new firms that are started merely imitate an existing product or service.

3. Surprisingly, hesitancy by long-term employees may slow a company's willingness to place bigger bets. Breakthrough companies indicated that they had to actively manage employees' appetite for new and bigger bets.

4. Though we expected that the presence of outside investors would make a company more likely to place big bets, this turned out not to be true all the time. Outside investors tend to make companies more or less likely to place big bets depending on where the investor is in his "fund cycle" and where the company in question fits in the investor's overall investment portfolio.

BREAKTHROUGH IN PRACTICE
Tips for Upping the Ante

1. Ask a group in your company to identify all the potential bets they can think of that they believe would best take the company to the next level. Next, ask the group to "peel the onion" on the top three to five ideas.

2. Choose two of the most promising bets that you believe your company might make in the next one to three years. Go to *www.breakthroughcompany.com/thegamble* and use the online "business poker hand" tool to compare and contrast the attractiveness of each bet.

3. Ask the group to identify three to five ways in which the company currently spends money that don't produce maximum possible strategic results. Cut those areas and redeploy the resources to your best bet.

5

BUILDING COMPANY CHARACTER

A man's character is his fate.

HERACLITUS

W HEN OUR RESEARCH team arrived at Paychex headquarters in Rochester, New York, the wintry weather was, as even full-time residents admitted, harsh. We were running late for our appointment and as we pulled into the parking lot, there wasn't an open spot for what seemed like miles. I shivered at the thought of scurrying into the teeth of that infamous Lake Ontario wind. Then we noticed a few openings, right up close to the main entrance. Alas, the spots were clearly marked: "For Expectant Mothers Only."[1] A quick poll of the research team revealed our lack of qualification, so we cranked up the heat and drove on. Never before had I wished to be one of those lucky expectant mothers.

If you pay attention to first impressions, companies tell you a lot about themselves. Want to know what a company considers to be important? Look around, the clues are probably right in front of you. Even the smallest details, like a parking policy, choice of receptionist, or a building's layout can reveal a company's priorities. If you notice things like a pricey art collection on the walls of the executive office wing, or a private dining room, or a line of prime reserved parking places a mile long—that company is telling you it honors its executives above all. Paychex sends the opposite message: No matter who you are, unless you are expecting a baby, get here early or walk. Even Jon Judge, a longtime IBM executive who succeeded founder Tom Golisano as CEO of Paychex in 2004, has to fight, just like we did, to get a choice parking spot.[2]

> At Paychex, a "nobody's special" ethic permeates the firm and helps to ensure that all employees feel that their contributions are important to the long-term success of the firm. It's tough to argue with its results; with only $1.8 billion in revenue, the company had a market cap at the end of 2006 of $15 billion.

And as we dug deeper by talking to the people at Paychex, it was clear that a nobody-gets-special-treatment ethic permeates the entire business. Consider that for the company's first thirty years, no one—including Tom Golisano, who is perennially listed on *Forbes*'s list of the richest Americans—was allowed to list a title on his or her business card. "We did this for a reason," Golisano told us. "Leaving off the titles emphasized humility and impartiality."[3] Given this foundation, it shouldn't be a surprise to learn, for example, that Paychex offers all its employees—executives and janitorial engineers alike—the same selection of benefits and healthcare packages. Walter Turek may be a major shareholder after heading up the company's sales and marketing efforts for the past two plus decades, but he gets the same number of vacation days each year as anyone with twenty-four years of service would.[4] The people at Paychex have embraced the idea that since everyone performs an important role in the company, each and every one deserves to be treated accordingly. "We spend a lot of time thinking about how to build an atmosphere of respect around here," Judge told us. "As adults, we spend the majority of waking hours at work and we deserve to do work that people think is valuable. And you don't have to give people carousels and free popcorn to do that. We are trying to build a place where people get up in the morning and get excited about what they are going to do that day."[5]

When you consider that Paychex employs more than 11,000 people to serve its 543,000 clients, the company's approach seems to be working.[6] From its humble beginnings in 1971, when most people scoffed at Tom Golisano's idea that there was a market for small business payroll services, the company has been setting records ever since. At the time of this writing, Paychex had posted sixteen consecutive years of record revenues, net income, and earnings per share, and could boast of a market capitalization of more than $15 billion. Perhaps even more impressively, the company earned $1.1 billion in gross profit on $1.79 billion in revenues in 2006; that works out to about $163,000 of *profit* per employee.[7] Those kinds of numbers will earn you some respect.

And the amazing thing is that of all the breakthrough companies, Paychex was the most difficult to find a comparison for. Why? Because Paychex doesn't often compete directly with either the literally thousands of mom-and-pop–style processors or the big corporate payroll providers like ADP and when it has come across rivals of a similar size, it has simply acquired them. Probably the best example of this was a Massachusetts-based company called InterPay. Also founded in 1971, InterPay was originally a family-run company that catered to customers in the northeast and middle Atlantic states. By 1995 it had expanded nationally, growing to be the fourth largest payroll processor in the country behind ADP, Ceridian, and Paychex. That expansion drew the attention of Fleet Financial Group, the multibillion-dollar bank, which bought the company with the idea of selling its services to its small business customer base. After InterPay's acquisition by Fleet made it a subsidiary mired in a corporate bureaucracy, the payroll processor struggled to find an identity and compete with Paychex. Even InterPay's big-name partnerships like the one forged with Staples in 1999 gained it little ground. In 2003, just eight years after Fleet bought InterPay, the bank, tired of battling and losing to Paychex, sold InterPay to its rival for $155 million and entered into a co-branding deal so that Paychex would continue to serve its small business customers.[8]

The manner in which a company's people behave and interact

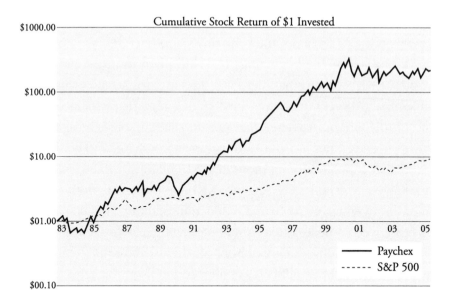

with each other, with customers, and even with visitors, is a significant clue as to whether that company can break through or not. You might think we're talking about a set of corporate values, but not quite. During our fieldwork, we noted that many of the firms we studied had hired consultants to help them define and articulate what would become their "core values." All too often, however, the resulting values statements were not only bland and obvious; they also seemed disconnected with how the company operated. Several of the breakthrough companies have written down their values as well, yet, as we explored what really made these companies tick, we often uncovered a foundation that was far more potent and dynamic than any words on a piece of paper.

> Anyone can write a values statement. Building a company with character is another thing indeed. We found a bedrock of character beneath the performance of all nine break-through companies—with a focus on lining up what people say with what they actually do.

Of course, lots of companies talk about values. What distinguishes the breakthrough companies from the pack is that they tend to focus on character instead. Companies can be said to have character in much the same way people do. And just like people, there are companies of high moral character and others that are completely lacking in character. Unlike values, which refer to what a person professes to believe in, *character* captures something more significant—how a person acts. The same definition applies to an organization: A company's character is measured not by what it says it stands for but by how it actually operates.

This distinction between a set of stated values and character is perhaps best expressed in this quote from the Dhammapada (Sayings of the Buddha):

The thought manifests as the word; The word manifests as the deed; The deed develops into habit; And habit hardens into character.

In other words, the values (words) that matter most in a company are those acted upon daily (deeds) and that "harden" over time into habits. Everything else is just PR. Here's a way to define a company's character:

Company Character = values translated into action

What is written in a statement of values is of little importance if those values are not powerfully reflected in how people in the company act. Companies may in fact be better off without any value statement at all because failing to act on those printed values could create unrealistic expectations and expose company leaders as hypocrites.

"NO SUCH THING AS CORPORATE CULTURE"

Some may wonder why we use the term "character" instead of "corporate culture"—it seems to us that the idea of a corporate culture brings with it too much baggage. Borrowing the term from the field of anthropology, many business observers have given the impression that culture is something largely beyond the control of individuals in an organization. Culture is viewed as something *out there*, to be studied and rectified by consultants. The idea of organizational character is different. Since character measures how we as a group of individuals act, we are reminded that each of us has an individual responsibility for determining our company's character. This point was driven home to us when, during our fieldwork, one executive told us, "There is no such thing as corporate culture, there is only how we treat each other."

We learned to distinguish between values and company character quite by accident during our research. Our favorite way to lead off an interview was to ask, "You've really built something special here. What makes this company so successful?" The question would light most people's faces right up and, without even a pause to think, they would start talking about the positive impact that the company has had on people's lives. Rather than talking about strategy, product development, or distribution systems as the key to the company's success, these folks focused first on the way their company treated its people and its customers. In other words, they began by discussing their company's character. Later in the interview, when we actually asked if the company had a statement of values, our interviewee's eyes often glazed over a bit in response. It was clear that to most people, talking about how the company acted was a lot more interesting than what its stated values were.

CHARACTER-ISTICS OF BREAKTHROUGH COMPANIES

Every breakthrough company approached the issue of company values in a slightly different way. When the Express organization gathers once a year for their annual meeting, they vote on what they call their "family values."[9] The Staubach Company has its constitution, and Fastenal hands out wallet-sized, laminated copies of its values. Paychex, on the other hand, doesn't have a printed list of values. Neither does Chico's or the SAS Institute. Similarly, when we talked to Bob Nygaard at Polaris about his company's value statement, he dismissed it with a wave of his hand, telling us it was something a consultant helped them draw up. "What I can tell you is that no one who works here would do anything to put our company in harm's way."[10]

Although each of the breakthrough companies had a unique approach to articulating values, they share several important character attributes when it comes to how they treat their employees and their customers, and even how they spend their money.

GIVE FOLKS A FAIR DEAL

When we interviewed Jim Goodnight, founder of North Carolina–based SAS, he told us that his two goals right from the company's start in 1976 were to make software that customers needed and, just as important, to create an environment that his employees would enjoy working in. "I wanted a place where life's distractions wouldn't get in the way so that the creative juices could flow," Goodnight told us.[11]

Goodnight was a graduate student at North Carolina State University when he and his SAS cofounders ventured out on their own after the academic funding for their statistical analysis software project ran out. In launching SAS, they sought to make their company more collegial than the corporate environment of General Electric, where

Goodnight worked on a project for NASA while finishing his PhD. While he found the work at GE stimulating—he was working on a project for the Apollo space program—he felt like someone was always looking over his shoulder. Things would be different at his company, he vowed, and one way he accomplished that was by giving most employees at SAS their own private office. "I know for a fact that most companies just give people cubicles to work in," Goodnight said. "What we tried to do was to treat people who joined the company as we ourselves wanted to be treated."[12]

SAS has become famous, among working mothers especially, for its vast array of benefits, which includes the private offices on a park-like, 300-acre campus, but also onsite doctors and nurses, a top-notch day-care facility, and even a hairdresser who takes walk-ins. Goodnight's goal of treating people fairly has also proven to be a great business strategy: SAS has increased its revenues every year since 1976 and is now considered the largest privately held software company in the world.[13]

Compare that performance with that of SPSS, a company similar to SAS in many ways, including its campus roots. SPSS got its start in 1971 at Stanford University, and later at the University of Chicago. The company's name is actually an acronym for Statistical Package for the Social Sciences. By the early 1980s, each firm was earning about $20 million a year. But by the early 1990s the two companies' paths diverged. Norman Nie, who cofounded SPSS, left the company in 1992, two years after a group of venture capitalists took a stake in the firm, and one year before SPSS went public. SPSS then engaged in a flurry of acquisitions to try to fuel its growth, shed a lot of skilled workers, and actually began reducing the amount it invested in R&D.[14] SAS, on the other hand, continued under the same management team, made few acquisitions, took no outside capital, and continued to increase its R&D investments, which equal, on average, 24 percent of revenue. The results are telling: While SPSS posted revenues of more than $261 million in 2006, SAS posted its thirty-first straight year of growth,

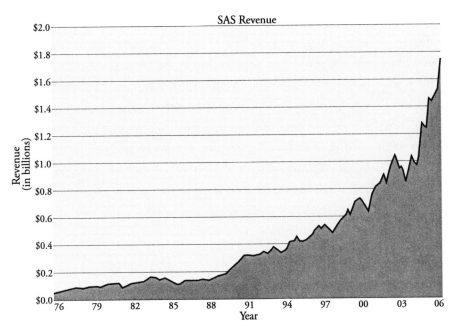

SAS is a private company that does not publicly share information on company profitability.

topping out at $1.9 billion in sales. Today SAS works with 96 of the top firms listed on the 2007 *Fortune* Global 500 list. "We continue to invest in our people so we don't need to make acquisitions," Goodnight told us. "While we have done a few, buying other companies is really about satisfying the CEO's ego more than anything else."[15]

This idea that people perform better when they are treated fairly may, in fact, have biological roots. In 2003, the science journal *Nature* published a study by Sarah F. Brosnan and Frans B. M. de Waal called "Monkeys Reject Unequal Pay,"[16] in which the scientists observed how brown capuchin monkeys reacted to unequal distributions of food.

Cucumbers, it turns out, are the meat and potatoes of the capuchin diet, while grapes are a decadent dessert. In their study, Brosnan and de Waal observed how the monkeys reacted to changes in the distribution of these treats. They taught the monkeys a basic exchange rate: The monkeys earned pebbles for good behavior, which they could then exchange for food. The results were fascinating: The monkeys quickly grew unhappy whenever the scientists gave them a piece of cucumber while their mates received a grape in a similar exchange. The scientists then watched the drama unfold as they handed a grape to a monkey who didn't even have a pebble to exchange. On these occasions, the researchers reported, the other monkeys, now irate, often went so far as to toss their cucumbers away and refuse to participate any further. "During the evolution of cooperation, it may have become critical for individuals to compare their own efforts and pay-offs with those of others," the researchers wrote. "Negative reactions may occur when expectations are violated."

> A sense of fairness may have biological roots. When brown capuchin monkeys think that other monkeys are receiving preferential treatment in an experiment, they will sometimes throw away food in protest.

Fairness, however, doesn't mean that all people expect to be paid equally. Workers understand that different roles in an organization merit different levels of pay. What really turns these workers off, it seems, is when executives rack up boatloads of options and enjoy gold-plated perks at the same time that everyone else's benefits are being cut. Companies that fail to strive for a level of fairness shouldn't be surprised to find that the "cucumbers" their unhappy employees are throwing away include the company's own competitiveness.

While each of the breakthrough companies strived for an environment of fairness, each had their own approach to achieving it. For example, Fastenal founder Bob Kierlin limited his own compensation to $125,000 per year, created an employee stock option program out of his own holdings, and built a compensation program that enables Fastenal employees to earn bonuses equal to or greater than 50 percent of their base salary.[17] Jim Goodnight created an almost utopian work environment, giving everyone at SAS access to an amazing array of benefits. Express cofounders Bob Funk and Bill Stoller both own Express franchises, and follow the same set of rules and guidelines as any other franchisee.[18] Not only does Paychex reserve parking spaces for expectant mothers, it makes every employee an owner through the distribution of stock options and grants. Tom Golisano, on the other hand, never received any options in his thirty-year term behind the Paychex wheel (he was already a big stockholder), and when he handed off the CEO role, in an era when severance packages run in the hundreds of millions of dollars, all he took were his desk and credenza, scuffs and scratches included. "I have always stressed how important it is that we consistently treat everyone the same," Golisano told us.[19]

Breakthrough companies also applied their fairness standard to their customers. Paychex customers, for example, don't have contracts: If they are unhappy with the company's service, they can leave without penalty.[20] If Roger Staubach's clients don't think their Staubach Company broker provided them with enough bang for the buck, they can reduce the fee paid to that broker by an amount they deem fair.[21] Scott Cook sent his engineers to customers' homes to see where they ran into problems installing and using products like Quicken and QuickBooks. "We wanted to ensure that we were always helping our customers solve their biggest problems," Cook told us.[22]

If you license SAS software, you are guaranteed unlimited technical support at no additional charge for as long as you do business with SAS. "It seems only fair to me that if someone pays us to provide them with software, it is our job to make sure it works for them," Goodnight told us.[23] So you can imagine Goodnight's shock when, in October 2006, he received a memo from his Oracle sales rep, noting that the Oracle tech support team had logged more than 300 bugs from SAS employees trying to get the Oracle system they had purchased to work correctly. The memo urged Goodnight and SAS to consider purchasing a premium support package that would prioritize those bug fix requests ahead of Oracle's other 300,000 customers. "They are suggesting we pay them more to get the bugs fixed sooner," Jim Goodnight wrote in response. "Why then are we already paying them an annual maintenance fee?"[24]

BELIEVE IN PEOPLE

When I was just starting out in business, I got to know the owner of a local company. I remember that shortly after I met him, he gave me some unsolicited advice. "The thing you need to know about business is that buyers are liars," he told me. "Don't believe anything they say to you. They are the enemy and you win when you get their money." I was jolted by this comment because it conflicted with my sense of how the world works. I have always believed that most people are basically honest and just want a fair deal. Then one day not long after that conversation, I discovered the following quote from Ralph Waldo Emerson:[25]

> *People seem not to see that their opinion of the world is also a confession of their character.*

At that moment I realized that the business owner's comment was a reflection of his own individual character and, over time, that point of view became the character of his company (which, incidentally, got stuck at under $10 million a year in revenue and never went anywhere). Imagine if Paychex, which gets two-thirds of its new customers through referrals, adopted such a mindset. Their referrals would trickle to nothing. If buyers were really liars, SAS, which gives away its tech support service, would go bankrupt running down their requests. When companies demonstrate that they believe in their customers and strive to cut a fair deal, their customers reciprocate.

When we asked Bob Kierlin about what made Fastenal so successful, he paused for just a moment and said, "We started by believing in what people could do. Then we figured out how to create an environment where ordinary people could do extraordinary things." That meant believing that he could hire people from just about any walk of life to first run Fastenal's stores and warehouses and then, perhaps, the entire operation. "We hired attitude and trained aptitude," Kierlin also told us.[26]

> A company's view of people is an unmistakable reflection of its organizational character. If it sees people as selfish, lazy, and unmotivated—that's the kind of people it will attract. If it believes in the potential of people to do great things, and has competent leadership, its people will rise to the occasion.

This key point Kierlin hit upon is another essential aspect of building a company's character: A breakthrough company believes in its people, and that people at all levels of the organization can and should be high performers. Those who fail to live up to those expectations don't last. Breakthrough companies refuse to limit their velocity to the speed of the slowest player on the team. Instead, breakthrough companies strive first to hire people of character, and the performance tends to take care of itself.

So how do you find the people with character? Lee Hein, a regional vice president at Fastenal who coaches some three hundred store managers from St. Louis to Denver, says that even after twenty-three years, he's still figuring that out. "The first thing I do in an interview is bore in on who they really are," he told us. "I've got a hundred questions I can ask that come from ten different directions. I've gotten to where I can figure out pretty quickly what makes a person tick." With that, he turned the tables on me and started an impromptu interview. "What's most important to you, Keith?" he asked. "Uh, my family," I stammered. "That's an interesting response. Why do you think you gave that answer?" he fired back. He continued peppering me with questions like these for about ten minutes, and then sat back in his chair and fell silent.[27] I was pretty sure he had my number.

In the end, because so many new employees come to Fastenal with little or no experience in the world of industrial distribution, Hein can't focus on a résumé. He looks to examples of someone's work ethic instead. That's also why some 30 percent of Fastenal's workforce is made up of part-time workers. The company brings potential store managers on part-time for up to six months so it can gauge their aptitude and hunger to grow within the company. "I want someone who is wired to act like an owner," he told us.[28] Other breakthrough leaders also told us about what they focused on when they look for new recruits. Tom Golisano values the ability to listen—even if no one is talking. "When Tom Golisano interviewed me, I was a bit uncomfortable at first," Laura Saxby Lynch, the corporate communications director at Paychex, told us. "There were long pauses when he was thinking and I kept quiet. When he finally asked me an accounting question and I admitted that I wasn't sure I knew the answer, I could tell he liked that I could admit that I didn't know something."[29] Roger Staubach told us he valued a person's consistency in behavior and the ability to persevere—even in a time of personal crisis.[30] And the reason is clear: The leaders of breakthrough companies put enormous faith—and power—in the hands of their employees. These leaders trust that their employees' actions will honor the company, not betray it.

Once you get people of character on board, you've got to do something with them, and the breakthrough companies we studied excelled at getting the most out of their people. We were struck by how carefully and precisely the companies had defined their business models so that they could build jobs in which people know exactly what was expected of them and also had the tools to achieve high levels of performance. Companies like Fastenal, Paychex, and Staubach have figured out intuitively what Claremont Graduate University scholar Mihaly Csikszentmihalyi learned when he asked thousands of people to log their mood as they went through the rigors of their day. He found that people tended to be most creative, effective, and connected to their work when they were challenged without being defeated. People flourish, he found, when they are given, "clear goals, unambiguous feedback, and a sense of control."[31]

There are times, of course, when the filter fails and people who just don't fit join the organization. They may actually perform well, but rub their fellow employees or customers the wrong way. "The hardest decisions are those that involve changes with top performers," Blair Bryan of Staubach told us, a problem of particular note in the commission-driven real estate industry. "If someone pollutes the organization and compromises its values and character, you have to have the courage to make those hard decisions even if, in the short term, it costs the company money. In the end, the organization is better off for it."[32]

BE A STRATEGIC MISER

Perhaps owing to their early years as cash-strapped start-ups, the breakthrough companies are a frugal bunch. Scan the balance sheets of breakthrough companies like Paychex, Fastenal, and ADTRAN and, aside from a mortgage or two, you won't find much debt. The folks at Fastenal, in fact, are quite famous for their penny-pinching ways. After seeing 1980s-vintage dot matrix printers and Formica-topped conference tables during our visit to Fastenal headquarters, we weren't surprised to learn that *Inc.* magazine and *The Wall Street Journal* each named Bob Kierlin the cheapest CEO in America.[33]

Fastenal built a package sorting system for its massive warehouse in Winona for just a few million dollars. When a team from FedEx visited to see the system, they said a similar system had cost them several times the amount Fastenal had spent.[34] Polaris, which invested twenty million dollars just five years ago to launch its new Victory line of motorcycles, is already operating in the free-and-clear and turning a profit. Compare that to the story of Indian motorcycles, a would-be competitor of Polaris, into which private equity investors plowed more than $100 million in a failed attempt to resurrect the brand.[35] Even SAS, which employs a staff of more than 120 specialists to operate and improve its employee benefits program, doesn't start a new benefit program unless it can show a return on investment.[36]

> Breakthrough companies pride themselves on finding ways
> to cut costs in areas that don't matter much, but generously
> ladle resources into areas they know will give them an edge.

But calling Kierlin and the other breakthrough CEOs cheap is an oversimplification: They scrimp on the frivolities so they can spend real money where it counts. Paychex has earned a coveted spot on *Training* magazine's list of the top 100 training organizations six years running,[37] and when you walk into the Paychex headquarters in Rochester, which doubles as the University of Paychex, you immediately see why. As you walk into the building, your eyes are drawn upward. The five-story interior is circular, like a tower, and is lined with a honeycomb of glass-walled training rooms. Almost every week of the year, Paychex flies employees from all over the country to receive training through some forty instructor-led programs, twenty-three of which cover the nuances of payroll processing and benefits management and are certified for college credit. About half of Paychex's 11,000 employees spend at least a week each year training in Rochester. All employees receive on average an astounding 121 hours of training each year. That's why, if necessary, a single Paychex payroll specialist can support more than 200 customers.[38]

Even supposedly cheap Fastenal offers college-level training to its employees through its Fastenal School of Business, which receives a budget equivalent to 2 percent of the company's payroll. The school, however, is not a money sinkhole. Peter Guidinger, a PhD who has been running the school since its start in 1999, says it produces a 10-to-1 return on investment for its two-week new-store-employee training program. In one study he ran, Guidinger found that managers increased store revenues by 10 percent on average after attending at least a week's worth of sales training.[39]

Investing in a company's people doesn't always have to involve classroom training, either. Consider again that Polaris keeps a fleet of dozens of snowmobiles and ATVs available for employees to check out on weekends—for free.[40] Not only has Polaris set aside the cost of the vehicles, it covers the cost of insurance as well. While that might sound like just a nice employee perk, it is actually an investment by the company. "When employees ride our products, they come up with great ideas on how to improve them," CEO Tom Tiller told us.[41]

MAKE YOUR WORD COUNT

When it comes to choosing our friends, we rarely stick with those people who consistently fail to follow through on what they say they are going to do, whether it be meeting up for a lunch date or even a promise of a phone call. Breakthrough companies are infused with a passion for following through on commitments. We were struck by the fact that, to the person, each of the breakthrough leaders was someone who chose their words carefully. It was easy to get the impression that when they said they were going to do something, they followed through. As the Buddhist text we referred to earlier said, what people say becomes what they do: the building blocks of character.

CASE STUDY IN CHARACTER: SHAMROCK FOODS
Making Your Word Count

Although Phoenix-based Shamrock Foods was already the biggest food distributor in its region, CEO Kent McClelland was worried: A few of his national competitors were using technology to radically drive down costs for national restaurant chains, and Kent believed that it was time for Shamrock to step up its game as well.

Kent asked us in early 2006 to help him and the top thirty people in his company put together a 36-month plan to significantly extend Shamrock's strategic lead. Specifically, the group decided that Shamrock needed to build a separate platform to service large national accounts and to radically optimize its logistics and warehousing processes. A year later, however, he was unhappy with the rate of change at Shamrock.

A quick survey in early 2007 of the top thirty-five people in the firm identified one of the problems: People in the firm weren't saying what they really thought. Perhaps owing partly to history (Shamrock is a 100-year-old firm still owned by the founding family), people at Shamrock are nice, sometimes too nice. And in the interest of niceness, sometimes people avoided confrontation. It turned out the team didn't agree as much as we thought about what the firm's key strategic imperatives should be, which caused a lack of focus.

We locked the team in a room for about sixteen hours, and put the key issue on the table: How could people at Shamrock learn to raise tough and controversial issues without losing the mutual respect and camaraderie that they so valued? How, in other words, could they better make their words count? A floodgate of discussion was unleashed. We learned that people in the divisions were concerned that if the national account business was pulled out of their regions and centralized, they might have difficulty rationalizing their costs over the lower revenue base. Others were concerned that the move would upset compensation systems at Shamrock. Still others felt that the company was pursuing too many priorities at once, and should set up the national accounts platform before seeking additional acquisitions. The problem was, people weren't saying what they were thinking. They weren't "making their words count."

Once these issues were out in the open, the group quickly came up with solutions to all of them. Four hours later, the senior executives gathered and hammered out a detailed plan of how to move forward, knowing that it had the full support of the leadership team. The team is now meeting all its milestones on the transformation plan.

One area where following through on commitments clearly serves companies well is in their relationship with shareholders. Board meetings and earning forecasts are treated with respect and energy, since what the company says at these events becomes a commitment to action. While many public companies complain that Wall Street's expectations trip them up, breakthrough leaders seem to embrace them. When we asked Tom Golisano if he thought it was a liability to be a public company, he scoffed. "It was the best thing we ever did," he told us. "Not only did we get the resources we needed, but it gives us credibility with our clients."[42] Indeed, when you are a company like Paychex, which holds billions of dollars of payroll taxes for its clients, doing what you say you are going to do doesn't just mean staying in business, it could mean staying out of jail.

And when breakthrough companies say they stand for something, they take action to back it up. For example, Roger Staubach talks about how his company, unlike many of its competitors in the real estate industry, will succeed only through exceeding its customers' expectations. To back that up, the company not only offers its money-back guarantee, it rewards its top employees each year—anyone from a broker to a receptionist—based on a number of criteria, including customer service and individual performance.[43]

> There is no substitute for doing what you say you are going to do. Aligning words and deeds is the single most important building block in creating strong company character.

Intuit cofounder Scott Cook told us a story about a team that worked for Intuit during the dot-com years, after the company had shed its start-up skin and become a force in the software world. The Internet revolution had caused upheaval in the company, with many executives, including this particular team, worrying that unless Intuit started launching new online products, the company would be lapped by the legions of new upstarts entering the market. So they rushed straight in, spending two years and several million dollars building the original version of Quicken.com. The project bombed. Intuit's customers had never asked for Quicken.com and they refused to use it: The project was a failure. "The problem," Cook told us, "was that this particular team chased its own dream and forgot to make good on the company's mantra of only delivering answers to the customer's biggest problems."[44]

LEADERSHIP AND COMPANY CHARACTER

What is clear is that character begins with the leader. Many of the leaders of our breakthrough companies believe that building character throughout their firms is their number one priority. CEOs like Jon Judge and Jim Goodnight continue to grow their organizations by surrounding themselves not only with talent, but also with character. As the business grows beyond the day-to-day reach of its leader, and as decision making is pushed down, the importance of the leader's setting an example regarding the firm's commitment to character becomes paramount.

> What one characteristic did all of the breakthrough CEOs we studied share? Charisma. But it turns out that the word "charisma" doesn't mean what many people think it does. Charismatic leaders inspire us with their character.

What quality is most important for breakthrough leadership? Our study suggests it may well be charisma. Wait, you say, hasn't it been shown that the stereotypical "charismatic" leader is actually bad for business? We would argue the contrary—charisma is in short supply today. Yes, narcissistic, selfish, greedy, and arrogant leaders are bad for business, but these characteristics are not the roots of charisma. The true definition of the word "charisma" has actually been mangled in modern usage. Most people use the term today to talk about people with celebrity appeal, people with George Clooney's good looks, Bill Clinton's ability to connect with an audience, or Sean Connery's suave demeanor. But the early-twentieth-century sociologist Max Weber meant something very different when he first used the term to help define leadership. Weber wrote that leaders get their power from three sources: (1) traditional sources (i.e., kings and priests); (2) rational sources (as in, it is my "role" in the company to follow this particular person); and (3) charisma, which Weber defined as "a devotion to the exceptional sanctity, heroism, or exemplary *character* of an individual person" (emphasis added).[45] People don't use the word "sanctity" much anymore, but it refers to something being sacred. As we wandered the halls of breakthrough companies and spent time with everyone from truck drivers to store managers to senior vice presidents, we learned that for each of the breakthrough companies, character is sacred.

As an ordained minister, Express Personnel Services cofounder Bob Funk knows something about the sacred. In building Express, he and his partner Bill Stoller have tried to put a commitment to character above all else. In the early 1990s, Funk and his management team decided that they needed to put in a new Microsoft Windows–based computer system that would not only be Y2K compliant, but would also improve communication and reporting between the home office in Oklahoma City and the franchise offices operating around the country.[46] Funk envisioned a system that let a franchisee type in information about a new job candidate on their end and that person's paycheck would spit out in Oklahoma City. Many franchises were still using manual time cards, and there was a lot of anticipation for this new system. At about the same time, Sam and Pam Higdon had just purchased their first Express franchise in Durham, North Carolina. They had heard rumblings about the new computer system, but were told they should just stick to buying equipment sufficient to run the existing Express software. "I was concerned that we would soon have to pay to upgrade our computers on top of the franchise fee," Sam Higdon told us. "But the COO at the time, Dave Gillogly, told me that if we needed new equipment when the new system came out, Express would cover it. I never got it in writing or anything, but I believed him."[47]

What Higdon didn't know at the time was that Express had spent years trying to perfect its new computer system. When the new system was finally completed in 1999, Bob Funk, Gillogly, and the other members of the management team learned that each of the franchisees would need to upgrade their computer hardware before they could install the new software. And with the unknown horrors of Y2K looming, the Express leadership knew that franchisees had to implement the new system fast. Rather than go back on their word to franchisees like Higdon and risk alienating them forever, Funk and partner Bill Stoller made the decision for Express to foot the bill—$11 million in total—to retrofit each franchisee's hardware. "It really was an example of how Express walked the walk," Higdon told us.[48]

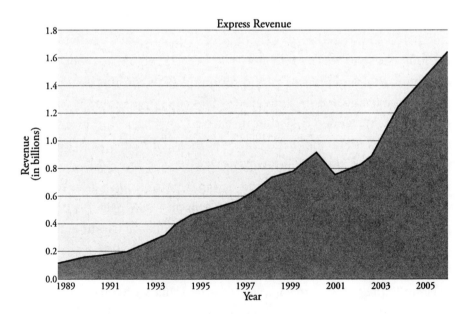

Express Personnel is a private company that does not publicly share information on company profitability.

Express Personnel was really the "accidental corporation." In February 1983, Acme Personnel Services CEO Bill Reiff suddenly passed away. Without Reiff's leadership and in the heart of an economic recession, Acme's fortunes quickly headed downhill. Still grieving the loss of their friend and mentor, Rieff, and disappointed at the fate of his company, three top Acme managers, Funk, Stoller, and James Gray, decided to strike out on their own. Funk, who had been running Acme's operations in Oklahoma City, bought up Acme's operations around the city while Stoller and Gray did the same in Portland, Oregon, and Boulder, Colorado.

What's interesting about Express's phenomenal growth is that it is one of only a handful of national staffing firms that are 100 percent franchised; most rival firms have either company-run offices or a mix of the two. One of the competitors that Express ran up against most often in its early years was Western Staffing out of Walnut Creek, California, which is now called Westaff. The company got its start back in 1948, but it wasn't until 1984 that Westaff began to face off against Express in courting franchisees. By 1988, the first year that Express made the *Inc.* 500 list, Westaff was already the largest privately owned temporary staffing company in the country—roughly four times larger than Express, and one of the five largest staffing companies overall, with 285 offices and revenues of more than $200 million. Eight years later, however, even as Westaff was preparing for its IPO, Express had caught up and both firms posted revenues in excess of $500 million. From 1996 to today, the story dramatically changes: While Westaff expanded slightly to some 239 offices and $600 million in revenue, Express blew by it, growing into a 588-unit organization that topped $1.8 billion in revenue in 2006—making it the fifth-largest staffing company in the United States.[49] Although Express asked us not to reveal its profit data, we can say that its profitability is as impressive as its revenue growth.

YOU CAN'T FAKE CHARACTER

When our research team traveled to Minnesota, we had the pleasure of visiting not one but two breakthrough companies: Polaris and Fastenal. Minnesota is the only state that produced two breakthrough companies. Our first stop on the trip was to Polaris headquarters in Medina, about a half hour outside of Minneapolis. As we were wrapping up our talk with CEO Tom Tiller, who capped a long day of interviews for us, he asked us where we were headed next. "To visit Fastenal in Winona," I told him, "about a two-and-a-half-hour drive away." "I love that company!" said a reenergized Tiller, who had been halfway out the door at the time.[50] He sat back down and told us about the twenty-three different Polaris vehicles he owns—from snowmobiles to ATVs to a Victory Vegas—and how he gets all his tools and hard-to-find parts from the Fastenal store in Plymouth, about nine miles east of the Polaris office on Highway 55. "I built a shop at my house to maintain all my vehicles and I stop by that store at least once a week to pick something up," Tiller told us. "If they don't have what I need, they always get it to me either later that day or the next. Amazing customer service."

Amazing customer service, huh? That got me to thinking: Time to try my "Closing-time Test" on Fastenal. If you show up at a store about ten minutes before closing time—when the staff is thinking about closing up shop and getting home to their families—you get the real story on how a company feels about its customers. So the team and I headed down the road and pulled into the Fastenal parking lot at just about 4:50 p.m. central time. The store was empty as we started wandering through the aisles, amazed at the variety of merchandise: not only hundreds of nuts and bolts but chainsaws, drills, and gift-wrapped knife sets. I grabbed the biggest nut and bolt set I could find—I honestly had no idea what one would use it for—and walked up to the counter where the store's assistant manager, Keith Henderson, greeted me. I asked a few dumb questions about the bolt and loitered around long enough to make sure I had become a nuisance. True to form, Henderson acted like he would be happy to spend the whole night there if that's what I needed. Finally, he shot me a quizzical look and asked, "You sure you found what you were looking for?" That got me to laughing and I confessed that I was writing a book on Fastenal and was there to do some research. Henderson then called over the store's manager, Eric Ruikka, who told me, "That's the first one-inch, top-locking lug-nut that we've sold in the eleven years I have run this store."[51] I handed over my credit card with pride.

As they rang up my purchase, Ruikka and Henderson couldn't stop talking about their company, even though it was past quitting time. They told us about how they often drive parts out to work sites to save their customers time, how often they attend training sessions at the home office, and about the first time they each met Bob Kierlin. "I love the fact that he wears secondhand suits," Henderson told us. "If you ran into him, you'd never think he is who he is."[52] That prompted me to tell them what Tom Tiller had said about stopping in at their store. "Oh yeah, I know him," Ruikka told us. "He comes in all the time, usually in the mornings. I remember I asked him once where he worked and he told me over at Polaris. Then I said, 'Are you a mechanic?' He said, 'No, I'm the CEO.' We had a good laugh about that."[53]

When I noticed that it was now closing in on 5:30, I started herding my team out the door, and asked Ruikka for his business card. He went to reach for one in a container on the counter, but it was empty. After digging out a spare from his wallet, he apologized: Apparently, the hardware aisle manager from the big-box home improvement store down the road had stopped in earlier in the day to grab a stack of business cards for himself. "He and I have a great relationship," said Ruikka; "he hands my cards out to his customers when they ask him for things he just can't get for them." Amazing customer service indeed.

BUILDING COMPANY CHARACTER
The Key Ideas

1. Breakthrough companies are built on a bedrock of company character. Values refer to what people in a company purport to believe, while character is more important; it refers to how people in an organization really operate.

2. Each breakthrough company we studied had its own special character, as unique as an institutional thumbprint. Of primary interest to breakthrough leaders was the degree to which their company goals lined up with how people generally behaved.

3. The quickest way for a person to get removed from a position of power in a breakthrough company is to act in a way that undermines the company's character.

4. Though the company character of the nine breakthrough companies varied significantly, all nine shared four character-istics: (i) give folks a fair deal; (ii) believe in people; (iii) be a strategic miser; and (iv) make your word count.

**BUILDING COMPANY CHARACTER
"SQUIRTS FROM THE GRAPEFRUIT"**
(Findings That Surprised Us)

1. When we asked people at breakthrough companies what explained their success, they invariably pointed to the company's character.

2. Some breakthrough companies had formal values statements and some didn't. The creation of a formal statement of values did not seem to be in any way related to the development of strong company character.

BREAKTHROUGH IN PRACTICE
Tips for Building Company Character

1. Hire someone who is a good listener (graduate student, university researcher) to ask a number of your people these two questions: (i) What explains this company's past success? and (ii) When the company fails to reach its potential, why is that?

2. Ask the interviewer to organize his/her notes according to themes, and use these themes to identify the major positive and negative aspects of your firm's character.

3. Get a group of people together and identify the three most important actions the firm could take to build company character.

6

NAVIGATING THE BUSINESS

BERMUDA TRIANGLE

We cannot direct the wind, but we can adjust the sails.
BERTHA CALLOWAY

JUST OFF THE COAST of Florida lies a half-million-square-mile portion of the Atlantic Ocean, known as the Bermuda Triangle. The region first made headlines in the 1950s after several airplanes and ships mysteriously vanished there, which fueled rumors of alien abductions, compass-defeating magnetic waves, deep ocean earthquakes, and ship-swallowing pockets of methane gas. When you travel through the area, which connects Miami, the island of Bermuda, and San Juan, Puerto Rico, you do so at your own risk, say wary observers.

During our in-person research at more than fifty different companies over the past five years, we accidentally happened upon a mystery of our own: Why was it that so many companies dropped off the map, so to speak, on their way to breakthrough? One thing we know for sure: This phenomenon, which we have labeled the "Business Bermuda Triangle," has nothing to do with aliens or methane gas. We think.

To unravel the mystery, we made a point of asking each of the almost 1,700 executives we interviewed during our research the same question: "What is your company's advantage over its competition?" That's when we began to notice something peculiar. While the executives who guided smaller companies all answered the question similarly—often citing their low-overhead and nimbleness in the market—we received much more nuanced and complex answers from the leaders of larger companies. That's when we began to posit that the difficulties companies experience in certain stages of growth might be linked with the notion that as companies grow to a certain size, they are forced to rethink how they compete. If a company fails to adapt and build on its advantages when it is small, it is likely to lose its way en route to breakthrough performance.

By definition, small companies tend to be lean, nimble, and close to their customers. When we asked the executives from smaller companies with annual revenues between $1 million and $50 million what made them successful, we invariably heard the same thing: (1) we are better at giving the customers what they want; (2) we are able to respond more quickly; and (3) we operate with lower overhead so we can compete on costs.

The Business Bermuda Triangle

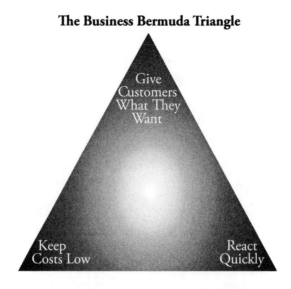

Give Customers What They Want

Keep Costs Low

React Quickly

But, as a company grows larger, adding overhead, management layers, and new customers along the way, how does it continue to give customers what they want, while at the same time keeping costs low and reacting quickly to changes in the market? To do all that, a company must navigate the Business Bermuda Triangle.

We found that the larger a company becomes, the more difficult it is to balance the three points of the triangle. Yet to stay on course, companies must continue to increase their mastery of all three, even though each factor has its own magnetic pull, which can cause firms to be stretched in several different directions at the same time. For example, a company that prioritizes cost containment above all can easily squander a great opportunity with its customers, and give its competition an advantage when it passes on investing in a new product feature. The company that guarantees its customers short delivery times may find that higher inventory holding costs have eroded its cost advantage. And the company that tries to please each of its customers by maintaining a large catalog of customized products may face skyrocketing costs, lengthy response times and, ironically, a decline in overall customer satisfaction.

Unlike these wayward examples, the nine breakthrough companies have learned to navigate the Business Bermuda Triangle. But how? After studying the course taken by our breakthrough guides, we learned that growing companies do not in fact have to develop whole new ways of competing. The key to navigating the Business Bermuda Triangle is to transform small-company advantages into what we call *sustaining* advantages.[1]

SMALL IS BEAUTIFUL, UP TO A POINT

As a kid growing up in Birmingham, Alabama, Mark Smith dreamed of a career building rocket ships. Smith even got the opportunity to shake hands with Wernher von Braun, one of the founding fathers of rocket science, after winning a blue ribbon at a high school science

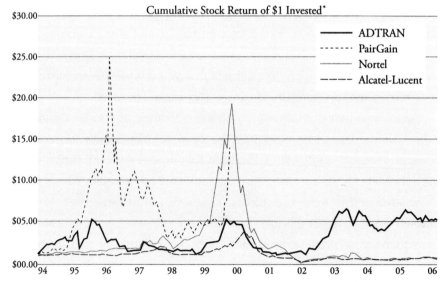

Cumulative Stock Return of $1 Invested*

─────── ADTRAN
------- PairGain
·············· Nortel
── ── Alcatel-Lucent

*ADTRAN is a perfect example of why it is important not to use stock price as the sole determinant of which companies are worthy of study. As the chart shows, beginning in about 2000 the telecommunications industry was pummeled on Wall Street, and has yet to fully recover. ADTRAN's stock was punished right along with the rest of the industry—yet when one looks at ADTRAN's growth rate and margins relative to the competition, it is clearly a top performer.

fair in 1958 for his invention: a digital device that measured distances using beams of light. Smith's love of science led him to study at the Georgia Institute of Technology, and later, to Huntsville to work on building rockets for NASA. A few years later, when the Federal Communications Commission forced AT&T to open its network to outside modems, Smith pounced, founding his own modem manufacturer called Universal Data Systems in 1970. Smith sold UDS to Motorola ten years later for $21 million, and after working for the company for six years, launched, along with six other partners, ADTRAN, his second high-tech venture.[2]

Under Smith's leadership, ADTRAN has grown into a key provider of networking and communications equipment, supplying more than 1,600 varieties of DSLAMs, multiplexers, multiservice access and aggregation platforms, high-speed routers, and solutions for IP telephony and Wi-Fi. ADTRAN products are used by all the major telecom providers including AT&T, Verizon, and Qwest as well as a growing list of enterprise customers outside the telecom sector. ADTRAN has faced off against giant competitors like Alcatel, Cisco, Nortel, and Lucent, and has prospered. Though the telecom industry meltdown in 2001 erased 30 percent of the company's revenues and led to the firm's stock plunging from $79 a share to less than $17 a share, ADTRAN has since rebounded in a big way. It has grown its annual revenues to more than $500 million, and because of its ability to win business with gross margins of nearly 60 percent earns more than $100 million in net income.[3]

> By definition, small companies tend to be lean, nimble, and close to the customer. The question is how to sustain these advantages and build on them as they grow?

When ADTRAN first opened its doors more than two decades ago, however, it was like any other start-up: understaffed, cash-strapped, and desperately needing to generate revenue quickly. With UDS and later as a vice president with Motorola, Smith had tapped the growing need for analog modems in the commercial sector. With his new venture, however, he wanted to avoid entering the same market as his former company. "You don't compete with your children," he told us.[4] While they didn't yet know much about the telecommunications market, Smith and his cofounder Lonnie McMillian knew there were new opportunities there. With the divestiture of AT&T in 1984 into the seven regional Bell operating companies, or RBOCs, and the proliferation throughout the country of dozens of independent and competitive local exchange carriers (called ILECs and CLECs), an entire new market had been created that was hungry for new equipment. Western Electric, which provided the equipment to the old AT&T, had long served a captive market and had become complacent. These new telecom providers, it turned out, wanted to move away from analog communications into the digital world and, in an era before fiber optic cable was commonplace, they were willing to pay for devices that could pump more bandwidth over the nation's existing infrastructure of twisted-pair copper telephone lines.[5]

HOW SMALL COMPANIES GIVE CUSTOMERS WHAT THEY WANT

So ADTRAN built just the thing customers wanted: a digital data service plug-in device that could crank data and voices along the pipe at the then-sizzling rate of 64 kilobits per second. The device wasn't rocket science—as a fledgling start-up, ADTRAN lacked the resources and R&D to do anything too revolutionary—but by assembling existing components and technologies into a new box that addressed this transmission speed problem, ADTRAN got up and running.[6]

Small companies, usually by definition, have very few customers. And for the first few years of its life, ADTRAN was no exception. It focused mainly on the seven RBOCs. Consequently, just about every employee was focused like a laser beam on making sure that customers like BellSouth, the local carrier in Alabama, were happy. If the company didn't service its customer well, employees knew it wouldn't be long before they were out of a job. That led to a lot of heroic efforts on the part of many ADTRAN employees who stepped in to save the day with a particular customer over a late delivery, a defective part, or an installation problem. Small companies are often good at this notion of "customer recovery," but as they grow, they need to build robust systems that can help ensure things don't go wrong in the first place.

Small companies also tend to focus their efforts on producing a narrow product line rather than taking a more shotgun approach favored by bigger competitors. ADTRAN couldn't afford to invest in a product that customers wouldn't buy: A failed product would be disastrous. But as the company began to add more customers in more markets across the country, the pressure to expand the product line increased. While the DDS device had been successful, new technology like DSL had emerged that threatened to make it obsolete. These RBOCs also wanted customized solutions, and if ADTRAN couldn't deliver, it would find someone else to make them.

ADTRAN, like most small companies, had excelled because of the growth of just a handful of products. How could it maintain its reputation for quality and yet remain on the cutting edge as their customers began to demand more and more from them, and as it radically expanded its product line and entered new markets? Over time, ADTRAN found itself drifting toward the Business Bermuda Triangle.

HOW SMALL COMPANIES KEEP COSTS LOW

ADTRAN, like most small companies, was cash poor at its inception, and ran the risk of burning through the $7 million in start-up capital that had come out of Smith's and McMillian's pockets.[7] But ADTRAN, unlike some of its larger competitors, could rein in its costs because of something financial consultant Doug Tatum calls "high performance, cheap labor."[8] The same high level of commitment—the "band of brothers" mentality that enabled ADTRAN to cement relations with customers in those early years—also helped keep costs low. Everyone, including Smith, worked around the clock, even on weekends, to meet product development deadlines and fulfill customer expectations. Staffed mostly with young engineers, many fresh from college, ADTRAN was able to get top talent by handing out stock options, which brought a sense of ownership, and by offering a chance to make a difference. "I took a pay cut to join the company, and everyone worked a lot of hours," Clint Coleman, now a vice president of engineering at ADTRAN, told us. "But I was also given a chance to take a lot of responsibility without having a lot of experience. We really knew we were a part of something special."[9]

> When companies are small, they often benefit from "high-performance, cheap labor." High levels of commitment ensure that people do whatever it takes to get the job accomplished.

ADTRAN, like most start-ups, also prized function over form and strove to save money wherever it could, buying used office equipment or cheap off-the-shelf components. Also, as a by-product of setting up in Huntsville, the company was able to lease office and manufacturing space at a fraction of what it would have cost in more well-known tech areas like Silicon Valley or Boston.

While these cost-saving methods were effective in getting AD-TRAN through its early years, the company still faced the challenge of sustaining this cost advantage as it began to face off with multibillion-dollar competitors such as Western Electric (later to become Lucent) and Alcatel. Could it continue to be a low-cost provider as it became a larger company? If ADTRAN failed to evolve its approach to costs as the business grew, it would eventually face a "cost squeeze" in which competitors with more sophisticated approaches to costs would price them out of the market.

HOW SMALL COMPANIES REACT QUICKLY

Small companies can move more quickly simply by virtue of their size alone. They have little, if any, organizational structure, and there aren't many layers of middle management to "check with" that can slow the process down. There is instead a lot of management by walking around, as McMillian calls it, where there is frequent contact between top management and frontline employees.[10] In ADTRAN's early days, Smith told us, he and McMillian would literally work side by side with their employees: There was no need for cubicle walls, let alone layers of management to stand between them.[11] A lean staff helps guarantee that the number of pointless committee meetings and oversight activities is kept to a minimum. At this stage in its development, a company feels and acts vulnerable, and as a result, employees tend to react quickly to problems and opportunities. Without the friction of an executive hierarchy to slow down the flow of information, management is often closely in touch with its customers' needs and problems, and can quickly allocate resources to please them.

Yet, as the company grows and begins to add staff and new management to meet customers' demands, how does it keep information channels flowing as quickly as before? As ADTRAN added staff and promoted its top engineers, how could it keep that same sense of "management by walking around"? ADTRAN knew that it couldn't rest on its small-company laurels. The company would have to focus on keeping speed and responsiveness high as it grew from a hundred-person operation to one that would eventually employ, in 2006, more than 1,600.[12]

FROM SMALL-COMPANY EDGE TO SUSTAINING ADVANTAGE

In its early days, ADTRAN clearly capitalized on the advantages of its small size to lay the foundation for its rapid growth. But what distinguishes ADTRAN from most other companies that enjoy a similar small-company edge is that its leadership team was engaged from day one in an effort to convert its early advantages into *sustaining* advantages.

ADTRAN's Small-Company Edge

Small-Company Edge: Customers
- *Few customers, products, and markets*
- *High commitment due to risks associated with losing a customer*
- *Excellent customer responsiveness and recovery*

Small-Company Edge: Costs
- *Low-cost, high-performance labor*
- *Everyone acts like an owner (strict cost control)*

Small-Company Edge: Speed
- *No layers to slow down the process*
- *High degree of focus on customer for sake of survival*
- *Fairly simple business in the early years— few products, markets, customers*

Give Customers What They Want

Keep Costs Low

React Quickly

As ADTRAN really began to take off in 1986, the telecommunications industry was awash in new trends. One thing was clear: There was a lot of money to be made in the coming wired world. While Mark Smith had correctly identified the big market demand for technology that digitized the existing copper wire infrastructure, he knew that ADTRAN lacked the resources to be the research and development leader in the field as newer and flashier technology arrived on the scene. With less than $1 million in revenue at the end of their first full year, and with an operating loss to boot, ADTRAN would be just a rounding error on the books of Motorola, Smith's former employer. Knowing his company could easily be crushed by larger competitors, Smith took a long look to determine what factors would drive success in the industry for the long run. He figured that the next wave in technology would be fueled by: (1) rapid product development cycles that made new products obsolete almost as soon as they were introduced; (2) demand for equipment customized to the specific needs of customers; and (3) tough price competition.[13]

With these predictions in mind, Smith and his management team set about structuring ADTRAN from its beginning so that its early small-company edge could be transformed over time into a sustaining advantage that addressed these trends. Here, in part, is how they did it.

EVOLVING FROM KEEPING COSTS LOW TO OPTIMIZING COSTS

Mark Smith and the other ADTRAN founders made a conjecture early on about what it would take for them to maintain the company's low-cost position relative to its competitors and still maintain close to 60 percent gross margins. They would need to replace their reliance on low-cost, high-performance labor with real structural cost advantages. And although ADTRAN led the industry trend toward outsourcing the final assembly of devices to low-cost plants in Singapore and

China, Smith knew that outsourcing alone couldn't guarantee lower costs. "The real costs in manufacturing electronics," he told us, "were the materials like silicon chips and components like microprocessors." Plus, since anyone could reap the same benefits from outsourcing, ADTRAN would need to be cleverer to maintain a cost advantage over its competitors. "Attempting to be a low-cost provider by controlling the assembly is a losing game," Smith told us.[14]

Where he could *win* the game, Smith decided, was in controlling costs on the design engineering side. "At most companies, the most talented engineers pursue the most fun and exciting projects, looking for a breakthrough technology," Smith patiently explained to us. "Product life cycles in electronics are so short, usually eighteen months. So by the time the new product comes out, the technology has already changed and the product is already obsolete. The engineering team then moves on to the next latest and greatest project, and the product never evolves beyond its first generation."[15]

> ADTRAN found a way to replace its reliance on "low-cost, high-performance" labor with real structural cost advantages.

On the other hand, when Smith assigned an engineering team to a product, they stuck with it, often for years at a time. The team's job was to incorporate the latest advances in component technology into the next generation of the product before the prior one even hit the market. Their role was, in other words, to make their own products obsolete almost immediately. Clint Coleman, for example, was one of the design engineers for ADTRAN's DDS plug, and he was personally responsible for overseeing many of the generations of its development. By revamping the product every eighteen months at a minimum, an engineer like Coleman could design the device to use fewer, more powerful components while, at the same time, incorporating the latest functional advances requested by its customers.[16]

Smith had also made the prescient decision to have ADTRAN invest in its own silicon semiconductor manufacturing facility. With the ability to design their own chips, ADTRAN engineers had much more control over the architecture and feature set than many of their competitors who actually bought cheaper, off-the-shelf components. And since engineering costs could be written off rather than capitalized, the chip itself, when manufactured in volume, would cost significantly less than if it came off the shelf.[17]

By rolling up silicon component development into the eighteen-month redevelopment process, ADTRAN pioneered something akin to the holy grail of manufacturing: Each new product generation offered more functionality and, since the devices used fewer parts, were cheaper to make. Not only did this make customers extremely happy, since they get more for less, it put extreme pressure on ADTRAN's competitors to keep up. Most could not: When ADTRAN entered a market, it usually gained control of the market within just a few product generations.

For example, ADTRAN waited until 1991 to enter the market for HDSL or high-speed digital subscriber lines, a market already dominated by Silcon Valley–based competitor PairGain. PairGain was a very technically competent player that also manufactured its own silicon. "They were the best competitor we ever had," Smith told us.[18] Yet, despite its two-year head start, PairGain slowly lost market share to its rival. Clint Coleman, who had moved over to head up the HDSL product development, told us that ADTRAN made up ground because, unlike PairGain, which had a more traditional approach to research and development, his team kept reengineering its HDSL modem, producing six generations in eight years and reducing costs at every step. By February 2000, ADTRAN had captured 85 percent of the HDSL market, forcing PairGain to enter new markets and to explore potential merger opportunities, which likely fed the run-up in its stock price in relation to ADTRAN in late 2000. "We're a company that's in transition from one product to another," Charles McBrayer, PairGain's chief financial officer, said at the time.[19] ADC, a larger rival, eventually did acquire PairGain in June 2000, all but ceding total control of the HDSL market to ADTRAN. "Once we were able to pull ahead, we stayed there," Coleman told us.[20]

SYSTEMATICALLY GIVING CUSTOMERS WHAT THEY WANT

Pleasing a single customer at any given time is relatively achievable; pleasing all of your customers all the time, almost impossible. One of the biggest struggles for companies trying to transition from small to large is pleasing their growing customer base. ADTRAN, for its part, made a systematic commitment to meeting its customers' requests that has allowed it to not only dominate the telecom access market, but make serious inroads into the nontelecom sector as well.

ADTRAN's investment in in-house silicon development and its commitment to continuously reengineer its products not only helped it compete on cost, it allowed the company to incorporate client feedback and requests into each subsequent generation of that product. For example, Mark Smith told us how Clint Coleman and the AD-TRAN team were able to incorporate an ingenious line testing capability into a later generation of its HDSL product. At that time, the installers working for the carriers often ran into problems with distortions and outages on the aging copper telephone lines, which were designed for analog transmission, not digital. Smith described it as being like a strand of Christmas tree lights: You would have to hunt by trial and error to find the dead bulb. To address this, Coleman and his engineers added a line-testing capability into its HDSL products that, by measuring the delay in the echo returned from its signal, pinpointed the exact location at the root of the problem. "The only reason we could do that was because we had our own custom chips," Smith told us. "Our competitors couldn't match our functionality because they were buying off-the-shelf components, and the installer would have to use separate equipment to test the line, which was an expensive proposition. This is how we began to build our competitive advantage."[21]

> Breakthrough companies eventually transition from "save the customer" organizational heroics to robust systems designed to constantly monitor and enhance the value they are providing their customers.

ADTRAN also added to its competitive advantage by eliminating the barriers between its engineers and the customers. From its very beginning, the company relied on the direct interaction between its design engineers and the end users to ensure that it was incorporating the customer's most highly valued feature requests. And where most growing companies begin to insert layers of management, sales, and support team to insulate its engineers, ADTRAN vigilantly kept to its flat structure so that when a customer like Verizon came calling, "I would encourage them to talk to our design engineers directly," CEO Tom Stanton told us. ADTRAN also tries to partner with customers whenever possible rather than trying to build products basically on spec, hoping customers will buy them. "When you have a customer with a vested interest in the development of a product, they will pare back their wish lists because they want you to succeed as much as you do," Stanton told us.[22]

ADTRAN's culture of ownership among its engineers also contributed heavily in its focus on customers. Rather than getting bored six generations into a product, engineers are motivated to keep improving their designs through customer input until they own 100 percent of the market. Clint Coleman told us that engineers to this day still come in on weekends to meet their deadlines because they take pride in seeing their work help ADTRAN gain market share. "It's more than just the stock options," Coleman told us. "Our customers are our partners, and at the end of the day, there is a real sense of accomplishment in building the best possible product that makes them happy because that means we will be successful."[23]

CREATING STRUCTURAL SPEED ADVANTAGES

Building the best product at the lowest cost won't help you much if you don't get it to the market before your competitor does. But as a company grows, often its ability to react quickly to customer needs and competitive moves deteriorates. Once aided by its small size, a company needs to build structural advantages that enable it to continue to outpace the competition. That's another reason ADTRAN continues to be so vigilant about churning out new product generations over eighteen months, a turnaround time that is basically unheard of in the industry. Bringing their silicon chip development in-house also gave ADTRAN engineers the ability to customize features far more quickly than if they had to wait for an outside vendor to do it for them. ADTRAN's willingness to put customers in direct contact with its engineers also ensured that when the next generation rolled off the assembly line in eighteen months, customers would know exactly what they were getting.

But ADTRAN has an even more powerful weapon that it uses to ensure speed: no rigid long-term roadmap for its products. Instead, it gives its engineers the leeway to adapt to what the customers are telling them, along with the time frame in which they think they can deliver the changes. "We make sure the decisions about new functionality happen at as low a layer as possible," Stanton told us. "Our priorities change monthly based on direct customer input, and our engineers have the freedom to come up with a better mousetrap without checking in with a lot of people. If you put too much weight on a roadmap, you may lose your speed and flexibility because you commit to moving in a certain direction."[24]

ADTRAN also encourages its engineers to be aggressive in setting time lines for developing a new enhancement, even if they are uncertain that they can deliver. Stanton explained to us that ADTRAN trusts that when engineers commit to a particular date, they will be motivated to make it, both to protect their reputation and to fulfill their word: By having an ownership stake in the success of the product, the

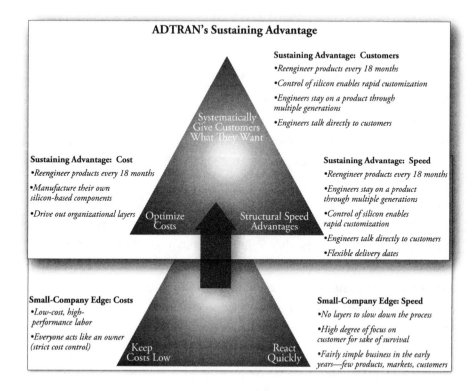

ADTRAN's Sustaining Advantage

Sustaining Advantage: Customers
- *Reengineer products every 18 months*
- *Control of silicon enables rapid customization*
- *Engineers stay on a product through multiple generations*
- *Engineers talk directly to customers*

Sustaining Advantage: Cost
- *Reengineer products every 18 months*
- *Manufacture their own silicon-based components*
- *Drive out organizational layers*

Sustaining Advantage: Speed
- *Reengineer products every 18 months*
- *Engineers stay on a product through multiple generations*
- *Control of silicon enables rapid customization*
- *Engineers talk directly to customers*
- *Flexible delivery dates*

Systematically Give Customers What They Want

Optimize Costs

Structural Speed Advantages

Small-Company Edge: Costs
- *Low-cost, high-performance labor*
- *Everyone acts like an owner (strict cost control)*

Small-Company Edge: Speed
- *No layers to slow down the process*
- *High degree of focus on customer for sake of survival*
- *Fairly simple business in the early years—few products, markets, customers*

Keep Costs Low

React Quickly

engineer is motivated to succeed. If an engineer does miss a date, on the other hand, they are not fired or reprimanded. In fact, ADTRAN's sales force has been trained to factor in this aggressive approach to product development. "We don't punish our engineers for missing dates, because when they see they have taken longer than they said they would, their efforts step up considerably to get the project done as quickly as possible," Stanton told us. He then asked us to consider the flip side: If he were to punish engineers when they missed deadlines, as most companies do, those engineers would compensate by padding their estimates, which would invariably push the delivery date further into the future. That's why, in the end, ADTRAN can churn out new products faster than anyone else in the telecom business. "Talk to any of our customers and they will tell you that no one gets new products out faster than we do," Stanton said.[25]

COMPASS HEADINGS FOR NAVIGATING THE BUSINESS BERMUDA TRIANGLE

While ADTRAN serves as an excellent example of how a high-tech manufacturing company can successfully navigate the Business Bermuda Triangle, there are key lessons for turning small-company advantages into sustaining advantages no matter what industry a company competes in. Here are a few:

Sometimes the best way to reduce costs is to spend some money

Early-stage and small companies often approach the subject of costs much too simplistically. Costs are bad, they say, and we need to reduce them whenever possible. As companies grow, however, they need to develop a more sophisticated approach to thinking about costs. They should begin to evolve their thinking from focusing on cost *control* to focusing on cost *optimization*.

Organizations actually have two classifications of costs: costs that directly add value for customers and costs that don't, often known by the dreaded term "overhead." The nine breakthrough companies, we found, understood that they need to focus constantly on optimizing their value-added costs while minimizing nonvalue-added costs wherever and whenever possible.

Just as some analysts on Wall Street probably raised their eyebrows when they learned ADTRAN wasn't outsourcing its silicon development, so too, some probably wondered why Fastenal, led by the supposed cheapest CEO in America, would not only build its own sorting facility, but build a distribution system to keep its growing number of stores in nine countries around the world stocked with its famously wide variety of products. Bob Kierlin is indeed thrifty—when it comes to keeping nonvalue costs to their absolute minimum. But when he saw the opportunity for Fastenal to build its own high-tech global distribution system, he jumped at it. Why not partner with a UPS or

FedEx like most other companies would?—control. By maintaining its own fleet of trucks combined with a high-tech inventory management system, Fastenal is able to guarantee delivery times for customers, ensure its stores are well stocked, and in the long run, actually realize a return on its investment. Fastenal's distribution has become so efficient that the company has considered offering the service to other businesses. "Why have the trucks returning to the warehouse empty when we might be able to make that trip profitable by carrying products for someone else?" Chris Duffenbach, Fastenal's national logistics manager, told us.[26]

CASE STUDY IN NAVIGATING THE BUSINESS BERMUDA TRIANGLE:
Western Wats

Western Wats got its start as a niche company that conducted telephone surveys for market research firms. It operated about ten "mini" call centers, mostly in small rural towns in Utah and Idaho. As the firm grew, it added new products and services, including Internet survey research capability, a teleservices division, and a full-service market research offering.

When David Haynes took over as CEO in 2001, he sensed that in order for Western Wats to reach its full potential, the company would have to change its approach. Though he didn't realize it at the time, his firm was entering the Business Bermuda Triangle. Here's how he helped his company safely navigate its way through:

1. Systematically giving customers what they want: From our discussions with key managers, it was clear that Western Wats was trying to do too much. In a spirited discussion late one evening, a group of twenty managers decided to idle the teleservices division, shut down the full-service research offering, and focus its resources instead on growing a survey research panel, which it turned out was what customers really wanted. With a narrowed focus, the company was able to build an Internet panel of 1 million respondents in just six months, an accomplishment unprecedented in the industry.

2. Optimizing cost: Western Wats realized that it simply could not scale its mini call centers model fast enough to keep up with growth. As a result, the company opened a call center and technology development center in Cebu, Philippines, that now employs more than 2,000 people and which enabled the company to cut operating costs by more than 30 percent.

3. Structural speed advantages: Instead of buying an off-the-shelf technology platform, Western Wats opted to invest $2 million over two years to develop WIRE, its proprietary research operating system. "We could respond to market opportunities much faster than waiting for the latest update from an outside software provider, and were able to respond with capabilities customers wanted, like support for integrated multimodal data collection," Haynes told us.

These changes helped Western Wats set its course well: The company is now the largest survey research data collection firm in the world.

Customers are happiest when you stay focused on the business you are already in

In their effort to please customers, many companies fall into the trap of prematurely diversifying their product lines. As a company grows larger and larger, there is a natural tendency for leaders to become bored with their firm's core products, and consequently, to push the company in new directions before current offerings have been fully exploited. If a company adds additional products and services too quickly, overwhelming personnel and internal systems, it may find itself slipping in terms of cost, speed, and even customer satisfaction.

This is not to say, however, that a company should limit itself to one product line. Quite the opposite. But breakthrough companies tend to follow this rule: Don't diversify before you own your existing market. ADTRAN, for example, waited until it owned the DDS plug market before moving into the HDSL business. Under Tom Golisano's leadership, Paychex waited for years to expand beyond the payroll processing business into new offerings like 401(k) administration, human resource compliance, and payroll tax collection and payment.[27] Polaris, as another example, has successively expanded from snow-mobiles, to ATVs, to watercraft, and most recently, to motorcycles. Each time it took a step into a new market, however, it had already established a dominant position with its existing products. And even with such caution, there is danger in product proliferation. Polaris lost market share in snowmobiles in 2006.[28]

> As a company grows larger, there is a natural tendency for leaders to become bored with their firm's core products and to push into new areas before current offerings have been fully exploited.

When you do diversify, let your customers lead you

While the phrase "Build it and they will come" might work for baseball fields in the movies, it is not a statement to live by when running a business. The only reason ADTRAN diversified into the HDSL business was because its customers, the telecom carriers, *asked* them to get into that business. If your company is at a point where it can diversify, let your customers lead you. For example, Scott Cook thought Intuit was in the personal finance business. His customers used Quicken to organize their monthly bills and balance their checkbook. What he soon found out, however, was that some of these customers were trying to run businesses using hybrid products, combining Quicken with, say, an Excel spreadsheet, to manage their inventory and payroll. Intuit got into the small business accounting world with *QuickBooks* because its customers asked them to.[29] Similarly, while Chico's has been wildly successful in the apparel business, stitching flattering varieties of slacks, shirts, and dresses, it wasn't until its customers started asking that Scott Edmonds pushed the company to provide nightwear and lingerie products under its Soma brand.[30] While Express began largely as a temporary staffing agency, it has added human resource capabilities, testing, and training, and Web-based reporting tools over the years—only because its customers have begged for them.[31]

LAYERS KILL

One of the most common ways companies inadvertently put the brakes on their speed and ability to react to the markets and customers is to add layers of unnecessary management. Think back to the lessons we learned about the value of flat organizations in chapter 3: Keeping management layers to a minimum not only empowers those employees closest to the customer, it also ensures that the entire company can react quickly and effectively to information learned on the frontlines. The more filters a company puts between its decision makers and its customers, the slower and more distorted the message becomes, which often leads to a company's embarking on the wrong products at the wrong time. ADTRAN's Tom Stanton equates this with a forwarded e-mail: An e-mail could have come out of a phone conversation between two people, yet as soon as that message is forwarded to someone else, the recipient loses that initial context and the message loses more and more of its context each time it is forwarded. "Our biggest challenge over the next five years is combating any sense of bureaucracy," Stanton told us. "We need more Indians than chiefs, and whenever we find a chief that isn't adding value, we turn that position back into an Indian. Our goal is to get engineers to be as close to the customer as possible."[32]

Despite all the mystery that surrounds the Atlantic Ocean's version of the Bermuda Triangle, the truth is, it is one of the most heavily traveled sections on the planet. Not only has the U.S. Coast Guard debunked the notion that the triangle is responsible for an abnormal amount of unexplained disappearances, Lloyds of London, the famous insurer of the uninsurable, doesn't charge a premium for travel through the area. Research by the Coast Guard reveals that most of the disappearances were actually the product of human error—such as instances when a ship captain or airplane pilot was simply too stubborn to steer around a coming storm system despite ample warnings.[33] As we looked more closely at the Business Bermuda Triangle, we began to understand that failure is not foreordained there, either. It is not inevitable that when companies grow, they must become fatter, slower, and less responsive to their customers. Ultimately, it is up to the captains and the pilots of growing companies to plot the proper course in order to safely reach their destination.

NAVIGATING THE BUSINESS BERMUDA TRIANGLE
The Key Ideas

1. Small companies, by virtue of their size, often have three major advantages. As a company grows, it must transform the characteristics that gave it its small-company edge into *sustaining* advantages. The difficult process of doing this is what we call navigating the Business Bermuda Triangle.

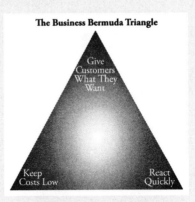

The Business Bermuda Triangle

Give Customers What They Want

Keep Costs Low

React Quickly

   a. As they grow, companies must find ways to move from dependence on "low-cost, high-performance labor" and low overhead to build structural cost advantages. We call this moving from cost reduction to cost optimization.
   b. Companies need to move from a focus on customer recovery to building robust systems that focus on monitoring customer relationships and anticipating customer needs.
   c. Companies must build speed and responsiveness into the very structure of their firms as they grow and become more complex.

2. Our study identified four "compass headings" for navigating the Business Bermuda Triangle:

   a. Understand that to build in structural cost advantages, you often have to spend some money.
   b. Avoid premature diversification of product lines: Companies often move on to the next product before fully mastering the ones they've already got.
   c. When it's time to diversify products or markets, let your customers be your guide.
   d. Nothing kills speed, hurts customer satisfaction, and erodes a cost advantage faster than unnecessary layers of management.

NAVIGATING THE BUSINESS BERMUDA TRIANGLE
"SQUIRTS FROM THE GRAPEFRUIT"
(Findings That Surprised Us)

1. Far from having to develop whole new strategies, breakthrough companies merely figured out ways to institutionalize the advantages that allowed them to prosper in the first place.

2. Sometimes the best way to save money is to spend money on developing capabilities that give you a long-term cost advantage.

BREAKTHROUGH IN PRACTICE
Tips for Navigating the Business Bermuda Triangle

1. Do a "cost audit." Identify three to five of the most important cost drivers of your business. Rate your business A to F in how well you do at optimizing costs across those drivers when compared with the competitors who are most likely to take business away from you. Identify specific ways you might increase your cost advantage.

2. Graph the development of your products and market over time, and ask yourself what kinds of opportunities might be generated by focusing more tightly on a few customer groups, needs, or markets.

3. Discuss in your company how your firm has built systems that monitor and optimize customer relationships that effectively replace the natural advantages you had in close customer contact when your firm had a smaller customer base. Look around your industry and related industries for ideas on how to do this better.

4. Discuss in your firm whether or not your growth is beginning to cause you to slow down your response time. Talk about ways you might build structural speed advantages into your company.

7

ERECTING SCAFFOLDING

Human beings, who are almost unique in having the ability to learn
from the experience of others, are also remarkable for their apparent
disinclination to do so.

DOUGLAS ADAMS

ROGER STAUBACH FACED perhaps the most critical "fourth-down and long yardage" play of his life in 1985, and he wasn't even on a football field. Years before he retired from professional football in 1979, he had started his brokerage business, owned part of a development company, and joined some partnerships to invest in Texas apartment buildings. However, when the Texas real estate market crashed in the mid-1980s, Staubach and his partners were left with assets of little value and a lot of debt. To make matters worse, Staubach soon learned that some of his partners had run out of cash and that, due to the intricacies of joint-and-several liability law, he was now personally accountable for the repayment of millions of dollars in debt. He wondered how he could extricate himself both financially and emotionally from this new crisis that threatened not only his personal finances, but also his real estate brokerage business. "Those were real dark days for me," Staubach told us.[1]

Fortunately, he knew where to turn to for advice: his YPO forum. YPO is a global network of more than 15,000 CEOs that was founded in 1950 with the idea that young executives need a supportive and confidential place to turn for advice in building their businesses. Staubach joined a YPO forum—a group of likeminded executives who meet monthly—not long after he founded his company. He says that joining his YPO forum, which included equipment leaser Robert Nichols, emergency room operator Dr. Leonard Riggs, serial entrepreneur Jim Gero, and real estate developers Bob Utley and Mike Prentiss, was the most important decision in his business career.[2]

The first thing his forum did was help him to accept the situation. "I think I was in denial at first because I only had 10 percent of the deal and I didn't feel that I should have to pay off all the debt," he told us, "but my forum really helped me put things in perspective." The forum went to work helping Staubach deal with the crisis, and hit on the idea of building up The Staubach Company to become an engine to help pay off his debt. It was through those forum discussions that Staubach decided to decentralize control of his company as a way of unleashing the entrepreneurial energies of his team. Not only did this switch help Staubach supercharge his company's performance so he could pay off the debt, it helped propel the company to its current status as an industry powerhouse with more than sixty offices nationwide. "That was a key decision in helping us grow as fast as we did," Staubach told us.[3]

SCAFFOLDING DEFINED

Staubach credits a lot of The Staubach Company's success to his early decision to establish links with people like members of his YPO forum, people who could help him and his team succeed. This willingness to go outside the company for help, it turns out, is also a hallmark of the other breakthrough companies we studied. Consider this: We selected our nine breakthrough companies purely on the basis of their longitudinal financial performance and *four of the nine* (Intuit, Express Personnel, Polaris, and Staubach) were founded by or are being run by members of YPO.

When we first launched our study, we expected to turn our microscopes on the nine breakthrough companies themselves. But, as our reporting began to give us a deeper understanding of how those companies operated, we began to see the outline of a bigger reality: Each breakthrough company was surrounded by a network of outside resources vital to its success. We call these resources "scaffolding" because, like physical scaffolding, they are *temporary structures that exist outside of the organization itself and enable the company to get to the next level*. While YPO and other peer networks can be important forms of organizational scaffolding, we found that breakthrough companies are also adept at using other forms of scaffolding, such as advisory boards, boards of directors, and customer or dealer councils, as well as investors, industry experts, consultants, and advisors. What sets the breakthrough companies apart, however, is not that they have these support structures (many companies have boards or hire consultants), but the optimal manner in which they learn from them. Just as breakthrough companies invest heavily in their employees and expect a lot in return (see chapter 5: Building Company Character), they have equally high expectations of outsiders upon whom they come to depend.

> Breakthrough companies build scaffolding, networks of resources outside the company that support their efforts to take the company to the next level.

The comparison companies we studied, on the other hand, appeared to be more insular and less eager to form real partnerships with people outside the firm. For example, while some of the comparison companies we studied formed customer councils or held regular user-group meetings, these meetings tended to be highly scripted broadcast events that involved one-way communication. Compare that to SAS, which allows its customers to determine its development priorities through a sophisticated customer poll—the

SASWare Ballot. SAS tech support reps listen to the kinds of things that customers want, and the top items get included in the ballot—which is sent out to the entire customer base. In this way, customers, not SAS engineers or marketers, determine the development team's priorities.

This is unheard of in the software industry. "I remember when we hired a sales manager from one of the other big software firms," Suzanne Gordon, SAS's CIO, told us. "He was completely dumbfounded by his first user-group experience. He told me that while his old company held user-group meetings, that they were viewed by customers as an obligation, or an opportunity to pick up some freebies. He was blown away by how we actually listen to our customers, and they love us for it. Our biggest risk is that we stop listening to our customers and start reacting to our competitors instead."[4]

CASE STUDY IN ERECTING SCAFFOLDING
Simms Fishing

When K. C. Walsh acquired Simms Fishing Products in 1993, it was a tiny, troubled Montana manufacturer of neoprene fishing waders. Over the next fourteen years, Walsh and his team have transformed Simms into one of the most respected brands in fly-fishing.

As a fly-fishing enthusiast myself, I wanted to learn more, so I called K. C. to ask him if I could feature him in one of my online columns for *BusinessWeek*. I discovered an impressive story. From Bozeman, Montana, Simms now sells into thirty-one countries and sources materials and finished goods from twelve nations around the globe. With fewer than 100 employees, Simms has grown revenues at over 25 percent growth per year, and now produces more than 120 products (1,200+ SKUs). The impressive thing is that they have accomplished this themselves, with little professional outside help and only traditional bank financing.

During our interview, it became clear to me that K. C. was at a turning point with Simms. "We have too many moving parts in this business for our size, and I worry about our ability to grow profitably from here. I'm also concerned about burnout among our best people." He was wrestling with management issues, strategic issues, and capital financing issues.

I shared the concept of scaffolding, and encouraged him to build a board of directors made up of people who had already faced the kinds of challenges that he was now facing. Within a month, he called to say he had secured two key people for his board, a recognized veteran in the outdoor apparel business and a leading private-equity investor. A couple of months later, I also became part of the scaffolding, as Simms engaged our firm to lead a strategy session with his team.

In a few short months, Simms now has an effective board, its revenues have exceeded forecast in every month since our session, and profitability has exceeded forecasts by 50 percent. In a recent conversation, Walsh summarized as follows: "We're reexamining every aspect of our business to make sure what we do is aligned with our core goals. There's still urgency in our business, but we already have a lot less firefighting." Simms is on target to achieve record profits, and is generating significant momentum for growth in 2008 and beyond.

So why aren't more companies adept at building effective scaffolding? Part of the blame may lie in the mindset of most entrepreneurial leaders. Recall from chapter 3 that entrepreneurial leaders tend to be great at figuring things out, and are supremely confident in their ability to find the right answer. That's great in a start-up environment, but as a business grows, leaders need to be willing to look outside their own four walls for people with the experience, connections, and perspective they may lack. If a leader is unwilling to look for outside ideas, people in the organization will follow suit and the company will become stuck. This was an all too consistent theme in the work we did with the fifty-two companies in our field study: Many would constantly "reinvent the wheel" unnecessarily, wasting precious time and resources in the process when a perfectly good solution to the problem was available "off-the-shelf."

THE POWER OF SCAFFOLDING

As we began to map the network of outside resources surrounding each of the breakthrough companies, we were struck by the myriad of ways that organizational scaffolding enhanced both the performance of a given firm and the individuals within it. We identified several distinct ways that outsiders contributed to a breakthrough company's success:

SUPPORT: SOMEONE TO LEAN ON

Roger Staubach's personal investment crisis points out a key way that scaffolding can help an individual and an organization. As human beings, we don't always think clearly in the heat of battle, and having someone in your corner can make the difference between making a good decision and a bad one. Everyone—whether they are running a company or simply climbing up the career ladder—should have people to turn to for support when they are faced with a challenge.

> Everyone—whether they are running a company or simply climbing the career ladder—should have people to turn to for support when they are faced with a challenge.

I learned this lesson myself early in my own career, when I was chairman of a technology firm that hit a crisis which nearly sank us. I agreed to step in as CEO, and at my first board meeting, I had to inform the board that the several million dollars of venture capital we had just raised was already spent (for more on this, see chapter 9: Graduating from Tough Times U). Board member Jose Collazo, then CEO of Infonet (who had put $400,000 of his own money into the firm), was the first to break the silence. I will never forget his words. "Keith, sometimes stuff happens that you don't control," he said.

"You've got what you've got—now focus on what needs to be done to fix it." That one small expression of support got me through the next month, the most difficult four weeks of my career. Just two board meetings later, I was forced to deliver even worse news: We needed to lay off 300 of our 390 employees. I didn't sleep at all the night before the meeting, so troubled was I by the pain I was about to cause those 300 people and their families. After the meeting ended, another board member, Steve Carpenter (former vice chairman of Security Pacific Bank and a member of the board of the Twelfth District Federal Reserve Bank), put his hand on my shoulder and gave me some advice. "You don't have the option of taking really good care of 300 people," he told me. "You can take terrible care of 390 people or take good care of 90." While that time remains one of the most difficult of my career, Collazo and Carpenter, by letting me know that they had been in similar situations, helped me keep faith in myself and my team, which was crucial to the eventual turnaround of our business.

PERSPECTIVE: ANOTHER SET OF EYES

Before joining Polaris in 1998, Tom Tiller was groomed in General Electric's famed management training program for fifteen years, culminating in a role as head of GE's billion-dollar silicone division. In his time at GE, Tiller came to rely on fellow division heads like Bob Nardelli (now CEO of Chrysler) and Steve Bennett (currently CEO of breakthrough company Intuit) for frank advice and feedback just a phone call away. After moving to Minneapolis to take the job at Polaris, however, Tiller realized that he had come to rely on his GE network more than he thought. "It was a big change for me," Tiller told us. "First as a thirty-seven-year-old COO and then as CEO a year later, I felt like I was always on a stage and needed to have the answers. While I had run a division, it was totally different running an entire publicly held company. You don't have peers anymore. I needed someone to bounce ideas off of when I didn't have the answers."

While he had a great mentor in former CEO Hall Wendell, he thought having additional support outside the company would be a good idea. That's when he turned to YPO as a way to help replace the support structure he relied on at GE. "I could take a business or personal idea and run it by people who have become close friends in a very trusting environment," said Tiller, who has been active in his forum for more than seven years. "It's nice to talk to people even if they don't have the answers."[5]

NEW IDEAS: FINDING THE WHEEL-MAKERS

Where does your company go for its best ideas? Intuit's Scott Cook says too many companies fail to look outside their own four walls. "You don't ever want to reinvent the wheel," Scott Cook told us. "Instead, go find the best wheel-maker you can and learn everything you can from them."[6] It's a philosophy Cook has lived by his whole life, and one that is embedded in the Intuit culture. Spend a few minutes with Cook and you realize instantly that his brain is like a radar screen, tracking developments in subjects as diverse as science and technology, management, sociology, and political affairs—always on the lookout for things that will help him and Intuit become more effective. That's also why some of the world's most successful companies, like Amazon, Procter & Gamble, and eBay, want Cook on their boards. When I first met Cook, in fact, I felt like he was sizing me up, wondering, "Is this guy worthy of adding to my wheel-maker collection?"

> Too many growing companies continually try to reinvent the wheel instead of seeking out the very best wheel-makers.

From the very beginning, Cook was determined for Intuit to be one of the most customer-centric firms on the planet, but he found that the bigger Intuit got, the harder it became to keep the company focused, especially after the company successfully went public in 1993. That's why, just two weeks after the IPO, he decided to get outside help. After renting out part of the San Jose Convention Center, Cook hired author Jim Collins and a strategic planner from Intel, which was celebrated within Silicon Valley for its effective planning processes, to lead his employees in a day-long discussion of their mission. By all accounts, the event—called VMOVA for vision, mission, operating values, and achievements—was a rousing success. "Having the whole company involved, wrestling with everyone's thoughts, made the process new, better, and fresh—far better than if the executive team had just done it themselves," Cook recalled about the event.[7]

Ten years later, Cook was again concerned: He thought that Intuit was losing touch with the real needs of its customers. As luck would have it, that's when he ran into a former colleague of his from Bain, Fred Reichheld. After hearing some of Cook's concerns, Reichheld, who had already published two books on the effects of loyalty in business, offered to teach Intuit a new program he had been working on, called Net Promoter Score, or NPS. The idea, which Reichheld later published in his 2006 book *The Ultimate Question,* was to ask customers, on a scale of one to ten, how willing they would be to recommend a company's product to their friends. A company's NPS was calculated by tabulating the responses and then doing a bit of math: Those who respond with nines and tens are considered "promoters"; sevens and eights are "passives"; and everyone else is a "detractor." NPS is the net of promoters minus detractors. "The key, therefore, is to zero in on those detractors and find out how to turn them into promoters," Reichheld told us.[8] Cook was thrilled when he heard how simple—and how powerful—NPS could be. After implementing the program and running it for about two years, Intuit's NPS scores, which were already solid, leaped up the chart. More important, by asking customers how they could do better, Intuit made improvements to products like TurboTax that helped it gain another 6 percent of market share, growing from 73 percent to 79 percent. "There are only two requirements for growth," Cook has said. "Happy customers and profitable customers. NPS was exactly what we needed to get back in touch with our customers and make the kinds of changes they wanted us to make."[9]

NEW TOOLS: ELEVATING YOUR GAME

Smart use of the right consultant can also provide an important form of organizational scaffolding. When Scott Edmonds took over as CEO of Chico's, he realized that the company had outgrown the "hub-and-spoke" style of management favored by founders Marvin and Helene Gralnick, especially since within 48 hours of being named CEO of Chico's, Edmonds announced the acquisition of another company: White House | Black Market. He knew he needed to change the way Chico's operated since he now faced integrating a new management team and ensuring a smooth integration of the new brand. Edmonds, however, knew that the transition away from the old way of operating would be extremely difficult, especially for those employees who'd grown accustomed to having the CEO weigh in on their decisions. That's when Edmonds decided to bring in a few external reinforcements. "I came to realize early on when I joined Chico's back in 1995 that the company wouldn't survive if the management team tried to tackle the women's apparel business on its own," Edmonds told us. "Instead, we need to use the best brainpower available on the planet to stay ahead."[10]

So Edmonds went looking for some outside expertise. First, he brought in an organizational psychologist to help him revamp his hiring process, which he felt was broken. While he had been working toward bringing in new talent to upgrade his management ranks, Edmonds was disappointed by some of the new hires. Rather than working toward the overall success of the company, these people seemed bent on personal glory instead. "It was the kind of thing where eight months after these people started, their heads would roll back, their eyes would go black, and we'd be left with a Great White Shark," Edmonds told us. "I wanted to bring in some help to develop some tests that would enable us to identify the best candidates, not only for their skills but also their personalities."[11]

One day Chuck Nesbit, Chico's COO, formerly of Sara Lee, charged into Edmonds's office. "Chuck told me that I needed to stop running the business from the hallways, it's too big and too complicated," Edmonds told us. "That's when he recommended a consulting firm out of New York City that has really helped us turn things around." The consultant helped Chico's to completely restructure the way its management team makes decisions and solves problems, thereby exploding the hub-and-spoke model in the process.[12]

ACCOUNTABILITY: TURNING UP THE HEAT

When you consider that most successful entrepreneurs are, at some level, competitive, it is not surprising to note that outsiders can play an important role in stoking those competitive fires. Researchers have recently been studying this very issue. One study found that one of the major reasons entrepreneurial leaders establish and maintain relationships with outside resources, such as peer groups, is to hold themselves accountable for improving the performance of their firms. "The motivational force of membership is embodied in members' desire to avoid inferior ranking in the group and the peer pressure to meet collective performance standards," the researchers wrote. In other words, entrepreneurs join these groups to feed their competitive juices and to gain recognition from their peers.[13]

> The research shows that one of the main reasons people participate in peer groups is to hold themselves accountable for improving the performance of their firms.

For CEOs like Roger Staubach, joining a peer group serves as both a sounding board and a chance to measure your success against that of your peers, which can be especially important for leaders of private companies that may not face the same scrutiny that public company leaders receive from analysts, boards of directors, and even the media. "The camaraderie keeps you going," Staubach told us. "Part of the drive to be successful is because you know you will be reporting back to your forum."[14]

Entrepreneurs can also build this sense of accountability through their choices of board members and mentors. When an entrepreneur taps a big name for help, the last thing he or she wants to do is let that person down in some way, either through the performance of the company or through their own personal conduct. When we asked Mark Smith of ADTRAN whether there were any people outside the company who were important to him, his eyes lit up. He pointed to two giants of the industry: Glen Robinson, founder of Scientific Atlanta, who served on the board of Smith's first company, UDS; and Bob Galvin, the former CEO of Motorola, who became a mentor to Smith after Motorola acquired UDS. "Both of those guys have been there and done that," Smith told us. "And more important, they were good people whom I had so much respect for." Smith said the last thing he wanted to do was let either of them down.[15]

TYPES OF SCAFFOLDING

After interviewing members of the breakthrough companies about the value of outside resources to their respective company's growth, one clear theme emerged: There are many different kinds of scaffolding. The following is a rundown of some of the most common forms we heard about.

PEER NETWORKS

Peer networks can provide executives with a confidential setting to discuss problems and share perspectives. Besides YPO, good options include WPO, EO, CEO, Vistage International, the American Leadership Forum, the Business Roundtable, the National Association of Women Business Owners, and the Forum for Women Entrepreneurs. Several of these organizations offer opportunities for small group discussions, often organized in such a way as to minimize competitive conflicts of interest and to assure high levels of confidentiality. One of the most common and effective forms of scaffolding we found in the breakthrough companies, as it turned out, was an early willingness to embrace peer-to-peer networks.[16]

In addition to the peer groups listed above, industry-specific peer groups can be found in a wide range of industries, from advertising agencies to car rental agencies and from car dealerships to office furniture distributors. When industry peer network participants were recently asked why they joined such a group, the most popular responses, in order, were to improve company performance; to obtain new knowledge and skills; to improve organization in their professional life; and to develop clearer performance benchmarks. Clearly, the results of this survey demonstrate that there's a great deal of appeal in reaching outside for help in growing an organization.

And peer groups are not just for company heads. When we conducted our non-CEO interviews at the breakthrough companies, we heard about all kinds of peer networks, ranging from groups of CFOs to a collection of young real estate professionals to the Product Management Association, a group that Scott Cook has challenged more Intuit employees to join. It is because they understand the value of these peer networks that leaders like Cook and Roger Staubach encourage their team members to join these networks on their own. Blair Bryan, who runs Staubach operations in the southeastern United States, for example, joined his local YPO chapter with Staubach's encouragement. "He has really emphasized to everyone in the organization how healthy it is to get input from sources outside the company," Bryan told us.[17]

CASE STUDY IN ERECTING SCAFFOLDING:
Eagle Global Logistics

Is it possible for a company to outgrow its need for scaffolding? Jim Crane, founder of Houston-based Eagle Global Logistics (EGL), doesn't think so. When we started working with him, EGL already had annual revenues of more than $3 billion and was providing outsourced supply chain management to two of the world's most demanding logistics customers on earth: Dell and HP.

We tasked EGL's top forty managers and key office managers to detail the most important issues facing the firm. In pointed discussions that went late into the night, the team grappled with strategic priorities and made tough choices. They then built detailed action plans for each of the company's regional business units. "The result," Crane told us, "was a retooled company capable of driving higher levels of efficiency and a much higher degree of alignment between operational units."

"I wanted a different set of eyes looking at the business," Crane said as he reflected on the six months we spent working together. "As a result of your work with us, I restructured the senior management in a way that now has all of my players playing to their strengths. We simply could not have accomplished that without someone from the outside coming in and looking at it with fresh eyes."

BOARDS AND ADVISORY BOARDS

Lots of companies have boards and advisory boards, but we noticed that breakthrough companies handled such boards differently: (1) they tend to set them up early; (2) they seek the very best board members they can find; and (3) they invite board members to really get to know the company and to take a "full swing" at the issues. Too many executives stock their boards with friends or country club cronies who are content to show up for a quarterly dog-and-pony show and some softball discussions.

When Hall Wendell led a restart of Polaris after he negotiated a buyout from its parent company, Textron, the first thing he did was build the strongest board he could find. Polaris was in tough shape when Wendell bought it, and things went from bad to worse; the company even dropped to an employee base of just sixteen full-time employees at one point. You would have thought that Bev Dolan, Textron's CEO at the time, would be wiping his brow with relief after selling the underperforming division to Wendell. Wendell, however, somehow convinced Dolan to join the Polaris board, where he served for twenty years. "Hall was only thirty-seven when he took over the company," Tom Tiller told us. "He and Bev had a good trusting relationship; Bev was his mentor just like Hall is mine today."[18]

Chico's is another company with an exceptionally experienced board composed of retail veterans like John Burden III, former chairman of Federated Department Stores; Verna Gibson, former CEO of The Limited Stores Division of the Limited; David Dyer, former CEO of Tommy Hilfiger and Lands' End; and Michael Weiss, former CEO of Express, a subsidiary of The Limited. "We purposely have a board filled with industry champions," Edmonds told us.[19]

More than one breakthrough CEO told us that he works hard to populate his board with the smartest and toughest people he can find, people who will really help raise the bar on performance.

Serving on other company's boards, it turns out, can also be a valuable way to extend your own company's scaffolding. Jon Judge,

CEO of Paychex, for instance, sits on the board of another public company and several boards of charitable organizations. He told us that after he and his fellow board members finish up the work at hand, they often stick around to swap experiences and bounce decisions off each other. "I learn so much from the fellow executives and businesspeople I serve on those boards with. I get the chance to see how other people react to similar problems that are crossing their desk," Judge told us. "I find it particularly useful for keeping up on new developments in things like Sarbanes and SEC regulations. I think that most thoughtful executives would admit that if they aren't continually in the learning game, they will quickly become dinosaurs."[20]

INVESTORS

Judge also told us about how valuable his relationships are with leaders in both the private and public investment communities. "These guys see tons of both start-ups and mature businesses, and a wide range of management styles," Judge told us. "I find it very useful to hear those stories and learn from them." Judge's point to us was that CEOs, especially public ones, often turn to the investment community for advice on anything from declaring dividends to their thoughts on a potential acquisition.[21] Chico's CEO, Scott Edmonds, for instance, told us the important role that the New York–based investment banks Peter J. Solomon Co. and Goldman Sachs played in his courtship of White House | Black Market. "I continue to rely on advice from the Wall Street brain trust," Edmonds told us.[22]

For private companies, finding the right financial partner at the right time can often be critical. Although Scott Cook bootstrapped Intuit's early years, he circled back around several years later and raised a round of venture capital, led by Kleiner Perkins Caufield & Byers and Technology Venture Investors, a move motivated in part by his desire to tap the breadth of knowledge that that these investors could bring to Intuit. Specifically, he wanted to add John Doerr of Kleiner Perkins and Burt McMurtry of TVI to his board. Both invested in Intuit, joined its board, and helped the company through its successful IPO. Even today, Cook continues to seek out knowledge from other Silicon Valley VC firms like Sequoia Capital. "You can see the guidance that they give their fund companies," Cook told us. "For the elite firms like Sequoia, it is not just about doing deals, it is about building a company for the long term."[23]

CUSTOMERS AND VENDORS

Examples like SAS's SASWare Ballot and Intuit's use of the Net Promoter Score show how customers also can play a pivotal role in a firm's scaffolding. By converting the outer wall of the company into a permeable barrier for customers, SAS and Intuit not only get productive feedback, they make more satisfied customers in the process.

Chico's, for example, lives and dies according to whether it can develop jackets, shirts, and skirts that its customers "have to have," in the words of Linda Costello, Chico's senior vice president of product development. That's why Costello works closely with people like Sher Canada, who runs Chico's 570 stores, to get feedback directly from customers. Chico's also invites longtime customers to visit its offices in tropical Fort Myers, Florida, to tour the facilities and give feedback on the latest fashions and fabrics. "We had a woman in recently named Bonnie who had been a customer since 1993," Costello told us. "And when we let her try on a pair of denim jeans we had just made, she was delighted. She told us she didn't think she would ever be able to wear jeans anymore because of their low backs and skinny thighs." Costello told us she and her product development team can then turn those new clothes out the door fast: Chico's churns out new items each month. Compare that to the J. Jill catalog, which, according to Costello, hasn't changed its product mix in years.

"They're still stuck in the same color palette and look they started with," she told us.[24]

Removing the wall that separates many customers from product teams within a company can prove to be a considerable strategic advantage for a firm. ADTRAN, for example, eliminated the middleman from its product management process long ago. Technical teams work directly with customers like AT&T, Verizon, and Bell South, not only to develop new products, but to keep enhancing existing product lines generations longer than their competition does. "We insist on getting direct customer input, which allows us to be diligent about removing bureaucracy in our decision-making," ADTRAN CEO Tom Stanton told us. "We talk to our customers early and often about what they need. We even encourage our customers to call up our design group directly. That means we get products to market 30 to 40 percent faster than our competition."[25]

Like ADTRAN, Polaris also has strong connections with customers and dealers, since many employees use the company's products and interact with other riders after work and on weekends. But Polaris has leaned in the other direction—toward its vendors—for support, as well. Polaris not only works very closely with its vendors to ensure lean manufacturing elements like just-in-time delivery of parts and equipment, it relies on its vendors to help push innovative features that keep its products ahead of the competition. Team Industries, which manufactures precision-machined components in Bagley, Minnesota, for example, played a key role in developing the automatic transmission and engine braking systems now used by Polaris ATVs, while another vendor, The Hilliard Corp., in Elmira, New York, holds four joint-patents with Polaris for the development of its all-wheel drive system, which is unique in the industry. "Our vendors are truly part of our support network," Mike Malone, CFO at Polaris, told us. "And the new technologies and ideas they provide us for our products are critical to our success."[26]

COLLEGES AND UNIVERSITIES

While it goes without saying that most fast-growing companies struggle to find good employees, the breakthrough companies have included colleges and universities in their scaffolding to facilitate talent pipelines for both graduates and top academics. SAS, for example, continues to maintain a strong relationship with North Carolina State University more than thirty years after Jim Goodnight left to found his company, while ADTRAN works closely with professors to identify top engineering talent at universities like Mississippi State, Alabama, Auburn, and Georgia Tech, Mark Smith's alma mater.[27] Fastenal not only maintains a relationship with the University of Minnesota, Bob Kierlin's old school, it has developed a strong working relationship with many technical schools whose graduates go on to work in Fastenal's retail stores or its custom manufacturing facility in Winona.[28] And the list goes on: Chico's works with colleges with strong schools of design, while Paychex seeks out the country's top accounting and finance talent.[29]

Today, at sixty-five, Roger Staubach is not eligible to be an active member of YPO. But that hasn't stopped him from regularly meeting up with four of his five original forum mates to talk shop, more than twenty years after he first asked them for help in sorting out his troubles with joint-and-several liability. Rather than focusing primarily on the future as they used to, Staubach and his forum mates spend their time together these days reminiscing about their achievements, as most have since successfully sold off their businesses. "My forum played a big part in helping me realize my dream of building a company of my own," Staubach told us. "Belonging to the forum with those guys has always meant reinforcing the right things and was often very therapeutic. Even as we get older, we all still mean a lot to each other."[30]

ERECTING SCAFFOLDING
The Key Ideas

1. Breakthrough companies are skilled at building scaffolding, networks of resources outside the firm that help propel the firm to the next level.

2. The breakthrough companies we studied tapped a broad spectrum of resources to help improve their operations, including peer networks, boards and advisory boards, investors, customers, vendors, and colleges and universities.

3. The value added by the resources these firms assembled was equally varied. These groups provided the company with support, perspective, new ideas, and tools, and helped hold the firm accountable to achieving its vision.

ERECTING SCAFFOLDING "SQUIRTS FROM THE GRAPEFRUIT"
(Findings That Surprised Us)

1. We were surprised to learn that four of the nine breakthrough companies were founded by or headed by people who belonged to the same executive peer group. This executive camaraderie counters the stereotype of the isolated and self-sufficient CEO. Leaders of breakthrough firms appear to place considerable importance on having people outside the firm they can talk to.

2. Far from this being an "executive only" trend, we found people at all levels of these companies engaged with people and groups outside the firm for the expressed purpose of improving their own performance or the performance of their division or department.

3. Rather than create "rubber stamp" boards, breakthrough companies attempt to build boards or advisory boards that challenge management's thinking.

4. While we were not surprised when breakthrough companies described the importance of forms of scaffolding like boards and peer groups—we *were* surprised that they put their customers in the same category.

BREAKTHROUGH IN PRACTICE
Tips for Erecting Scaffolding

1. Across the top of a sheet of paper, write the following words: Support, Perspective, New Ideas, New Tools, and Accountability. Now list the people or groups you currently go to for these things. Decide whether you need to develop some new scaffolding to support you in any of these areas.

2. If your company doesn't have a board or advisory board, talk about getting one. Fill it with highly experienced members, preferably ones who have successfully navigated whatever transition your firm is currently facing. And encourage board members to take a full swing at the issues—to challenge the organization's thinking. Give board members plenty of time with managers in the firm, and invite them to your strategy retreat and arrange opportunities for them to have contact with customers.

3. Explore what peer groups are available for a person in your position. Research those that are available, being sure to talk to current members of any groups you are considering joining—to get the real story on the level of value provided. If you don't find a peer group that meets your specific needs, start your own! If you set up your own peer group, be sure to build it in such a way as to minimize conflicts of interest and assure confidentiality.

4. Make a list of key people in your organization who will need to increase their skills or abilities over the next three years. Sit down with these people to discuss the areas in which they need to grow, and then assist them in finding outside resources that will help them grow in those particular areas.

5. Organize a meeting of key people in your organization who are in roles that put them in regular contact with customers. Evaluate how well your firm effectively taps the knowledge of your customers, and identify the two or three most important ways you can improve your organization's use of customer knowledge to improve your business.

8

ENLISTING INSULTANTS

It is difficult to lay aside a confirmed passion.
CAIUS VALERIUS CATULLUS

WHY DO SO many once promising companies get left in the dust by the competition? It turns out when a company botches strategy or misses out on the industry's next big thing, the executive team probably fell victim to one of two common human afflictions—at least that's what two researchers at the MIT Sloan Business School believe.[1] The researchers call these two ubiquitous management traps "myopia" and "inertia." Myopia, or short-sightedness, refers to a company's inability to see the forest for the trees. Myopic executives tend to focus more on fighting fires and tackling projects close to home, and forget to watch for tectonic changes reshaping the industry. Similarly, executives suffering from inertia fail to take advantage of new opportunities, choosing instead to stand pat in familiar markets, finding comfort in doing business the way they have always done business.

Examples of these twin traps of myopia and inertia are splashed across the front pages of the business press almost every day. Consider Sony, which dominated the portable music player business for decades, then ignored the digital revolution, and is now forced to play catch up with Apple. Or Ford and General Motors, which, unlike Toyota and Honda, discounted the potential of investing in hybrid technology. Even MTV, once beloved by advertisers as the hippest brand around, has struggled to stay relevant in the face of competition from online networking and video sites like MySpace, FaceBook, and YouTube.

How do company leaders avoid falling prey to myopia and inertia? The nine breakthrough companies, at least, all shared a similar strategy: They created companies where people are encouraged to question the fundamental assumptions of the business. Breakthrough companies, in other words, want people to buck the system when the system is wrong. We heard so many stories of people bucking the system during our interviews with employees at all levels of breakthrough companies, in fact, that we started calling these people "insultants." I first heard the term "insultant" when my friend Ichak Adizes used it to refer to a person who "consults from the inside." I use it to describe someone willing to ask the tough questions that cause a company to think critically about its fundamental assumptions.[2]

> Not only are they open to people questioning the fundamental assumptions of the business, breakthrough companies encourage people to buck the system.

The value of insultants is that they will go to great lengths to get their companies to reevaluate a position or adapt to a changing environment. Remember the story of Chuck Baxter, the former engineering chief at Polaris, who was the key driver in getting Polaris into the ATV business in 1984. At the time, Polaris had just begun its restart after Hall Wendell's buyout from Textron and possessed few resources, financial or otherwise, to spare on anything except its snowmobile business. Baxter, however, was not someone to sit still when he saw an opportunity. He observed the kinds of products the Japanese manufacturers were churning out and he thought he could do better. And, while never receiving official approval, Baxter began developing prototypes in the company's tool shop. "Chuck Baxter got us into the ATV business," Bob Nygaard, head of sales operations at Polaris, told us. "Sure, he got his hand slapped a bunch of times, but he saw an opportunity and he went after it. We wouldn't be the company we are today if he hadn't."[3] And Baxter didn't stop there: Jeff Bjorkman, now VP of operations, told us that the Ranger, a utility ATV that is now the best-selling vehicle in the Polaris fleet, was also developed in Baxter's so-called *skunk works* garage. "Chuck was always challenging why we did things the way we did," Bjorkman told us. "A group of us agreed that there wasn't a need to build something like the Ranger, but he went ahead and did it anyway. He had a challenging personality that drove you nuts a lot of the time. But that kind of attitude toward innovation continues to be a big part of what makes us successful today." The key, Bjorkman says, is that while Hall Wendell or Tom Tiller may never give their official approval for a project, engineers know they don't risk their jobs when they follow their own instincts.[4]

CASE STUDY IN ENLISTING INSULTANTS
o^2 *ideas*

It had been almost five years since I had last talked to John Zimmerman and Dr. Shelly Stewart, leaders of the then tiny Birmingham, Alabama–based ad agency, o^2 ideas. They had asked for our help in 2002 when their sales hit a plateau and their profits were declining.

I called up Zimmerman to tell him I was writing a book and to get an update on o^2. "I hope you'll tell the story of how you insulted me out of a job," he said with a laugh. I had no idea what he was talking about, so I asked him to explain.

"The last time you were in my office," he reminded me. "You told me that you thought I was a creative genius, but I was making myself and the company miserable by trying to be the CEO. You told me that I should do what I do best, and let someone else handle the day-to-day management of the agency."

He said that at first the idea didn't sit well with him, but that after a couple of months he sat down with his then sixty-eight-year-old partner Shelly Stewart to discuss it. They agreed that Shelly would step in and run the firm so that Zimmerman could focus on providing creative leadership.

What has happened since? In the past four years, o² ideas has doubled in size, and has inked major deals with leading national advertisers such as Intuit, Home Depot, and Verizon Wireless. More important, Zimmerman said, the structure and process accountability that Shelly brought to the business has actually *increased* the company's entrepreneurial spirit—something that he was worried about when he stepped down as CEO. "Sometimes you need someone from the outside to point out what is right in front of you," Zimmerman said. "This change ended up being the best thing our company has ever done."

WHY COMPANIES NEED INSULTANTS: THE PROBLEM OF DEFERENCE

Think your company is a place where folks are encouraged to take a full swing at the issues, especially if they think the leader might disagree? If you could really get into the minds of your troops, you might be surprised. It is an issue that Intuit's Scott Cook, for one, is fascinated by. That is why, back in the spring of 2006, he conducted a two-question survey of the winners of that year's *Inc.* 500 class who would be attending the magazine's conference, held in Savannah.[5] That survey, which went out to about 1,000 CEOs and their direct reports, asked the following two questions:

1. ***Ideas the CEO initially doesn't like are regularly implemented at our company:***

        ____*True* ____*False*

2. ***Our CEO encourages thinking that challenges our current beliefs:***

        ____*True* ____*False*

When Cook revealed the results of the survey during his keynote speech, there was more than one audible moan from the audience. While 90 percent of the responding CEOs answered "true" to question one, indicating that they felt that their companies regularly implemented ideas that they, as CEOs, initially disagreed with, only 60 percent of the non-CEO executives felt the same. The results of the second question were even more unsettling to the audience: While 77 percent of the CEOs reported that they encouraged their employees to challenge beliefs, only 47 percent of their managers agreed. And the results of the survey were somewhat skewed, Cook reminded the audience, since he only polled CEOs and their direct reports. Wouldn't the differences have been even greater, Cook asked, if he had surveyed the folks working outside of headquarters, on the front lines?

> Ninety percent of CEOs believe that their companies regularly implement ideas that the CEO initially doesn't like. Only 60 percent of their direct reports agree. It doesn't take much imagination to guess what the view of the people on the frontlines would be.

How could these leaders of such great growth companies have such a different view of these questions than their direct reports? Here again, part of the answer may lie in the psychological wiring of the entrepreneurial leader. Entrepreneurial leaders tend to be imbued with a strong sense of optimism and self-efficacy that may enable them to, at times, view the world through rose-colored glasses (a useful characteristic during their firm's difficult start-up years). And when it comes to people disagreeing with them, entrepreneurial leaders sometimes think they want disagreement more than they actually do.

Another reason for this disconnect may lie in the tendency of most humans to defer to authority. When, in an experiment, military fliers were asked to solve a series of logic problems, researchers found that navigators almost always acquiesced to the solutions provided by pilots, even when they believed the pilot's answer was incorrect.[6] Why? Since the pilots outranked them, the navigators (wrongly) assumed the pilots knew better. You could readily substitute a CEO or vice president for the pilot and a frontline employee for the navigator in such a study and, no doubt, get the same results. People defer to authority or rank because they assume that person, the person in authority, is likely to have more information or clearer perspective. But often authority figures are wrong, and if an organization doesn't have a strong insultant culture, errors are likely to be propagated throughout the company.

It is also true that often candor tends to flee authority. In far too many companies, the CEO receives filtered or packaged information that emphasizes good news and camouflages the bad. If leaders don't work hard to build an environment where it is okay to bring up potentially bad news, it will get buried. In the words of Polaris CEO Tom Tiller, "Good news rises and bad news sinks like a rock."[7]

WHY COMPANIES NEED INSULTANTS: THE PROBLEM OF HERDING

A second reason companies need insultants is that people, like animals, seek safety in numbers. This has been emphatically demonstrated by University of California researcher David Romer in his study of decision making by professional football coaches.[8] Romer wanted to find out whether the commonly accepted practice of punting away the ball on fourth down was the best strategy for winning football games. To do that, he studied every play of the more than 700 National Football League games played between 1998 and 2000, and used a dynamic points system to assign a value whenever a team had possession of the ball. The closer a team got to the end zone, the higher the value of the possession became. Having a first down at the one-yard line, for instance, was worth far more than having possession at mid-field on third down.

What Romer concluded was that coaches didn't go for a first down on fourth down as often as they should. This is probably because, as any NFL fan can tell you, whenever a coach decides to run a play on fourth down rather than punting or trying for a field goal, he sets himself up for criticism. The "herd" (in this case, other football coaches, fans, and pundits) believed, as gospel, that you punt or go for a field goal on fourth down. Romer's study established that coaches would actually win more games if they went for touchdowns and first downs instead of punting or attempting a field goal. His findings, not surprisingly, were largely ignored in the NFL until one coach, Bill Belichick of the New England Patriots, started winning championships by applying some of Romer's principles.[9]

> Romer's study established that coaches would actually win more games if they went for touchdowns and first downs instead of punting or attempting a field goal—results that were largely ignored in the NFL.

This same kind of herd behavior happens in the business world all the time. CEOs, like coaches, can avoid the rebuke of Wall Street by playing it safe and following the path traveled by others, even if their company's performance suffers. Similarly, a company's top salesperson can avoid conflict if he follows the herd and avoids pointing out that competitors are steadily eroding his company's position. It is only after someone like Coach Belichick is successful that people begin to take notice. Remember the case of ADTRAN. Back in 1986, the contract silicon manufacturing business exploded. While most of ADTRAN's competitors in the telecommunications industry at that time took advantage of this trend by outsourcing the production of their silicon chips, ADTRAN veered from the herd's course. CEO Mark Smith was prompted to take this course by Lonnie McMillian, his chief engineer and cofounder. "Rather than save costs in the short-run," McMillian argued, "ADTRAN could control its own custom silicon design, which would pay off not only in reduced long-term costs, but in gaining independence from outside vendors."[10] Just about fifteen years later, the telecom industry collapsed, and while most of AD-TRAN's competitors were squeezed out, ADTRAN survived, largely because it controlled its own silicon design.

Similarly, if Polaris's Chuck Baxter was more concerned with fitting in or pleasing Hall Wendell rather than challenging the conventional thinking of the time that Polaris needed to save money wherever it could, Polaris might not have leaped into the ATV market when it did.

GETTING YOUR IDEAS HEARD

Insultants like Polaris's Baxter are often the first members of the organization to spot a development that will require a business to reconsider its direction. Just having the idea, however, isn't enough; insultants must also be adept at presenting and championing their idea throughout the company, especially to a particularly charismatic or forceful authority figure.

Take, for example, the case of Walter Turek, the longtime sales and marketing head at Paychex. Throughout the 1980s, Turek had watched one of Paychex's rivals, ADP, expand rapidly into the business of collecting and paying its clients' payroll taxes. Though ADP serviced clients far bigger than those targeted by Paychex, Turek felt strongly that Paychex needed to also extend its product line to include a payroll tax payment service. At the same time, he also understood that such an endeavor would be an uphill battle: Founder and CEO Tom Golisano was determined to keep the company focused on its bread and butter, processing paychecks. "Tom's whole philosophy was that until something changed, the past would be the future," Turek told us. "He said that he would expect the same results year after year unless you could prove that something had changed."[11]

Golisano, for his part, had already heard just about every other pitch imaginable on how Paychex could expand its services. He just considered them distractions. And who could blame him: By 1989, Paychex was processing payroll for some 100,000 small business customers and revenues topped the $100 million mark. Golisano was determined that Paychex should continue to fulfill its primary role—processing accurate payroll—not trying to sell credit cards, banking relationships, software systems, or a host of others services to his customers who, on average, employ just seventeen people. "If you had ideas about changing that model," Golisano would tell people, "you had to prove, with numbers, that Paychex would lose customers if it didn't add that feature."[12]

Even though Turek knew his boss's mindset, he couldn't keep silent about the potential he saw in collecting payroll taxes. He wasn't surprised, then, when Golisano reacted coolly to the pitch. "Why in the world would somebody want us to pay their taxes for them?" Turek remembers Golisano saying. "People don't want us to hold their money when they can invest it for themselves. All they have to do is fill out some simple paperwork." Turek, however, was undaunted; he decided to let the numbers make his case.[13]

> Insultants are masters at getting their ideas heard, and they never resort to insulting someone. They work quietly within existing systems to get the organization to question its assumptions and change its thinking.

Every week, Paychex executives reviewed something prepared by Turek's sales team called the Weekly Activity Report, a summary of sorts of new business prospects, business won, and business lost. And each week, Turek accumulated more and more evidence for his case: Paychex was losing prospects because it wasn't offering a payroll tax service. "That weekly activity became our market research," Turek told us. "Turns out small businesses and their certified public accountants wanted this service. Consider someone like a welder. The government wants him to collect and pay taxes in a sophisticated manner and if he doesn't, he goes to jail. He wants us to do it for him because the interest on the amount of money we collect is insignificant to him." For Paychex, however, those monies today are far from insignificant: As of May 31, 2006, 92 percent of all the firm's 500,000 clients were enrolled in the Taxpay service, which allowed Paychex to earn more than $100 million in additional annual interest income from safekeeping their clients' money.[14]

INSULTANT'S STYLE GUIDE

Be empathetic. Your point of view is shaped by the information and experience you have. Others have different perspectives that also deserve consideration. Intuit cofounder Scott Cook is fond of quoting the proverb "It's helpful to walk a mile in another's shoes—and remember, first you must remove your own shoes."

Don't attack. Questioning the assumptions upon which the business is based is the job of insultants—finger pointing is not. Too many people don't understand the difference. Nobody likes to be told that their assumptions are wrong, that their department is focusing on the wrong thing, et cetera. Good insultants, therefore, work hard to avoid such blaming. The most powerful tool in the insultant's arsenal is the question—and knowing how to ask the right question at the right time.

Don't triangulate. Most people find talking behind someone's back to be insulting—so effective insultants avoid it at all costs.

Don't kid yourself—your real motivation will be obvious. According to Chris Argyris at Harvard, a person's effectiveness as a change agent is impacted by his or her real motivation for effecting change. If you are intent on ax grinding, people will figure it out. If you mean to embarrass, demean, or criticize another person, while you might succeed in that goal, you will have unnecessarily sacrificed any opportunity you had to contribute to change.

Be a grown-up. Your perspective is just one person's perspective—keep that in mind. There is usually more than one way to achieve a goal. Effective insultants don't fall in love with their own solution to a problem; they work instead to make sure that problems are raised and discussed by as many people as is feasible. An insultant's job is to make sure an issue gets a thorough vetting, not to convince everyone to see the world his or her way.

Be assertive and persistent. Not everyone will be receptive to the hard truth, so an insultant must be both assertive and persistent, returning to the issue as often as he or she thinks is necessary to get the point across.

Implementing Taxpay in 1989 also marked a key inflection point for the company. Not only did it add another important revenue stream, it demonstrated that customers did indeed want services in addition to payroll, paving the way for the company to introduce key services like direct deposit and a human resources division in 1992. Fueled in part by this product expansion, Paychex then posted ten consecutive years of net income growth in excess of 30 percent, helping drive the stock price from $0.90 a share in May 1991 to $38.43 in May 2001. "I have to admit, I didn't think Taxpay would go," Golisano told us. "It took Walt Turek and the sales force to slap me around a bit to get me there."[15]

CREATING AN ENVIRONMENT WHERE INSULTANTS FLOURISH

Because most folks tend to both defer to authority and make up their minds based on the opinions and actions of those around them, building an organization that tolerates, much less encourages insultants, can be tough. Here are a few lessons we learned from watching breakthrough companies in action.

CELEBRATE PRODUCTIVE FAILURE

If your employees are afraid to fail, or are punished when they do, you can bet you aren't breeding any insultants in your company. To question the assumptions upon which a business is based is to run the risk of being wrong. People will only do that when they feel safe to do so. It's important because if people stop questioning the status quo, the company's gears of learning will seize up. Any company that is experimenting with new ideas is bound to fail at least some of the time. What breakthrough companies emphasize is that when you do fail, learn from the experience: Use the failure to create new knowledge that moves the company ahead.

Rather than punish failure, Intuit celebrates it. Consider the case of the former head of Intuit's TurboTax division. This manager led a marketing effort called "Focus on the Young" to get young people to use TurboTax to prepare their tax returns. Intuit had high hopes for the campaign and plowed millions of dollars into promoting it through high-profile celebrities and hip-hop acts. As the 2005 tax season came and went, however, the results were in: The campaign was a complete failure. Now, if this manager worked for another software company, he might have expected a visit from the human resources department. At Intuit, on the other hand, he got back to work to see what had gone wrong. And, using a page from Scott Cook's handbook, he went directly to the customer to get the answers. That's when it hit him: Young people don't care about filing their taxes—they care about their tax *refund*. The manager used this bit of "aha" intelligence to flip-flop the focus of his campaign: Now young taxpayers could visit a Web site to file their taxes, rockyourrefund.com, where they could elect to receive their refund amount via a gift card to retailers like Best Buy or travel sites like Expedia. And the higher the refund amount got, the bigger the bonus the retailer would add to the card, adding, for instance, another $200 in store credit to a $1,000 refund. This time, because Intuit listened to its customers, the campaign was a big hit.

> Rather than punish failure, Intuit celebrates it. Each year, the company gives an award to the team member responsible for the "Failure of the Year."

Despite his initial ill-fated campaign, not only did this manager keep his job, he was honored with Intuit's annual Best Failure award. "At Intuit, we celebrate failure," said Cook. "Because every failure teaches something important that can be the seed for the next great idea."[16]

GIVE PEOPLE ENOUGH INFORMATION TO BE GOOD INSULTANTS

One way many businesses unintentionally limit the growth of insultants is by running operations on a need-to-know basis. If the only information people receive is that which relates to their functional silo, they'll never develop a 360-degree understanding of what the business is trying to accomplish. That's why breakthrough companies like Fastenal encourage active strategic debate at all levels, from the retail store to the sorting room to the boardroom. One of the introductory courses at the Fastenal School of Business, in fact, is a discussion of Fastenal's various roles in the industrial distribution business. By providing information and education, Fastenal helps employees understand what their business is trying to accomplish, as well as the strategy it's using to get there. As a result, Fastenal employees are always in a position to identify where and when that strategy can be tweaked.[17]

Many companies also make the mistake of cutting off the flow of information to their board of directors, often seeing the board more as a constituency to be "managed" than as a strategic asset. Breakthrough companies like Chico's, on the other hand, treat their board members as trusted advisors, counting on them for objective advice and getting them deeply involved in the business so that they can truly add value. Scott Edmonds, for instance, could have simply filled his board with people he knew would support him at all costs. Instead, he recruited the highest caliber and most experienced board members from the women's apparel world, to keep him honest and on an even keel. In keeping these board members involved, Edmonds knows he'll be able to learn from their past experiences and get their proactive thoughts on new trends he might have missed.[18]

Many firms fail to tap people who gather information on the front-lines, especially salespeople. Too often, companies fail to cultivate a deep understanding of the business model within their sales teams, which often results in these teams tracking down the biggest commission, rather than a customer or line of business that might be a better strategic fit for the company. A company that's avoided this mistake is Express Personnel: By training franchisees about how the company has fueled its growth by focusing more on temp-to-perm placements in fast-growing companies, rather than on one-time, national contracts for large corporations, Express has been able to sidestep many of the traps that have taken down so many staffing companies over the past decade.[19]

Fueled in part by this notion that the power of insultants is directly proportional to the free flow of information in a company, we experimented with a new model of strategy development with our fieldwork companies. We encouraged these companies to expand beyond the CEO and senior management team, adding to the mix board members, select managers, and members from the sales team, up to twenty-five to sixty people in all, when setting the firm's direction. We found that the resulting groups created strategy faster and with much higher levels of commitment and followthrough than if strategy were formulated in a more traditional manner. (For more on this approach, see chapter 10: Building Breakthrough Capabilities.)

FOCUS ON YOUR DEFECTORS

Another source of insultants that most companies ignore, to their peril, are customers and employees who walk out the door. Making time to talk to employees and customers about what the company could have done differently can be invaluable, as these people are natural insultants: They have little reason not to tell you the truth. They may, in fact, tell you things you might have been reluctant to consider otherwise. Consider again the example of Intuit's use of Net Promoter Score to identify dissatisfied customers. Rather than rely on traditional market research, Cook favors getting out in the field to find out how customers are using his products and, in that way, learning firsthand how to make them better. By using NPS to identify unhappy customers, Intuit is able to use these folks to help improve its products. Similarly, when Chico's found its sales slipping in the past, it made efforts to talk to unhappy customers about what had changed. By asking questions, Chico's learned that it went wrong by veering away from its flattering cut and by replacing its stylish solid prints with garish floral designs.[20]

DON'T LOSE YOUR SENSE OF HUMOR

One of the unexpected findings from our exploratory fieldwork was the importance of humor. Many companies take themselves and their work very seriously; others are quick to enjoy a laugh at their own expense. When we started paying attention to this attribute, we noticed that the companies that were imbued with a sense of humor tended to embrace new ideas and modes of thinking more readily than their more serious counterparts. This sense of humor also seemed to fuel an insultant-friendly atmosphere, as team members, in general, seemed less defensive and more proactive.

> "A good laugh sends a reassuring message: We're on the same wavelength, we get along."

New developments in brain science suggest that laughter and a sense of humor may in fact be much more important than many have thought in creating an environment of openness and trust. Daniel Goleman, the noted psychologist who popularized the notion of emotional intelligence, writes in his book *Primal Leadership* about the benefits of a hearty chuckle. "A good laugh sends a reassuring message: We're on the same wavelength, we get along."[21] In other words, humor creates an atmosphere in which insultants can do their best work.

Spend even a short time with Paychex founder Tom Golisano and you'll realize that he's as quick to laugh as fix you with a stare. While he's a serious man—you can't make a serious bid for the New York governorship if people don't take you seriously—he also loves practical jokes. He told us, for example, about the time that longtime friend and fellow Paychex executive Gene Polisseni came back from a lunch meeting to find his car hanging from a crane in the employee parking lot, courtesy of Tom Golisano himself. As he related the scene to us, Gene's Mercedes convertible dangling precipitously from a metal wire, Golisano could hardly stop laughing. Is it any wonder sales head Walter Turek felt confident he could debate with his boss?[22]

ENLISTING INSULTANTS
The Key Ideas

1. When companies lose their way strategically, it is usually because of two management traps:

   a. Myopia—a tendency to focus on the familiar and local at the expense of exploring new territory.

   b. Inertia—a tendency to stay with proven markets and approaches at the expense of developing new capabilities.

2. Breakthrough firms counter myopia and inertia by cultivating "insultants," people willing to work within the system to get the firm to question existing assumptions and ways of doing business.

3. Insultants are necessary because:

   a. People naturally tend to defer to authority for important strategic perspectives.

   b. People are "wired" to follow the herd, sometimes relying on what psychologists call "social proof" (the fact that everyone else believes something to be true) rather than their own critical thinking.

4. The best insultants are careful never to insult anyone. They are skilled at getting the company to question key assumptions in a way that values everyone's perspective and that keeps the focus on what is best for the organization as a whole.

5. Breakthrough companies work hard to create an environment where insultants flourish. Specifically, they:

   a. Celebrate productive failure.

   b. Involve people enough in the issues that they can make intelligent contributions.

   c. Focus on defectors—both employees and customers.

   d. Use humor to encourage frankness and trust.

ENLISTING INSULTANTS "SQUIRTS FROM THE GRAPEFRUIT"
(Findings That Surprised Us)

1. Every breakthrough company has at least one story of how a single individual, often several layers down in the organization, was the first to see the need for change, and tirelessly pursued that change until he got senior management's attention. Insultants are common in breakthrough companies, and are seen as making an important contribution.

2. Many CEOs believe they are far more open to ideas that "go against the grain" than others in the organization think they are. If leaders don't make a concerted effort to continually surface different points of view, they probably are unlikely to hear much controversial thinking.

3. Far from being the stereotypical rabble-rousers, the best insultants we met were quiet, curious, and extremely open to the input of others. They were careful to share credit, and to raise controversial issues in a way that made others feel safe and that focused discussions on what was best for the organization as a whole.

4. We were surprised to learn that Intuit gives an annual "Best Failure" award, and were impressed by how the award helps take the sting and stigma out of failing, thereby encourages people to try new things.

BREAKTHROUGH IN PRACTICE
Tips for Enlisting Insultants

1. Prior to your next strategy retreat, set up a Web page or blog, and ask people throughout the organization to post what they believe are the two or three most important issues facing the firm. Invite people to either post their own issues, or to comment on the posts of others. Examine the themes that emerge from these posts and use them to structure your strategy discussions at the retreat.

2. Identify the times in your company's history when individuals, other than the senior managers, have identified a key opportunity or challenge and have been responsible for bringing that issue to the attention of the organization. Talk often about what an important contribution these people have made. Give an annual Insultant of the Year award to the person who most helps the organization revisit its assumptions in an important way.

3. When making a key strategic decision, assign a person or group of people the role of playing devil's advocate as you deliberate.

9

GRADUATING FROM TOUGH TIMES U

Adversity has the effect of eliciting talents, which in prosperous circumstances would have lain dormant.

HORACE

VIVIDLY REMEMBER the day we received the letter; it was an otherwise beautiful Southern California morning in February 1996. I was serving as chairman of Collectech, a technology company in Los Angeles, and times were good. The company's revenues had doubled for fifteen straight years, which helped us earn spots on two *Inc.* 500 lists and expand our customer base to some 3,500 clients nationwide. Our next step seemed obvious: We were about to close on a first round of venture capital to fuel our push toward a splashy IPO. That all changed, though, after our CEO handed me the letter from the Business Software Alliance (BSA).

The BSA is a consortium of law firms, charged by software vendors like Microsoft, Oracle, and Symantec to prosecute any illegal copying and use of software for products like Microsoft Office or Norton Utilities. As I scanned the letter, my eyes fell on the words "federal criminal action pursuant . . . fine of up to $250,000 and imprisonment of up to five years." They wanted $2 million to settle a suit that alleged that some of our employees were using pirated software, a demand that I feared would spook our prospective investors and kill our IPO prospects in one fell swoop.

It was devastating to discover that employees in our firm had illegally made copies of software. Little did I know that we had yet to hit bottom. While we were able to settle the suit and close the badly needed round of funding, just weeks later, things went from bad to worse. Our largest client, responsible for the biggest chunk of our annual revenue, began its own financial tailspin, and, overnight, cut its spending on our service to nothing. It was as if someone had thrown gasoline onto our burn rate, prompting our bank to demand immediate payment of a $2 million outstanding loan, under threat of their own lawsuit. Meanwhile, after seeing two-thirds of the money they had invested evaporate in less than ninety days, our investors began discussing the possibility of a lawsuit of their own. In an emergency meeting of the board of directors, I was asked to assume the role of CEO, a move that led to the most difficult two-year period of my career. Collectech and I had just enrolled in Tough Times U, and the tuition was going to be steep. Over the next few months, I would learn just how badly my firm had fallen prey to myopia and inertia traps, and how difficult it was going to be to climb out of the hole.

> As any leader who pushes his organization to achieve breakthrough performance can tell you, tough times are inevitable—they just come with the territory.

As any leader who pushes his organization to achieve breakthrough performance can tell you, tough times are inevitable—they just come with the territory. When you empower people to think and make decisions, mistakes will result, some big enough to trip up the organization. A company that systematically places bets, attempting to up the ante in its industry, will occasionally lose a hand. However, when companies with character face off against tough times, giving in or giving up is not an option. Rather, they embrace these moments as opportunities for learning and improvement. In fact, in my more than twenty years as an executive, the most important educational experience of my life was the two years I spent at Tough Times U. Those two years transformed our company in a way that unleashed its true potential.

Likewise, we found that Tough Times U reshaped each of the breakthrough companies in important ways. When the telecom industry collapsed in 2001, for example, ADTRAN found its key customers canceling orders left and right. Sales decreased by 30 percent, and Wall Street punished the firm's stock price. At the same time, ADTRAN had to follow through on purchase orders it had signed in the high times of the late 1990s. Frustratingly, the company found itself obligated to buy a six-month supply of parts that it couldn't sell. While it was forced to lay off some 100 of its 1,500 employees, ADTRAN largely coped by leaning even more heavily on its design and manufacturing teams to shave costs, and by continuing to innovate and improve its core products. As a result, ADTRAN emerged from the industry's rubble four years later leaner and stronger, and more independent than ever. And as Smith told us, now wiser: No matter how hot the industry gets and no matter how many customers start doubling their orders, ADTRAN will never entangle itself in another fixed contract with a supplier again. "What we learned is that you need to be very apprehensive when times are too good," Smith told us. "You can't get caught up in it. We were lucky because we could move and see change. While we may have ignored the changing environment for sixty days, we saw it within six months. A lot of our competitors didn't."[1]

WHAT DIFFICULT TIMES CAN TEACH

As ADTRAN's example shows, even breakthrough companies experience tough times. But it is not the surviving of tough times that defines a breakthrough company; rather, a breakthrough company is defined by how it uses those tough times to adapt, learn, and redefine its thinking. Specifically, difficult times represent the perfect environment for the organization to be awakened to insights that can help combat myopia and inertia. Here are just some of the ways that time spent in Tough Times U can have positive results.

FORCES YOU TO FACE THE FACTS

As we learned in chapter 8, during a company's good times, people and organizations tend to operate like they have everything figured out. And they resist changing things: If it ain't broke, don't fix it, they say. In these good times, even companies that have cultivated insultants may tend to ignore any suggestion of trouble ahead. But when the going gets rough, on the other hand, there is usually a renewed willingness to question the assumptions upon which the business is based.

At Collectech, for example, we had been featured on the cover of *Inc.* magazine during our *Inc.* 500 run, which led to a lot of backslapping and overconfidence.[2] But as we started bleeding cash, we were suddenly forced to question all of our assumptions: Were we really on the right path? After taking a hard look in the mirror, we recognized that we had diversified across too many markets too quickly, and as a result, we weren't making enough, if any, money on a per-customer basis in several of these markets. To compensate, we shut down the line of business that represented the majority of our customer base, and shifted our entire focus to serving only one industry. This seemed counterintuitive to many at the time, but this narrowing of focus was the real reason we were able to exponentially grow revenues and profits over the next few years.

When a company hits rough water, its leaders need to remember that perhaps more than at any other juncture, tough times represent an organization's greatest opportunity for learning. At the same time that Mark Smith pledged to limit ADTRAN's exposure to long-term supply contracts, the firm also began moving more aggressively to expand its client base beyond the telecom sector, where it now competes with companies like Cisco, to supply routers and other providers of communications equipment to large corporate clients. That way, Smith told us, even if the sector hits another low, ADTRAN will have a more diversified client base to soften the blow.[3]

PROMPTS YOU TO RIGOROUSLY PRIORITIZE

During times of smooth sailing, companies implement good ideas by the bucketful. What gets lost along the way is a sense of priority, a focus on the 20 percent of the activities likely to generate 80 percent of the results. Tough times often require a management team to choose between competing good ideas, and to select the ones that are most crucial to the company's strategic success. When Scott Edmonds was promoted from president to CEO of Chico's in 2003, for example, the company had been struggling to reinvigorate its newest brand, Pazo, which had been launched just a year earlier by founder Marvin Gralnick. While the company's core brand, Chico's, was doing well, management knew it needed to expand its offerings to keep fueling the company's phenomenal growth. Edmonds, however, didn't believe Pazo had the upside of another brand, White House | Black Market, that he had his eye on. So Edmonds decided to close Pazo and shift those resources into integrating White House | Black Market into the Chico's family instead. The result: While Pazo had been losing cash, the new acquisition brought in more than $350 million in revenues in 2006, with substantial profits, and has become a big driver in the company's overall growth.[4]

During times of smooth sailing, good ideas accumulate like barnacles on the hull of a ship. But too many good ideas can slow a company down. What gets lost along the way, unfortunately, is a sense of priority, a focus on the 20 percent of the activities likely to generate 80 percent of the results.

REMINDS YOU THAT YOU CAN COUNT ON PEOPLE

Nothing quite brings out the truth about one's character like difficult times. Tough times generally prompt a fight-or-flight response from the troops: Some will dive under their desks or head for the exits, and others will square their shoulders and ask what they can do to help. The latter are the kinds of folks on whose backs breakthrough companies are built. When they sign up to support the organization during these tough times, they are, in essence, renewing their commitment to its success. When Hall Wendell led the buyout of Polaris from Textron, for instance, he knew he might have to rebuild his workforce from scratch, especially because he had decertified the union and had asked each and every employee to take a 30 percent pay cut. But he had a plan for keeping the people who would commit to the future success of the company. "Hall knew he needed to operate lean to survive," CEO Tom Tiller told us. "So, in return, he told anyone who would stay that they'd get a share of the profits. These were hardworking Midwesterners, and they trusted him." And they were right to: Those employees who stayed earned a small profit-sharing check the very next year. Today, those checks have grown by a factor of twenty-five, to about $4,000 for the average hourly employee.[5]

CLIFFS NOTES FOR GRADUATING FROM TOUGH TIMES U

Merely facing off against tough times doesn't necessarily mean that the company and its people will learn anything from the experience; a lot depends on how the leadership team responds to the challenge. Just showing up for class at Tough Times U doesn't guarantee that you'll graduate. What we learned from talking to breakthrough leaders like Bob Funk was that tough times are opportunities to put to work all the homework the organization has done during the good times. If your company finds itself facing a difficult challenge, you should:

USE YOUR SCAFFOLDING

When we enter crisis mode, we often lose our objectivity and the ability to look at all the sides of an issue. Tough times are often the best opportunities for leaders to reach outside the organization for help. Recall the story from the early days of Staubach, when Roger Staubach reached out to his YPO forum for help in solving his debt problems, or when Scott Cook turned to his old Bain colleague Fred Reichheld for help in driving a customer focus in the TurboTax division. While a company's scaffolding often serves as a means of getting a company to the next level, it can also be invaluable during darker times.

> Not every company that enters Tough Times U will graduate. How a team *responds* to a challenge determines whether it will be a source of growth or nothing but trouble.

For example, two days after I was named CEO of Collectech, following the collapse of our biggest client and our troubles with the BSA, it was clear to me that the only way the company would survive was to complete a major restructuring. Rather than attempting this on my own, I hired Steve Hauck, a veteran turnaround specialist who had safely returned more than twenty struggling firms to financial stability and health. I worked closely with Steve for eight weeks: He helped me objectively evaluate our various product lines, negotiate with frustrated banks and investors, and perhaps above all, instill a sense of confidence throughout the company that we would get through this challenging time. And we did, thanks largely to the experience and insight Steve brought with him.

GET TO THE ROOT CAUSES

Just as we lose the ability to think objectively in times of stress, we also tend to gravitate toward those things we know best, or look for a single root cause of the problem. The answer is usually more complex than a single issue, and is often the result of multiple factors. My friend

David Garrison, CEO of IBAHN, uses the story of an American Airlines jet that crashed in Little Rock, Arkansas, in 1999 to illustrate. As David tells it (he also happens to be a pilot), it took ten different things to go wrong for the MD80 to overshoot the runway on landing. If any one of those things hadn't gone wrong, the plane would have arrived safely. When companies go looking for a single culprit, they often oversimplify the situation and fail to rigorously address the true root cause. This is, of course, where the value of insultants can become paramount.

Think back to how Polaris shifted from seasonal manufacturer of snowmobiles to full-time manufacturer of ATVs. Textron had divested itself of snowmobiles partly because of an unprecedented string of record-low annual snow levels. There was probably more than one executive at Polaris who attributed the company's struggles to that lack of snowfall when, in truth, there were many problems afoot, especially the lack of a product that could be sold year round. What would have happened if Chuck Baxter, the chief engineer at Polaris, hadn't kept pushing to develop the ATV, even though the prevailing attitude at the time was that the fledgling company needed to clamp down on costs, not expand into an entire new market? Baxter opened the company's eyes to the fact that more than just a lack of snow threatened the company.

COMMUNICATE, COMMUNICATE, COMMUNICATE

During difficult times, many leaders tend to hunker down, cutting off communications with the rest of the folks in the company. And they usually mean well: They are afraid that if they share any shred of bad news, it will spook the troops. Ironically, by dramatically decreasing the amount of information they share, some leaders virtually guarantee the very problems they're trying to avoid. Everyone lives each day on the edge, and rumors fly around the water cooler and coffee room. When you cut off the flow of information to the troops in difficult times, you leave them to develop their own negative fantasies about what's happening, and they often dream up doomsday scenarios that are far worse than the reality. Company leaders who communicate often and honestly, on the other hand, can convey both the gravity of the situation along with the confidence that the firm is working toward a solution—and could sure use the rest of the company's support to get there.

> Ironically, by dramatically decreasing the amount of information they share, some leaders virtually guarantee the very problems they're trying to avoid.

In 1989, just about six years after the company was founded, Bob Funk and cofounder Bill Stoller faced dire circumstances: They had just received a $5 million bill from the insurer who covered their worker's compensation policy, and they didn't have the money to pay it. "The problem was that about half a dozen of our franchisees had been placing work with light industrial companies like oil refineries, where there were a lot of injuries," Bob Funk told us. "And since we were basically self-insured, and all the franchisees paid the same amount to the premium, our claims exceeded the amount we paid in premium by $5 million, and the carrier wanted the balance paid by June. We only had about $400,000 in the bank, so we were in trouble."[6]

Most companies, especially franchisers, might have been tempted to keep this news quiet. Funk and his management team did exactly the opposite: They convened emergency meetings with several of their franchisees, including a few of the worst offenders when it came to filing the worker's comp claims. The result of the meetings was that the franchisees agreed to implement a self-rating system that would assign costs to individual offices based on the number of worker's comp claims filed by each location every ninety days. With the new system in place, the number of claims filed from the field fell dramatically—

one office even unloaded 90 percent of its existing business with industrial clients—and by June 1, Express had collected enough in extra
premium payments that it could pay its bill to the insurer. "We asked
our franchisees how they could help us," Funk told us. "And they
came through."[7]

TOUGH TIMES DEMAND ACTION

Not only do most companies initially underestimate the magnitude
of the difficulty they may be facing, they frequently fall prey to inertia,
underestimating the level of response that will be required. If the quarterly numbers suggest a drop in profitability, for instance, companies
will often recast their future revenue budgets in a way that suggests
they will simply grow their way out of the problem. While this approach can work sometimes, the company may just be delaying its
need to restructure or resize the business in a way that sets it up for
profitable growth. This scenario can be further compounded if these
same leaders are blinded by their optimistic forecasts, and make the
mistake of not restructuring correctly or reducing headcount effectively the first time through. As the tough times continue, the company
can be pushed into a "death by a thousand cuts" trap in which it has
to make several subsequent rounds of layoffs, each round cutting
deeper and deeper into survivors' morale.

When Mark Smith and others at ADTRAN saw piles of inventory
stacking up at the same time their customers were cutting back on orders in 2001 and 2002, it would have been easy to plow forward, pro-
jecting that the telecom market would soon turn around. Smith
understood, however, that ADTRAN needed to restructure to become
more independent of these market swings, and he wanted to get it
right the first time. So while cutting almost 15 percent of his workforce
was painful at a personal level, ADTRAN emerged leaner and more focused on diversifying its customer base.[8]

COURTING PARANOIA

Scott Cook from Intuit made a curious statement at the end of our first interview with him: "Anyone can run a company during the tough times—it's the good times that actually challenge leaders the most."[9] What great leaders like Cook understand is that rather than coast during the times that the business is flying high, the company should continue asking hard questions about where it is going, digging more aggressively for ways to tap its latent potential. While companies should certainly celebrate periods of success, breakthrough leaders understand that they need to build some paranoia into these periods as well, keeping the company alert for signs that its key assumptions may be becoming outdated. The cost of questioning these assumptions ahead of time is far less than trying to unravel them after the tough times have already steamrolled in.

> It is during the good times that a company is most at risk. When times are tough, people tend to focus. But without outside pressure, organizations can become complacent and lazy.

When the dark days set in at Collectech, I feared our company, which was already on life support, would end up dying in a court battle. So I booked rooms at a local hotel for our top five executives and hired a facilitator to lead us through a discussion of our options. After the smoke had cleared on three brutal days of shouting, blaming, and denying, I agreed to step into the CEO role, and our former CEO became chairman. And at the next board meeting, we presented a plan to stop the bleeding. The board signed off on the plan, though they gave me just ninety days to turn the company around. Tough times indeed.

In the end, we spent about two years fighting our way back to financial health, and it was a true team effort. Since we could no longer avoid the issues that had seemed too sensitive or intractable to confront during the good times, everyone throughout the organization—folks from middle management all the way to the frontline—began talking openly and aggressively about how to turn the company around. The emotional costs of righting the ship, however, were high: In the three months during which we cut headcount from 390 to 90, we had to replace or shift to other positions eight of our top eleven executives. We were so caught up in the turmoil that we inadvertently announced our biggest layoff on February 14, in what the survivors eventually came to call the St. Valentine's Day Massacre. As painful as the changes were, they saved the company. In the four years following the turnaround, Collectech grew to more than 2,000 employees and became an industry leader in providing specialized services to the telecommunications industry.

Looking back, the experience was both the high and low point of my business career. It was a low point because I was part of an executive team that had become complacent, which resulted in 300 lost jobs and required heroic efforts on the part of everyone else to save the company. It was a high point because I learned perhaps the most important lesson of leadership: When it counts, people and organizations are capable of far more than we imagine. Anyone who has ever successfully navigated a business crisis knows that given good leadership, people rise to the challenge. Nietzsche was right: That which does not kill us does, in fact, make us stronger.

GRADUATING FROM TOUGH TIMES U
The Key Ideas

1. To achieve breakthrough performance requires a company to "push the envelope" and stretch its capabilities and its people. Tough times are a natural by-product.

2. When a company hits a difficult stretch, it is important for leaders to remember that challenges can actually bring out the best in an organization by:

   a. Forcing it to face facts
   b. Encouraging the prioritization of competing good ideas
   c. Reminding the organization of the potential of people to pull together and overcome obstacles

3. To successfully navigate through difficult times, leaders need to keep a cool head. They should also:

   a. Use their scaffolding—get outside perspectives
   b. Be aware of the complexity of the situation and avoid the tendency to find the "one" solution
   c. Communicate often and openly in a way that both assures people that leadership understands the gravity of the situation, and that reassures people that the right steps are being taken
   d. If painful steps are required, make sure to correctly estimate the level of restructuring required and attempt to "consolidate the pain" so that multiple rounds of cuts are not required

4. The real challenge of leadership is teaching the organization to keep the pressure on, even when times are good.

GRADUATING FROM TOUGH TIMES U
"SQUIRTS FROM THE GRAPEFRUIT"
(Findings That Surprised Us)

1. Many breakthrough companies actually view difficult times as key opportunities to reorient their thinking in ways that make them stronger.

2. When we asked breakthrough company executives what one factor was most important in helping them deal with difficult times, many cited a vigilant attempt to make sure the focus stayed on solving the problem and not on finding someone to blame.

3. Breakthrough leaders worry more about keeping their companies on their toes during the good times than they do about dealing with adversity.

BREAKTHROUGH IN PRACTICE
Tips for Graduating from Tough Times U

1. Benchmark your company's key capabilities against top performers inside and outside of your industry. If you are not the best on some dimension that is critical to your success, encourage people to try to get there.

2. Simulate stress through scenario planning. If it's all smooth sailing for your company, ask your team to look at how the organization would respond to some challenging scenarios—like a sudden drop in revenue of 20 percent or the loss of a key customer. This can help identify gaps that can be shored up before the fact.

3. If you are currently in a time of stress—remember the #1 and #2 responsibilities of a leader during difficult times: to absorb anxiety, and to provide the structure through which the team rigorously prioritizes issues and solves problems.

10

BUILDING BREAKTHROUGH

CAPABILITIES

It is not the strongest of the species that survive, nor the most intelligent, but the ones most responsive to change.

CHARLES DARWIN

W HEN I STARTED this project, I didn't intend to write a book. Instead, I was looking for answers to tough questions I had faced as a CEO of a growing company. I wondered why so few companies break through the entrepreneurial stage of development. More important, I wanted to understand *what a leadership team can actually do* to make sure a company has a shot at being one of those rare breakthrough companies.

While our empirical study of nine breakthrough companies and their competitors helped us with context, it was working in the field with fifty-two companies of all sizes and shapes that taught us how to actually build breakthrough capabilities. While we were struck by the power of breakthrough company ideas like crowning the company, upping the ante, and enlisting insultants, it was seeing these concepts come alive in the day-to-day operation of a business that convinced us of their unequivocal importance.

To conduct our fieldwork with the fifty-two companies, we traveled to four continents over a five-year period. We worked closely with the top twenty to sixty people in each of the companies—1,441 managers and executives in all. We sought to identify the key opportunities and challenges facing these organizations, and to understand how an environment could best be created to address those issues effectively. From our perspective, this fieldwork experience was invaluable as it enabled us to, as Peter Drucker had urged, "live in the world of the people we were studying."

For the most part, we weren't dealing with companies with an overwhelming competitive advantage: We met normal, everyday people running normal, everyday businesses, each trying to forge a set of capabilities that just might offer them a clear path to sustained growth and profitability.

THE THREE LEVERAGE POINTS OF LEADERSHIP

After about a year in the field, we began to notice a few common threads in all the companies we were working with. For instance, there appear to be three key ways a leader can influence a business: crafting and adapting strategy, getting the most out of people, and driving execution. We began to think of these three activities as the three fundamental leverage points of a business. We also began to see how these three factors were connected. One of the best ways a company can improve its strategy, for instance, is to focus on people, either by increasing the level of strategic understanding of an existing team, or by recruiting new people capable of crisp strategic thinking. On the other hand, if people know that a company's strategy is inherently flawed, they are unlikely to be motivated to put forth their best effort. Fixing the company's strategy first, therefore, can sometimes be the best way to get the most out of people. Effective execution can impact a company's ability to both craft strategy and to motivate employees. A company that does what it says it is going to do (effectively executes) is "making its word count" (chapter 5), and is thereby directly building company character. Effective execution can improve the quality of a company's strategy because people and companies learn best by doing. The faster and more effectively a company executes, the faster its "store" of learning increases—and strategy is nothing but the sum total of what a company has learned about itself and its environment.

> There are three places a leader can have the greatest impact on an organization: strategy, people, and execution.

Once we came to understand how important crafting and adapting strategy, growing people, and driving execution are to the success of a firm, we knew where to look for the keys to building breakthrough capabilities.

REINVENTING STRATEGY

Traditional strategic planning is dead. Strategy has never been more important. Leaders who fail to see the difference between the two are unlikely to harness the true power of strategy to transform their business. The purpose of crafting a strategy is not to create a detailed plan for where the company is headed five or ten years into the future: In today's fast-moving environment, it is impossible to predict that far into the future. Instead, the purpose of strategy is to help the members of an organization learn to triage issues, to sort out what is truly essential to the firm's success. Building an effective strategy is the process through which a team learns how to evaluate potential "big bets," how it might best "up the ante" in its industry. It also involves learning how to reconcile the dilemmas of the Business Bermuda Triangle, where the team must learn to balance costs with customer needs and the need for speed.

> Traditional strategic planning is dead. Strategy has never been more important.

A strategy is, after all, nothing more than a collection of ideas about how a company intends to win. The act of strategizing is the process by which, if aided by good insultants and support from scaffolding, a company can replace old ideas with new and improved ones. And when a leadership team realizes that strategy is really the single most important opportunity for learning within a company, it is free to drop some of the more cumbersome trappings of traditional strategic planning, and reinvent strategy processes around the objective of learning.

We met Amercable, an El Dorado, Arkansas–based manufacturer of heavy-duty industrial cable, early in our fieldwork. In 2002, the company had just been spun out of a large, public company through a management buyout. Facing an economic recession and a rather mature industry, its sales had stalled at around $50 million. Not only was CEO Bob Hogan eager to show his new equity investors that his company had what it took to be a successful, independent company, as a part-owner in the company he now had a strong incentive to turn things around. But how to get there, he wondered, since the traditional strategic planning process the company had experimented with in the past had become obsolete. "We need an approach that is light on theory and heavy on action," Hogan said at the time.

Just six weeks after going independent, however, Hogan received letters of resignation from just about everyone working in his oil-and-gas division, which was based in Houston. Even worse: They told him they were leaving to join a competitor. Hogan and his executive team found themselves suddenly enrolled in Tough Times U. Amercable shifted into crisis mode, as ten of Hogan's managers began commuting every week from the plant in Arkansas to Houston to hold the oil-and-gas business together for a few months until they could hire replacements. I called Bob and suggested that we put off my visit to talk strategy until after he got things under control. Instead, he asked if there was any way we could move it up. "There's nothing more important right now than getting our strategy right," he told me.

MAKING STRATEGY EVERYBODY'S JOB

Bob was determined to set Amercable on a path of dramatically improving performance. And, since strategizing is really about teaching an entire company how to learn, we decided to blow up Amercable's old executive-centric model of strategic planning and involve a lot more people. We identified twenty-nine key Amercable managers—more than 10 percent of the company at the time—folks from the shift supervisor on up, and invited them all to attend a three-day strategy conference at a ranch in central Texas. Besides Bob and the three people who reported directly to him, this was the first time most of the twenty-five other people present had played a role in corporate strategy. Hogan also invited two representatives from Amercable's new equity investor, Wingate Partners. "Are you sure you want your new investors to see the real Amercable right now, warts and all?" I asked.

"How can they help us if they don't see the warts?" was his swift reply, and he continued, "If we are going to be partners in this, we should really be partners." Only later on would I realize that Bob was showing me the power of insultants and scaffolding in transforming a business.

> Executives kid themselves that they are better at strategy than their troops, but fail to recognize that they have one key advantage—they are drinking from a very large data pipe. Give people on the frontlines access to key strategic information and train them how to use it, and they'll surprise you every time.

Rather than call that meeting in Texas a "retreat," we called it a strategy "advance" to reflect the need for a new aggressive vision for Amercable. We worked closely with Bob to build an intensive three-day process that we hoped would flesh out the major important strategic issues facing the company. We made sure the bulk of the time would be spent discussing those items the group saw as the most vital to Amercable's long-term success, and that everyone in attendance would have an equal chance to voice their opinions. The response was even better than we expected: The meetings, which went on until nearly midnight each night, were so animated and productive that we had to chase people back to their rooms to get some sleep.

Just before noon on the third day, the group locked in on a strategy. The vision called for Amercable to grow from $50 million to $120 million in just four years, while increasing annual profits from $5 million to $15 million. To reach those numbers, the team decided to push aggressively into international markets, reinvigorate growth in its struggling petroleum and mining businesses, and break into new industrial markets like automobile manufacturing and robotics.

As I walked out to my rental car following the meeting's wrap-up, a couple of Amercable employees approached me. "I don't see any way in the world this will be a $120 million business by 2007," one confessed. Today, with a little hindsight, I can say that the guy was right: just not in the way he expected. Amercable not only exceeded its goals—it did so a year early—posting revenues for 2006 of $150 million and net profits of $25 million. In the wake of that trip to Texas, Amercable was so successful that Wingate sold its interest to another private equity firm after just 2.5 years, having already quadrupled its initial investment. If you ask CEO Bob Hogan or the folks from Wingate what enabled Amercable to post such an incredible performance over the past few years, they'll tell you it was in large part because they got the entire organization involved in building the strategy.

Amercable's success story points out some of the many advantages of broadening involvement when setting strategy. The more people the company gets involved in asking questions and sharing insights, the better decisions it will make. Enrolling people from all functional areas and levels of the firm on the strategy team helps assure that a firm's perceptions, especially those of its executives, match reality. There is also no more effective means of moving a company toward organizational sovereignty than to equip people throughout the organization with the skills and knowledge necessary to contribute meaningfully to strategy discussions. In the words of Nobel Prize–winning economist Herbert Simon:

One does not live for months or years in a particular position in an organization, exposed to some streams of communication, shielded from others, without the most profound effects upon what he knows, believes, attends to, hopes, wishes, emphasizes, fears, and proposes.[1]

Participating in the strategy process enables people to transcend their normal "streams of communication" and come to better understand the organization as a whole. Armed with a holistic view of the firm, people can go back to their jobs better able to identify and focus on those priorities that promise the biggest strategic payoffs. An effectively run strategy process also provides a key forum to encourage the active involvement of insultants, where people are able to take a full swing at the issues, and help uncover unnoticed errors or emerging opportunities not yet on the firm's radar screen. And letting people in on strategic discussions is a great way to build company character. A properly designed strategy process signals to people that the company believes in them and has an interest in investing time and resources to help them become more effective contributors.

COMPRESSING STRATEGY CYCLE TIME

Strategy making represents a key learning opportunity for an organization. But leaders of companies headed for breakthrough should be just as concerned about the *velocity* of strategy learning as they are about the quality of that learning. We observed that the best companies shaped strategy moment by moment, day by day, as they learned from their customers and from their competitive environment. In our work with more than fifty companies, we found that most can create a strategy in three days that is 90 percent as good as one it might create in three months—if the strategy process is designed correctly. But why would a company be willing to settle for anything less than 100 percent? Simple: Because of the rapid pace of change that shapes most industries, it doesn't make sense to spend the extra time to get the game plan perfect. Spending three months crafting a strategy pretty much guarantees that it will be obsolete before the ink on the final report is dry. We call our approach Rapid Enterprise Development, or RED, modeled on approaches such as Rapid Application Development (RAD) and Agile development in the software world. Companies can't wait months, let alone years, to release new versions of software anymore. If they do, they risk delivering a product that is already out of date. The same principle applies to strategy: Companies simply cannot afford the delays that come with trying to produce the perfect strategic plan. Instead, they need to make some key assertions, start driving action, and iteratively adapt the strategy as they go along.

> In today's competitive environment, leaders need to be as concerned with the velocity of strategic learning as they are with the quality.

Companies are strategizing all the time; they just don't realize it, and they don't pause often enough to organize their thinking. The strategy cycle usually starts with someone in the organization seeing something that people haven't noticed before. At Amercable, for instance, people had been too focused on the domestic mining market, where the company already held a 60 percent market share. "How can we expect the company to grow significantly when we already have such a high market share?" many on the team asked. Then, during the meeting in Texas, Amercable sales head David Nasky had an epiphany. "Why are we so focused on the domestic market?" he asked. "The global mining business is going to explode in the next decade. The question we should be asking is, how can we get a big share of *that* market?" Some of his colleagues rolled their eyes and countered that a little cable company from Arkansas had no business competing in the global cable market. They were wrong. Today, 20 percent of Amercable's business comes from overseas, and that is expected to double over the next three years. But Nasky's insight was only the beginning of Amercable's strategy shift. People sometimes confuse strategy with generating ideas, and mistakenly think that just because they see something, that counts as doing something. Amercable succeeded because the people in the room believed Nasky's idea had merit, and they decided, right there in the room, to push into global markets. Soon, they translated that decision into action—hiring new staff and shifting Nasky's duties to focus exclusively on developing international markets. This story illustrates how organizations learn in the strategy process: First they see something, then they decide something, and then they do something—then they apply what they learned in the next round of seeing. The most important step in the process is pausing to analyze the results of taking action, and using the perspective gained to forge new strategic insights, at which point the learning cycle starts all over.

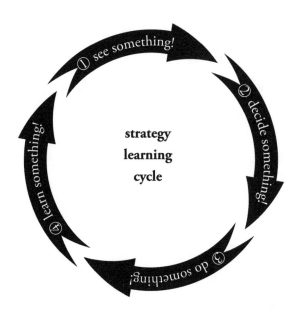

Successful companies taught us how essential it is to keep this strategy learning wheel spinning as rapidly as possible. The faster a company can accumulate and prioritize insights, convert the most important insights into decisions, and translate those into actions, the more readily it will outpace competitors.

With this insight, we recognized the need for a new strategy model that would enable companies to compress the amount of time it takes to create and adapt strategy, and increase the frequency of strategy discussions. We spent several years refining a design for a three-day strategy "advance" process—eventually testing and adapting it with the fifty-two fieldwork companies. We also continued to work with Hogan and Amercable in a process that brought the same group of twenty-nine managers (with a few additions each time) back together every quarter over a four-year period, to rapidly and continuously refine strategy. Each quarter, we would focus on the following three questions:

1. What have been our most important *strategic* accomplishments during the past ninety days?
2. What are the most important ways we *fell short of our strategic potential* during the past ninety days?
3. What are the most important things we have *learned about our strategy* during the past ninety days?

This strategy reset discipline helped Amercable to ensure that insights like those contributed by sales head David Nasky at the first meeting were constantly being highlighted, tested, and acted upon far more frequently than with the once-annual strategic planning approach taken by most companies.

FOLLOWING THE INSIGHTS

We quickly learned that there is no way to predict beforehand where the insights generated by this rapid strategy development process will come from, nor where they will lead. What is predictable, however, is that when companies work hard to manage strategy dynamically, their rate of learning improves, and as a result, so does their performance. An early insight at Amercable was that it needed to move out of the safety of its core domestic mining niche and expand into new markets both at home and abroad. When we worked with Vans, the legendary apparel and sports equipment maker in California, the strategy team realized that their core market had abruptly moved in a new direction. Then a public company, Vans had seen its stock fall to just $5 a share in 2002. The culprit? For fifteen years, Nike had set the pace in the athletic footwear market with an emphasis on performance and endorsements by pro athletes, then suddenly, fashion and lifestyle became important to athletic shoe buyers. Brands like Skechers and Puma burst onto the scene, growing from nothing to annual sales of up to $1 billion in sales in just a few years. Retailers made room for these new, innovative brands and designs, which cut into Vans's revenues and profits. During a three-day strategy meeting, the Vans team identified the problem and laid out a plan to invigorate its product design, merchandising, and marketing efforts to beat back these competitive attacks. In addition, the team revamped Vans retail stores in a way that made them the premier destination for the brand. These moves caught the attention of apparel titan VF, which purchased Vans in April 2004 for more than $20 per share—a 300 percent premium over the price of the stock when the Vans's team sat down to rethink their strategy, just two years earlier.

When companies shift to a dynamic model of strategy, their rate of strategic learning, as well as their performance, improve.

GETTING THE MOST OUT OF PEOPLE

Another important way a leader can impact the trajectory of a business is by continuing to find new ways to get the most out of the company's people. We found that all nine of the breakthrough companies cultivated exceptional levels of commitment and performance. In our fieldwork, we observed companies take a variety of approaches to this issue, and we helped them experiment with several more. For example, we found that when we enrolled people from all levels of the organization in crafting a strategy, those people invested more of themselves in making sure the company reached the goals it outlined. Because people better understood what the firm was trying to accomplish, and why, they tended to throw themselves more fully behind the firm's most important initiatives.

Involving people in strategy is just one of a number of things a business can do to drive commitment. As we noted in chapters 3 and 5, the breakthrough companies we studied continue to be obsessed with creating an environment in which, in the words of Fastenal founder Bob Kierlin, "ordinary people can do extraordinary things." Unfortunately, most companies fall victim to symptoms of the "grass is greener" complex where they look outside to fill key roles, rather than develop the talent they already possess in-house.

Whenever I travel and speak to businesspeople, I usually try to steer the conversation toward getting them to tell me about their priorities. "What's your biggest challenge these days?" I usually ask. Over the past five years, I have been surprised at how often I get the same answer. "Getting the right people on the bus," I often hear, an obvious nod to Jim Collins's book *Good to Great*. Now there's nothing particularly disturbing about the idea that executives across the country are focused on recruiting great people—who could possibly argue with that terrific idea? The disturbing part comes when you probe a little bit deeper. "You're obviously referring to Jim Collins's book," I usually say in response. "Tell me, since you first read *Good to Great,* what have you been doing differently to make sure you *get* the right people on the bus?" And that's when I get the blank stares. It turns out that a lot of people *talk* about getting the right people on the bus, but few have spent much time thinking about how to actually do it.

I think some leaders may be using "the right people on the bus" idea as an excuse for their own failure to get their own companies performing, not exactly what Jim intended when he coined the phrase. After all, it's a lot easier for a leader to blame lackluster performance on the people on the bus than it is to take responsibility for creating the kind of place that gets the most out of the people it already has. Strong people tend to gravitate to strong organizations, and as the nine breakthrough companies have shown us, the best way for a leader to get the right people on the bus is to create a bus worth riding on. Companies like Fastenal, Polaris, and Staubach hardly ever have to recruit: The best people find them.

> Maybe the best way to "get the right people on the bus" is to create a bus worth riding on in the first place.

All this begs the question: Who exactly is the "right" person for this hypothetical bus? In the two decades that I ran organizations, I had the privilege of hiring some terrific people, but I don't know that any would qualify as perfectly "right." As good as they were, and some were outstanding, everyone I've ever hired has had some area they could improve upon, or could use help in developing new skills that would contribute to taking the business to the next level.

And the right person today could very well be the wrong person tomorrow if he fails to grow along with the company's needs. Clearly, you can't reshuffle your staff every time the rules of the game change. Companies, especially fast-growing ones, can barely keep up as it is. So what's the answer?

In talking to the nine breakthrough companies, we learned that they never dwelled too long on trying to hire the right person for a particular position. What they tried to do instead was hire people they thought could scale. "Paychex hires attitude and trains aptitude," founder Tom Golisano told us. Fastenal looked for hardworking young people to manage its stores, and Intuit went to the colleges for its programmers. In the end, the breakthrough company leaders understood it was their responsibility to develop these new hires into the right people. But just how does a leader go about developing members of his team? We were impressed with how Olympic teams and elite military units use the TAIS Inventory mentioned in chapters 3 and 4 to help people improve their performance—so impressed that we developed our own version of TAIS designed specifically for growth company managers (for more information go to *www.breakthroughcompany* *.com/red*).

THE NO. 1 JOB OF A LEADER: COACHING

If managers focus too much on getting the right people on the bus, and not enough on developing the people they already have on the bus, you can bet that bus is headed for some kind of fender bender or worse. Consider an example from outside the world of business: the ultracompetitive ranks of collegiate basketball. John Wooden accomplished what few coaches in any sport could even hope to aspire to: ten national championships as coach of the UCLA Bruins, including seven in a row from 1967 to 1973. "The Wizard of Westwood," as Wooden was known, seemed to have a knack for attracting talented players like Bill Walton and Lew Alcindor (who later changed his name to Kareem Abdul-Jabbar). What most people forget about Wooden, however, is that it took twenty years for him to win his first championship at UCLA, years he used to perfect his coaching and teaching skills. In the early years, talented players were drawn to UCLA less for its track record than the opportunity to play for the best coach in the nation, a coach who would make them better. And as a college coach, Wooden knew he had only four, sometimes five years at most, to work with his players before they graduated. It would have been understandable if Wooden had devoted most of his effort each year to recruiting the best high school talent in the country to restock his roster. But Wooden's real genius was his ability to get the most out of every one of his players, especially the ones who weren't destined for a career in the NBA. "A player who makes a team great is more valuable than a great player," Wooden once said. "Losing yourself in the group, for the good of the group, that's teamwork."

The best college coaches, regardless of the sport, know that recruiting the right players is critical to winning a championship, but they spend far less time recruiting than coaching. Business leaders would be well served by following this example. Amercable, for one, succeeded because Bob Hogan is a superb coach. He was able to double revenues and quadruple Amercable's profits, not by replacing his Arkansas crew with a bunch of Harvard MBAs, but by growing his people right along with the business. He didn't just include them in the strategy advance meetings, he also took his entire management team outside the company to programs sponsored by General Electric, the Army War College, and—yes—even Harvard.

> The breakthrough companies we visited were filled with great coaches—people skilled at helping people do their very best.

There are, of course, many approaches to help executives improve their coaching skills. The critical aspect is not the specific approach, but rather the commitment leaders make to grow people right along with the business. I remember receiving a call one day from Steve Olson, CEO of The Olson Company, a real estate developer in Seal Beach, California, whom we worked with for several years. "Do you know anyone who heads up a marketing department at a company with revenues of over $100 million and has experience in brand marketing?" he asked. "Why, are you trying to recruit someone?" I wondered. No, he explained, he wanted to find a mentor for his head of marketing. "She does a great job now," said Olson, "but she'll need to keep expanding her skills if she's going to lead marketing for us when we're a half-a-billion-dollar company. I want to find someone who can help her prepare for the new responsibilities she'll need to take on as our company grows." Now *that's* what it means to be focused on growing your people.

DRIVING EXECUTION

The final leverage point for leaders seeking to nudge their businesses toward breakthrough performance is a relentless focus on improving the company's ability to execute. Even with the greatest strategy and the most committed people in the world, if a company fails to execute, its efforts will be for naught. Effective execution is vital to breakthrough, and it was through our fieldwork that we learned that companies fall roughly into two categories: those that do what they say they are going to do, and those that don't.

One of the most powerful aspects of an effective strategy is that it allows a company to choose between initiative A and initiative B. Companies can then effectively assign resources to higher-priority items. But just assigning priorities isn't enough: The company must still take action on those initiatives.

Some companies are great at "seeing" themselves and the world around them, but have a hard time making a decision. Others can make a decision, but don't effectively follow through on those decisions. Regardless of where the strategy cycle breaks down, if insights don't quickly get translated into decisions and then transformed into actions, the organization will be at a disadvantage.

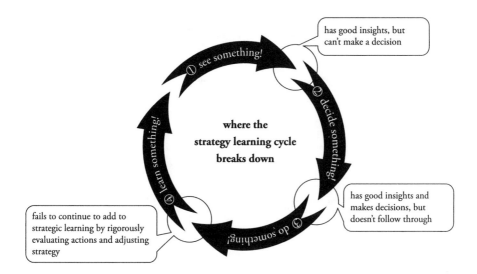

We have encouraged companies we have worked with not to wrap up their strategy meetings until they've distilled their top priorities into specific, measurable initiatives and action plans, ones that have both a deadline and a person responsible. If members from each of the company's major departments and regions have participated in the creation of the strategy, it can be relatively easy for them to break up into their departmental groups, and reflect on how their departmental priorities should be reordered as a result of the meeting. To stimulate their thinking, we generally ask each department to reflect on the following question: "Given the strategy we have just created (or adapted), what are the 20 percent of the activities in your department that are likely to create 80 percent of the results?" The heads of those departments are then asked to lead the creation of detailed ninety-day action plans that reflect the new strategic priorities.

CASE STUDY IN BUILDING BREAKTHROUGH CAPABILITIES
House of Blues

Running a House of Blues location is like running a small city. As part of the operation, many managers have to juggle retail sales of apparel and souvenirs, restaurant operations, a large bar business, a private club (The Foundation Room), as well as the live-music performances that made the venue famous.

Dolf Berle, the former COO of House of Blues, believed that location managers were pulled in so many directions that they often didn't have time to adequately focus on improving the performance of their individual clubs. We brought together the top three managers from each of the House of Blues locations nationwide for a three-day strategy advance.

Working together, the group identified the major opportunities for improvement across the company, and prioritized them based on their impact on the brand and the bottom line.

We tracked down Dolf nearly five years after we worked with him, and here's what he said in an e-mail reflecting on the process:

> The ninety-day action planning discipline became a part of who we were at House of Blues. People feel involved in developing the strategy, feel invested in executing it, and therefore create even better plans in the next cycle because they know whether they have been successful or not in the last ninety days. They learn quickly whether they have a tendency to under- or overresource initiatives and just how important it is to involve colleagues in the creation and execution of any strategy. It was a key method in helping us drive the double-digit same-venue EBITDA growth every year for five straight years.

Powerful online collaboration tools such as Microsoft Sharepoint and others make it possible to aggregate these action plans on the Web, in a way that enables team members throughout the organization to share information, integrate interdepartmental efforts, and keep the focus on the most important priorities. To view a demonstration of such a system, go to *www.breakthroughcompany.com/red*.

Revisiting strategic assumptions every three or four months can also help a company move toward more effective execution by forging a tighter link between strategy and execution. If, for instance, certain initiatives are found to be less productive than others, resources can be quickly shifted to maximize effect rather than be suboptimized until the next annual budget cycle. Even more important, when a company revisits its strategy every ninety days, it creates increased opportunities for organizational learning. As we said earlier, companies learn best by taking action and learning from the results. The faster an organization learns, the faster it can adapt. The U.S. military has long seen the value of this approach and uses a discipline called After Action Reviews (AAR) as a learning tool. After every major engagement, soldiers gather to discuss what went wrong, what went right, and what should be done differently next time. The results of these AARs are then forwarded to places like the Army War College where they can be analyzed so that national military strategy and tactics can be constantly updated and improved.

THE STRATEGY CYCLE AT WORK

Our five years of working in the field with dozens of companies has shown us that companies that adopt a dynamic approach to strategy, focus on getting the most out of its people, and drive effective execution are at a significant advantage. What's more, we continue to be amazed at how the companies we have worked with continue to refine and improve on these basic ideas. When we led our first strategy meeting for The Olson Company in 2002, it had revenues of slightly over $200 million, and we could tell it was poised for dramatic growth. When CEO Steve Olson called us a year later and asked us to facilitate a second strategy meeting, he made a strange request. "This year, I want the people in the regions to drive the strategy for the company," he told me. "So I am not attending the meeting and I am barring any of my corporate officers from attending as well." I was stunned. "Have you lost your mind?" I asked. "How can you hope to build a successful strategy if you don't let the corporate officers participate?" He chuckled patiently. "Our regional people won't take ownership of the strategy unless we give them a chance to make it their own," he explained. "Our job at headquarters is just to make sure we clear a path for them." As it turns out, Steve hadn't lost his mind at all. Today, The Olson Company has annual sales of more than $500 million a year, boasts a multibillion-dollar construction backlog, and is one of the most respected creators of affordable in-town housing in the nation.

BUILDING BREAKTHROUGH CAPABILITIES
The Key Ideas

There are three areas in which a leader can most powerfully impact the trajectory of a firm: strategy, people, and execution.

1. Strategy: Our fieldwork taught us that the real value of strategy isn't the plan itself but rather the process, which, if managed correctly, teaches an organization how to triage issues. To achieve its full potential, a strategy process should be dynamic and closely linked to execution, involve people from a variety of areas of the firm, and focus on both the velocity and the quality of learning.

2. People: Some firms focus too much on finding the "right" people and not enough attention on developing the people they have. The most neglected skill in business today is coaching.

3. Execution: By instituting a dynamic approach to strategy, companies can more closely link strategy and execution. Web-based collaboration tools can help a firm stay focused on the 20 percent of the activities that, if executed effectively, will produce 80 percent of the results.

BUILDING BREAKTHROUGH CAPABILITIES
"SQUIRTS FROM THE GRAPEFRUIT"
(Findings That Surprised Us)

1. Strategy is usually thought of as the purview of the executive suite. We were amazed in our work with companies by how quickly people at all levels of a business can grasp the key dimensions of strategy and can begin contributing meaningfully to strategic decisions.

2. When we first began our fieldwork, we greatly underestimated the power of tightly linking strategy with execution. When we began tying the two together with Web-based tools, the performance of the companies improved markedly.

3. Like the breakthrough companies we studied, the top performing companies in our fieldwork were able to keep their teams together for long periods of time. They stressed the need for "more blood" over the need for "new blood." They appeared to have accomplished this by constantly pushing people to keep growing.

BREAKTHROUGH IN PRACTICE
Tips for Building Breakthrough Capabilities

1. Expand the strategy development team to include key middle managers, up-and-comers, nay-sayers, and key salespeople. Encourage the group to tackle the toughest strategic issues facing the firm.

2. Replace large, annual, formal strategic planning processes with more frequent and nimble strategy skull sessions. Hire an experienced strategy facilitator to make sure everyone's voice is heard and that the process is streamlined and effective (for more of our thoughts on strategy process design, go to *www.breakthrough-company.com/red*).

3. Develop detailed professional development goals for each of your direct reports, and meet with them quarterly to review their progress. Use tools like TAIS to help identify potential areas for improvement. For more information, go to *www.breakthrough-company.com/red*.

4. Make sure your strategy is translated into specific and measurable goals, and that goals are translated into initiatives, and that initiatives are supported with detailed action plans. For an example of how to use Web-based technology to link strategy and execution, go to *www.breakthroughcompany.com/red*.

AFTERWORD:
POST-BREAKTHROUGH—
AVOIDING BREAKDOWN

The art of progress is to preserve order amid change and
to preserve change amid order.
ALFRED NORTH WHITEHEAD

'M SITTING ON my deck overlooking the snow-capped Wasatch
Mountains, reflecting on my five-year expedition in search of the secrets of breakthrough. It's a beautiful spring day and the book is
nearly completed, but I'm distracted by one question that keeps resur-
facing: What will become of these nine breakthrough companies? Will
the same characteristics that fueled their breakthrough performance
sustain continued upward trajectories, allowing them to one day take
their place among the nation's best large companies? Or will they
stumble and fall, discovering that it takes one set of characteristics to
break through and quite another to battle over the long term with the
global titans? In other words, once a firm has achieved breakthrough,
how can it make sure it doesn't break down?

The nine breakthrough companies all starkly distinguished themselves from their more than 7,000 *Inc.* 500 company peers. But now, as much larger and more complex organizations, they all face new challenges that may test their ability to sustain their remarkable past performance. Polaris has soared to become a market leader in two segments—snowmobiles and ATVs. Can it now conquer a third, as it squares off in the motorcycle market against the likes of Harley-Davidson? Will ADTRAN be able to build on its success selling into the more monopolistic telecommunications industry and become a player in the commercial markets fiercely guarded by companies like Cisco? How much of Express Personnel Service's past success was the result of the inspired hands-on leadership of founders Bob Funk and Bill Stoller, and what will happen to its band of energetic franchisees when Funk and Stoller are no longer at the helm? And what about Intuit? How will this firm, whose founding goal was to solve the pain of the average bill payer, fare as it integrates new businesses like the recently acquired banking software company Digital Insight?

Sitting here on my deck thinking about the hundreds of people I've met at these companies, I realize I'm generally confident about the fate of these nine breakthrough firms. Perhaps not all will continue to shatter records as they did in the past, but many figure to have great years ahead. One of the reasons I'm upbeat on their futures is that for the most part, they're led by people who still worry a lot. It's been said that if you know what kinds of things a person worries about, you know a lot about who that person really is. I believe the same can be said of companies. With that in mind, we closed each of our interviews with the same question: "As you look to the future, what worries you?" Nine times out of ten, we got an answer that went something like this: "The greatest challenge will be to maintain and nurture those organizational qualities that have allowed our company to succeed in the first place." These executives didn't seem concerned about their companies' ability to *learn new things*—but they worried a lot about the possibility that their people might *forget the old things* that made them so successful early on. I always remember something Scott Cook told me in our very first interview for this book: "Remembering the stuff that made you successful as a start-up is a lot more important than any of the new stuff associated with getting big."

Much of organizational life tends to draw our attention to the "shiny new things"—whether they be a sophisticated new activity-based costing system, a new class of products, entry into international markets, or a new specialized staff to integrate acquisitions. But these may not be the things that ultimately determine a company's success. Perhaps one of the central challenges of leadership is to ensure that the complexities of running a bigger and bigger business don't distract people from the fundamentals determining long-term success. Maybe the key job of a leader is to be an amplifier: to magnify those entrepreneurial qualities of risk-taking, character, commitment, unselfishness, and collaboration, and make sure they're not drowned out by the increasing noise associated with scale and scope.

If we've learned anything in this process, we've learned that breakthrough is a journey, not a destination. There are no permanent breakthrough companies—only companies that engage in practices leading to long-term success. And just as it's possible for an everyday company to achieve breakthrough performance, it's equally possible for a breakthrough company to, without realizing it, fall back into life as an everyday firm. On the day that the emphasis swings from crowning the company to crowning individuals, the company's future becomes less certain. The moment the firm begins to rest on its laurels and starts playing it safe, organizational entropy kicks in. If a company's character gets reduced to a set of platitudes no one really believes in, much less acts on, the passion and commitment will fade away. If a firm isn't continually finding new and better ways to meet customer needs, reduce costs, and increase speed, it will soon be overrun by competitors that *are* doing those things. Peril lies ahead for the breakthrough company that forgets how important an outside perspective can be, or that forgets the value of constantly questioning the assumptions upon which the firm is based. Leaders who allow their firms to be distracted from the handful of fundamental disciplines that enable breakthrough performance will likely find their organizations enrolled in Tough Times U—where they'll be prompted to either re-learn the lessons of breakthrough, or find themselves and their companies enrolled in an even less desirable class of institution.

Will our nine breakthrough companies continue to achieve stellar performance? There is, of course, no way to predict the future. But if they stay committed to the fundamentals of breakthrough, I wouldn't bet against them.

RESEARCH NOTE A:

EXPLORATORY FIELDWORK

A CRUCIAL FIRST STEP in our research was getting out into the field and working closely in a variety of settings with companies widely ranging in size; a decision prompted by my experience studying under Peter Drucker. What impressed me most about Peter was his ability to quickly spot patterns in complex, dynamic situations. It was as if he possessed an innate ability to see more deeply into an issue than the rest of us. The contrast between Peter and the average person formulating opinions may be likened to that between two people standing on a river bank, only one of whom is equipped with polarized glasses. The one relying on the naked eye alone sees merely riffles and currents while the other sees the contours of the river bottom that create those currents.

Much of Drucker's ability was due to his monumental intellect, but when he was asked one day in class how he did this, he gave a curious answer: "Most researchers are not willing to go to the trouble of seeing the world through the businessperson's eyes," he told us. "My consulting allows me to do that. I would never try to interpret what I see without spending some time living in the world of the people I study." I remember smiling when he said this: It was an insight as simple as it was profound. An anthropologist wouldn't parachute into New Guinea, distribute and collect some questionnaires, and expect to learn anything meaningful about a particular tribe. Instead, he'd move into the village and live among its people for months, learning the language and discovering the meaning of its customs. Only after conducting this kind of deep research could the anthropologist hope to discover the deep currents that move a group of people to do what they do.

With this important insight in mind, I was determined to begin our study, as Drucker would have said, "in the world of the people I was studying." Like Drucker, I'd become a student by becoming a consultant. Over a five-year period, my team and I conducted field studies in fifty-two companies in a variety of industries and with annual revenues ranging from $6 million to $5 billion.

Field Study Companies

Company Business	Firm Size	Ownership	Study Term
Commercial interior design	0–$10 million	Private/Family	1 year
Food manufacturing	$50–$100 million	Private Equity	3 years
Food manufacturing	$25–$50 million	Private Equity	1 year
Food distribution	$1–$5 billion	Private/Family	2 years
Paper distribution	$10–$25 million	Private/Individual	1 year
Industrial cable manufacturing	$50–$100 million	Private Equity	4 years
Real estate developer	$100–$250 million	Private/Individual	1 year
Real estate management	$10–$25 million	Private/Individual	6 months
Real estate mortgage/residential	$25–$50 million	Private/Closely Held	3 months
Real estate mortgage/commercial	$0–$10 million	Private/Closely Held	1 year
Real estate mortgage/manufactured homes	$25–$50 million	Private Equity	1 year
Health professional staffing	$250–$500 million	Private Equity	3 months
Wealth management (studied one division)	$1–5 billion	Public	9 months
Wealth management (studied one region)	$5 billion	Public	6 months
Craft supply manufacturer	$50–$100 million	Private Equity	6 months
Packaging manufacturer	$25–$50 million	Private/Individual	6 months
Pipeline maintenance	$100–$250 million	Private Equity	9 months
Apparel manufacturing and retail	$50–$100 million	Private/Individual	6 months
Logistics management	$25–$50 million	Private/Individual	6 months
Logistics management	$1–$5 billion	Public	6 months

Company Business	Firm Size	Ownership	Study Term
Plastics manufacturing	$50–$100 million	Private/Individual	6 months
Hedge fund	$1 billion (assets)	Private	2 years
University	$50–$100 million	Private (Nonprofit)	6 months
University (proprietary technical school)	$0–$10 million	Private Equity	6 months
Automobile components manufacturer	$250–$500 million	Private	1 year
Automobile components manufacturer	$10–$25 million	Private/Individual	2 years
Computer network storage	$10–$25 million	Private Equity	3 months
Computer network storage	$10–$25 million	Private Equity	9 months
Software	$25–$50 million	Wholly-Owned Sub.	1 year
Law firm	$10–$25 million	Private/Partnership	2 years
Book publishing (Australia)	$25–50 million	Private/Individual	3 months
Hospitality	$250–$500 million	Private Equity	3 months
Hospitality	$10–$25 million	Private/Closely Held	9 months
Commercial insurance	$50–$100 million	Private/Closely Held	1 year
Commercial insurance	$0–$10 million	Private/Closely Held	2 years
National laboratory (studied one division)	$1 billion	Private/Nonprofit	1 year
Metal fabricator	$10–$25 million	Private/Individual	3 months
Emission control device manufacturer	$10–$25 million	Private/Closely Held	2 years
Pet supplies distributor	$250–$500 million	Public	6 months
Regional bank	$1 billion (assets)	Private/Closely Held	2 years
Chemical manufacturer/distributor	$500 mil–$1 billion	Private/Closely Held	1 year
Advertising agency	$0–$10 million	Private/Closely Held	9 months
Advertising publishing	$50–$100 million	Private/Individual	1.5 years
Contract software developer (Canada)	$10–$25 million	Private/Individual	3 months
Recreational equipment and apparel mfg	$250–$500 million	Public	6 months
Recreational equipment and apparel mfg	$10–$25 million	Private/Individual	1 year
Recreational equipment and apparel (retail)	$250–500	Private/Closely Held	3 months
Residential window manufacturing	$25–$50 million	Private Equity	1 year
Mobile Internet technology	$10–$25 million	Private Equity	1 year
Market research	$25–$50 million	Private/Individual	2 years
Market research	$25–$50 million	Private Equity	3 months
Customer service outsourcing	$10–$25 million	Private Equity	3 months

The objective of this first exploratory phase of our study was to gain real-world experience in a wide range of business types and sizes, and in so doing, to identify the key themes that arise as a company grows and develops. Further, we wanted to work shoulder to shoulder with managers as they attempted their own versions of breakthrough so that we could get some sense of the internal and external obstacles likely to arise.

Our team conducted an initial ninety-day analysis of each company and its financial and market performance. In addition to industry research, we talked with twenty to sixty key members of each firm (1,441 in all), including all of senior management, as well as key middle managers, sales people, first-line supervisors, board members, and industry experts. We made sure to involve people from all of a firm's functional areas, including marketing, sales, operations, human resources, finance and accounting, product development, and customer service. Each of these representatives was invited to share with us, in strict confidentiality, what they viewed to be the most important issues currently facing the firm.

FIELD STUDY INTERVIEW/DISCUSSION QUESTIONS

The following questions were used to secure and refine information from field study companies:

1. *What are the four biggest challenges currently facing your firm?*
2. *List the five most important measurements of success for your company and indicate how your firm has performed against those measures over the past two years.*
3. *List the four most important external factors likely to affect your firm in the next three years.*
4. *What do customers most want from your class of product or service?*
5. *What customer segments offer you the greatest opportunity over the next three years?*

6. *What are your most promising product/service categories over the next three years and why?*

7. *What advantages does your firm have over the competition?*

8. *What advantages do your competitors offer that your firm does not? Which are most important to the long-term success of your firm?*

9. *How do you want your customers to differentiate you from competitors?*

10. *What is it that your firm does better than most firms? Which of these items are most important and why?*

11. *If your firm lived up to its full potential, how would it be different three years from today? five years from today?*

12. *What are the three most important things that your firm needs to accomplish in the next twelve months to assure that your firm reaches its full potential?*

13. *Are there things that your firm is currently doing which are lower priority that you could stop doing and redirect the time, energy, and resources to items of greater strategic import? What are these, and if your firm ceased these activities, to where would you redirect the resources freed up?*

14. *What most worries you about your firm's future?*

15. *What principles guide the day-to-day operation of your firm?*

FIELD STUDY COMPANY ISSUE REVIEW PROCESS

Once we received input from the twenty to sixty people in each firm on the questions above, we facilitated an average of twenty-five hours of small-group discussions per company to help the group reach consensus on the most important issues facing the firm, and on what the firm should do about them. We made sure everyone's voice was heard, and we encouraged groups to use the strategy wheel described in chapter 10 as a tool to help them turn insights into decisions, and then to turn decisions into actions. The work of these small groups was then integrated into discussions involving the larger group. We kept detailed notes on discussions and decisions, and were later able to create detailed process comparisons between the companies that participated in the fieldwork studies.

We recorded all of the major decisions that were made in the process, and we captured the detailed departmental action plans for each firm on a custom-designed Web community. We were then able to track on a weekly basis each company's progress in achieving key milestones.

Our fieldwork enabled us to create a large database of information on companies, all along the company's growth curve. As our work progressed, patterns began to emerge that would later inform and direct our analysis of the nation's best-performing growth companies.

I've been asked on several occasions whether it was worth spending as much time and effort as we did in the exploratory fieldwork phase of our study, and my reply is always the same: The fieldwork provided a crucial foundation for our study: It gave us a framework with which to approach the selection study of breakthrough companies. It didn't give us the answers, but it gave us something even more important: a context for our questions.

RESEARCH NOTE B:

THE BREAKTHROUGH STUDY

ARMED WITH THE real-world insights provided by several years of fieldwork, we were ready to return again to the three questions that provided the impetus for our study:

1. *Why do most companies start small and stay that way?*
2. *What is special about the handful of companies that successfully "break through" the entrepreneurial stage of development?*
3. *What can a leader do to ensure that his company maximizes its chances for breakthrough?*

To answer these three questions, we first needed to isolate a population of companies likely to contain firms that had achieved breakthrough. Then, we needed a way to cull from that group firms meriting rigorous study. Our goal was not to identify *the* definitive list of breakthrough companies; rather, we wished to identify a population of companies likely to possess breakthrough characteristics. Then, through a comprehensive study of those companies, we sought to identify some of the key factors that might possibly fuel a company's trajectory toward breakthrough. We were impressed by aspects of Jim Collins's research methodology for *Built to Last* (with Jerry Porras, HarperCollins, 1994) and *Good to Great* (HarperCollins, 2001), and where appropriate, we sought to adopt aspects of his approach. One key difference: Because we were studying the dynamics of breakthrough, we couldn't limit ourselves to the study of public companies. We spent considerable time and energy building a research database of some of the top private companies as well.

STAGE 1: SELECTING THE POPULATION

We chose *Inc.* magazine's annual list of the 500 fastest growing companies because it is one of the most comprehensive and recognized sources of information on growth companies (for more information on the *Inc.* 500, see Research Note C: *Inc.* 500). We created a database of every company listed on *Inc.*'s annual list from the first year *Inc.* published the list (1982) up to and including the 2004 list. This yielded a list of 7,233 companies (some companies made the list more than once).

Next, we cross-referenced this database of 7,233 companies with information provided to us by Dun & Bradstreet. D&B is the world's leading source of business information, and its databases contain more than 100 million unique business records. Our analysis of the D&B data determined that of the 7,233 *Inc.* 500 companies, 5,251 were still viable business entities as of 2004 (the remaining 1,982 firms had either gone out of business, been sold, or were for some other reason not present in any of Dun & Bradstreet's databases).* We elim-

---

*The possibility exists that certain companies might have failed to report accurate data to D&B over the years—thus skewing the data for those firms. For public companies, such errors are readily corrected using publicly available data, but with private companies, we had a more limited set of sources to confirm or correct erroneous data. We sought to verify financial performance of all private company finalists, by comparing D&B statistics with those published in industry studies and reported in the press. We sought and received confidential financial performance data from twenty-four of the top-ranked finalist companies—including all three private companies that were included in the final list of nine breakthrough companies.

D&B utilizes more than 2,000 quality checks, audits, and other statistical and quality-control techniques, and makes more than one million updates per day to its global database. Furthermore, D&B scientists tell us that as the size of the company studied increases, the reliability of the data increases significantly. Because we limited our study to firms with 2004 annual revenues of $250 million or more, we have been assured that the data we used to initiate our study is highly reliable. Still, the possibility exists that a company may have been inappropriately excluded from our study if its actual financial performance was, in reality, better than reflected in the D&B numbers.

inated any firms from our study that had been sold to other entities. We did this *not* because we believed it's impossible to achieve breakthrough performance as a division of another company, but rather because we believed it would be too difficult to isolate the influences of the acquiring company.

This approach led to some difficult decisions. For example, the St. Louis Bread Company made the *Inc.* 500 list in 1993, but was purchased later that year by Au Bon Pain. In May of 1999, Au Bon Pain spun out the Au Bon Pain part of the business and refocused on what had been the original St. Louis Bread Company business under the new corporate moniker, Panera Bread. Panera Bread grew rapidly to some 1,020 bakery cafes in 38 states, earning recognition in 2006 by the *Wall Street Journal* as the top performer in the restaurant category for one-, five-, and ten-year returns for shareholders. Panera's performance would likely have put it in our list of breakthrough companies, but since the original company that had made the *Inc.* 500, the St. Louis Bread Company, had been purchased and its operations combined with Au Bon Pain between 1993 and 1999, we decided it would be impossible to adequately isolate the key drivers of the original business in our analysis.

STAGE II: NARROWING THE FIELD BASED ON FIRM SIZE

As we learned in chapter 1 and chapter 2, most companies start small and stay that way. Since we wanted to study firms that had successfully broken through the entrepreneurial stage of development, we required that firms included in our company study set have 2004 revenues of at least $250 million. We wanted to make sure that the companies we studied had achieved the scale and scope necessary to have encountered most of the issues associated with breakthrough. Of the 5,250 *Inc.* 500 firms still in business in 2004, we identified ninety-four *Inc.* 500 firms that had achieved annual revenues of $250 million by 2004—fifty-three public firms and forty-one private. We confirmed/updated information on public companies using Compustat, and we did extensive background research on private companies, including contacting those identified in our research as top performers and asking them to disclose confidential financial information under a nondisclosure agreement.

One might think it odd that of the 7,233 firms listed on the *Inc.* 500, over a twenty-plus year period, only ninety-four (1.5%) have reached revenues of $250 million. But according to the 2000 U.S. business census, only 0.11% of U.S. employer firms have revenues of $250 million or more. Since the *Inc.* 500 award focuses on the nation's fastest growing firms, it is reasonable to assume that a greater percentage of these firms would reach $250 million in sales than the population of U.S. firms in general. Our analysis found that *Inc.* 500 firms are more than ten times more likely to reach revenues of $250 million than companies in general—a conclusion that struck us as reasonable.

Next we eliminated the seven *Inc.* 500 firms that had 2004 revenues of greater than $2 billion (two examples are Oracle and Microsoft). Our fieldwork suggested that when a firm reaches revenue levels of about $2 billion, it's more likely to have grown so large that the "artifacts" of breakthrough are more difficult to isolate and study. This is not to say that the characteristics of breakthrough might not be important as a firm grows beyond $2 billion (in fact, we think they are: see Afterword: Post-Breakthrough—Avoiding Breakdown). Rather, we chose to focus on firms in the size range where we believed we could more readily identify the key drivers of breakthrough performance.

STAGE III: IDENTIFYING BREAKTHROUGH COMPANY CANDIDATES

As previously mentioned, of the ninety-four firms with 2004 revenues between $250 million and $2 billion, fifty-three were public companies and forty-one were private. We were not surprised to learn that such a high proportion of these firms had gone public during the study pe-riod—the public markets are keen to invest in rapidly growing compa-nies—particularly when they're highly profitable. Since most private companies guard the confidentiality of their revenues and profits, we do not reveal the names of the private companies in our research ex-cept for the three companies that were finally selected for inclusion on the final breakthrough company list.

To make sure the companies we selected for our final list were the best-performing companies on the *Inc.* 500 list, we applied three filters to eliminate companies whose recent performance had declined or whose long-term performance was below average, relative to their industry.

Filter Stage 1 required that to be considered for the final list, the profitability of the company must exceed the average profitability for the industry. We utilized comparative data furnished by Dun & Brad-street to determine the median return on sales (ROS) and return on eq-uity (ROE) for each industry.* If either a firm's average return on sales (ROS) or its return on equity (ROE) during the study period was below the median or comparable, it was eliminated from the list. Of the ninety-four companies, thirty-six companies (21 public and 15 private) were eliminated by this criterion established in Filter Stage 1.

Filter Stage 2 was put in place to ensure that a firm's profitability had not materially declined. Each company's average ROS perfor-mance during the period 2002–2004 was expected to exceed the in-dustry historical median. Thirteen additional public companies and ten additional private companies were eliminated by the Filter Stage 2 criterion.

---

*Where reliable comparison data was not available from D&B, we calculated the average Return on Sales and Return on Equity for comparable public companies.

Filter Stage 3 was used to ensure recent sales performance was positive. Each company's average annual growth rate for sales during the years 2002–2004 was expected to be positive. Three additional public companies and four private companies were eliminated by this filter stage.

The table below outlines which public companies were eliminated as a result of our filters. (Information provided here is for public companies only, since we agreed to keep all performance information gathered on private companies strictly confidential.)

Results of Filters 1–3 for Public Companies

Public Company	Filter Outcomes
Administaff	Eliminated, Filter Stage 1
ADTRAN	Included in Stage 4: Breakthrough Ranking
Advance Digital Information	Eliminated, Filter Stage 2
Advanced Energy Industries	Eliminated, Filter Stage 2
BMC Software	Eliminated, Filter Stage 2
Catalina Marketing	Eliminated, Filter Stage 3
Chico's	Included in Stage 4: Breakthrough Ranking
Clean Harbors Inc.	Eliminated, Filter Stage 1
Coldwater Creek	Eliminated, Filter Stage 2
Compuware	Eliminated, Filter Stage 1
Credence Systems	Eliminated, Filter Stage 1
Domino's	Eliminated, Filter Stage 1
Fastenal Company	Included in Stage 4: Breakthrough Ranking
Franklin Covey	Eliminated, Filter Stage 1
Gartner	Eliminated, Filter Stage 1
Heartland Payment Systems	Eliminated, Filter Stage 2
Herbalife International	Included in Stage 4: Breakthrough Ranking
Hypercom	Eliminated, Filter Stage 1
Intuit	Included in Stage 4: Breakthrough Ranking
Itron	Eliminated, Filter Stage 1
Kronos	Included in Stage 4: Breakthrough Ranking
McDATA	Eliminated, Filter Stage 1

Public Company	Filter Outcomes
Medcath Corporation	Eliminated, Filter Stage 1
MTS Systems	Included in Stage 4: Breakthrough Ranking
National Instruments	Included in Stage 4: Breakthrough Ranking
Orbital Sciences	Eliminated, Filter Stage 1
Papa John's	Eliminated, Filter Stage 3
Parexel	Eliminated, Filter Stage 1
Paychex Inc.	Included in Stage 4: Breakthrough Ranking
PC Connection	Eliminated, Filter Stage 2
Pemstar	Eliminated, Filter Stage 1
Physician Sales & Service	Eliminated, Filter Stage 1
Plexus Corporation	Eliminated, Filter Stage 2
Polaris Industries	Included in Stage 4: Breakthrough Ranking
Progress Software	Included in Stage 4: Breakthrough Ranking
Respironics	Included in Stage 4: Breakthrough Ranking
RF Micro Devices	Eliminated, Filter Stage 1
Russ Berrie and Company	Eliminated, Filter Stage 3
San Disk Corporation	Eliminated, Filter Stage 1
Select Comfort	Eliminated, Filter Stage 1
Sharper Image	Eliminated, Filter Stage 1
Simple Technology	Eliminated, Filter Stage 2
TeleTech	Eliminated, Filter Stage 2
Tessco Corporation	Included in Stage 4: Breakthrough Ranking
Timberland	Included in Stage 4: Breakthrough Ranking
U.S. Xpress	Eliminated, Filter Stage 2
Unisource Energy	Eliminated, Filter Stage 2
Vector Group	Eliminated, Filter Stage 2
ViaSat	Eliminated, Filter Stage 2
Wabash National Corp.	Eliminated, Filter Stage 1
Wild Oats	Eliminated, Filter Stage 1

As a final step in the culling process, we wanted to make sure that for each of the remaining firms, the company founder and a significant portion of the senior management team would still be available for interviews to shed light on the company's breakthrough years. We eliminated Herbalife from consideration because Mark Hughes, Herbalife's founder, passed away in 2000 and few of the original management team were still at the company. We make no judgments as to whether Herbalife's performance should be considered breakthrough performance. Rather, we eliminated the company from the study because our initial analysis suggested that we wouldn't be able to reach the people in a position to comment on the characteristics that contributed to the firm's success. On the other hand, we decided to include Polaris in our study, which appeared on the 1986 *Inc.* 500 list. Polaris was an independent company from 1954 until 1968, when it was purchased by Textron. It was taken private again when, in 1981, Hall Wendell led a management buyout of the company. Although Wendell was not Polaris's founder, he was at the helm when the firm first appeared on the *Inc.* 500 list. Since Polaris was near bankruptcy when Wendell bought the business from Textron and since he and his leadership team obviously turned things around following the buyout, we treated Polaris as a "restart."

We then rank-ordered the two groups of firms (public and private) based on four criteria: (1) the firm's average annual rate of revenue growth from the time it first made the *Inc.* 500 to December 31, 2004; (2) the firm's return on sales (ROS) compared with the median ROS for its industry segment; (3) the firm's return on equity (ROE) compared with the median ROE for its industry segment; and (4) the firm's relative size. We then sorted the list from best to worst average performance. From this list of rank-ordered firms, we selected our nine breakthrough companies, selecting six top-ranked public companies and three top-ranked private companies.

SELECTING THE COMPARISON COMPANIES

Some of our most important insights came when we related the performance of breakthrough companies to that of close competitors. We found Collins's model (*Good to Great,* HarperCollins, 2001) for selecting comparison companies to be an excellent model, and we adapted it for our own study. The criteria we utilized to select the comparison companies are provided below:

Line of Business We selected companies that, at the time the breakthrough company made the *Inc.* 500 list, were in similar lines of business and offered similar products or services.

Size of Business We attempted to select comparison companies that were about the same size or bigger than breakthrough companies at the time the breakthrough companies made the *Inc.* list.

Age of Business We attempted to identify and include as comparison companies those competitors that were about the same age or older than the breakthrough companies.

We also tried to find comparison companies that would generally be deemed *more* successful than the breakthrough companies at the time the breakthrough companies appeared on the *Inc.* 500.

We considered comparing our breakthrough companies with other *Inc.* 500 companies that made the *Inc.* list around the same time, but we quickly realized that comparing breakthrough companies with direct competitors of similar size, age, and strategy was far preferable. We also rejected making comparisons based solely on stock performance for public companies or revenue growth for private firms. We expended the extra effort and time required to secure detailed financial performance information for both public and private firms so that we could truly understand the dynamics of performance for each firm.

In the end, we found nine comparison companies that at one time performed as well, if not better than, the breakthrough company itself. Of course, at a later point, the breakthrough company pulled ahead. We then conducted interviews with both breakthrough company executives and with executives from comparison companies to understand what caused the performance levels of breakthrough companies and comparison firms to diverge.

Comparison Companies

Breakthrough Company	Comparison Company	Comparison Company Current Status
ADTRAN	PairGain	Acquired
Chico's FAS	J. Jill Group	Acquired
Express Personnel	Westaff	Public
Fastenal	Endries International	Acquired
Intuit	Meca Software	Acquired
Paychex	InterPay	Acquired
Polaris	Arctic Cat	Public
SAS	SPSS	Public
The Staubach Company	Studley Inc.	Private

ANALYZING THE BREAKTHROUGH COMPANIES

With our nine breakthrough companies and nine comparison companies identified, we were ready to begin our in-depth analysis of the dynamics of breakthrough.

Background Research We collected a small library's worth of annual reports, newspaper and magazine articles, books, company reports, presentations, industry and analysts' reports, and consultant white papers. We accumulated more than 20,000 pages of materials—and every document was reviewed, categorized, and cataloged. The research team used this information to prepare background reports on both the breakthrough companies and their comparisons prior to our visits during the interview stage of our research.

Financial Analysis Utilizing publicly available resources and confidential audited financial reports, we conducted a comprehensive longitudinal analysis of the performance of the breakthrough companies, and when possible, the comparison companies (in some cases, the comparison company was either private and would not make its data available to us, or had been sold to another entity and could no longer provide the information). In addition to a careful analysis of each firm's growth and profitability compared with industry averages, we looked at each firm's use of debt, its credit-worthiness, its dividend payout rate, and its sales and profits per employee.

Product/Market Analysis We also collected the available information on the industry that each breakthrough company operated in. This involved speaking to analysts in the investment community who covered the industry. They were able to provide us with comprehensive statistics and trends on the products and services offered by our breakthrough companies and their comparison companies as well.

Company Visits and Interviews We visited the headquarters of each of the nine breakthrough companies, where we interviewed executives, managers, and front-line employees. We then supplemented those visits with additional phone calls to key managers, executives, and employees when necessary to meet our goal of conducting a minimum of ten in-depth interviews per company. Provided below is the list of interview questions.

1. *Tell us the story of the history of your organization.*
2. *How has leadership changed over the history of the company?*
3. *How do decisions get made in the organization? How has decision making changed over the years?*
4. *What has made your organization so successful?*
5. *How does your company measure its success?*
6. *Who is your customer? Why did you choose to serve those particular customers over others?*
7. *Why do your customers do business with you?*
8. *What have been your most important products and services? Why?*

9. *How does your firm know when it is time to add a new product or service?*

10. *Who is your most important competitor? Why?*

11. *What advantages does your firm have over the competition?*

12. *What are people in your firm most proud of? What are you most embarrassed by?*

13. *What have been the most difficult times in your organization's history? Have those times had any impact, positive or negative, on the organization?*

14. *How do you believe you are most different from other firms in your industry?*

15. *What have been the most important investments that your firm has made over the years? Tell us about some that have succeeded and some that have failed.*

16. *Have people in organizations outside your firm impacted your firm's history? If so, how?*

17. *Has your leadership team ever been wrong? If so, how did it discover its mistake and what did it do about it?*

18. *What are the most important things your firm has learned? What are the most important things you have learned while working for the company?*

19. *Does your firm have a set of guiding values or principles? If so, what are they?*

20. *As you look to the future, what worries you?*

We also identified and interviewed industry experts in each of the industries of our breakthrough companies and asked them to comment on the relative performance of breakthrough companies and comparison companies. In addition, we contacted employees and former employees of comparison companies to get their insights into the dynamics of the industry and the relative performance of the breakthrough and comparison companies.

RESEARCH NOTE C:

THE *INC.* 500

INC. MAGAZINE HAS BEEN publishing its list of the 500 fastest growing private companies since 1982. The magazine has a circulation of nearly 1 million, has consistently ranked highly in magazine industry rankings for the reach and quality of its growth company audience. Today, the *Inc.* 500 is the oldest and best-recognized national ranking of private growth companies. While the rules have changed slightly over the years, the basic criteria for earning a spot on the *Inc.* 500 have remained consistent for more than twenty-five years: Rankings are based on four-year revenue growth (it was five years up to and including the 2004 list), with a company needing five years of operating history and a minimum of $200,000 in the base year of the comparison.

We considered other data sources besides the *Inc.* 500, the most promising of which would have been a comprehensive list of companies that have successfully completed an initial public offering (IPO). An obvious strength of such an approach would have been the easy access to the significant amount of information publicly disclosed at the time of an IPO. But since public companies make up such a small percentage of U.S. corporations, we decided that the *Inc.* 500 list would be a far more representative population for our study, despite the fact that it required considerably more effort on our part to build the database and to gather additional data from third parties.

While we deemed it to be the best option overall, the *Inc.* 500 list was not without its disadvantages. The *Inc.* list is created based on revenue growth, so we had to invest considerable time and effort collecting other relevant financial data. While companies that apply for the list must provide tax documents or audited financial statements, and *Inc.* does perform periodic audits of these financials, the information is still self-reported and potentially flawed or inaccurate.

Companies must apply to be on the *Inc.* 500, so it's possible there were firms in the United States during the study period that generated performance levels equal to or even in excess of that achieved by the breakthrough companies. Finally, while being a more representative sample of the overall population of U.S. companies than many other lists, the *Inc.* 500 list tends to overrepresent or underrepresent certain industries. Examples of underrepresented on the list include food service, building construction, and healthcare. Building construction and healthcare are industries dominated by very large and very small companies with fewer mid-size firms. Examples of industries overrepresented on the *Inc.* list include computers and electronic manufacturers, information services, and administrative and support services, all of which are high growth industries.

ENDNOTES

CHAPTER 1: INTRODUCTION

1. The eleven companies profiled in *Good to Great* (New York: HarperCollins, 2001) had mean annual revenues in 2005 of $32 billion. The median for the group was $22 billion.
2. 2000 U.S. Census Data.

CHAPTER 2: THROWING THE DYNO

1. The revenue growth chart presents the summed revenues for the nine break-through companies during the first fifteen years following the year that each was listed on the *Inc.* 500. Source: Compustat and confidential company annual reports.

   The Return on Equity and Return on Sales comparison charts compare the aggregated average ROE and ROS performance of the breakthrough companies to the aggregated average performance for their respective industries.
2. Sources: *Inc.* 500 Lists 1982–1995, Compustat, and company annual reports.
3. Assumes that $1 was invested in each of the six breakthrough companies that went public during the study period 1982–2004. Also assumes that the investment was made on the day of the IPO, and that all dividends were reinvested in the security immediately upon payment. Cumulative returns are calculated based upon the thirteen years following the IPO of each company (thirteen years was selected because the last company to go public, ADTRAN, went public thirteen years ago). The average S&P performance was derived by calculating the average returns of the S&P across all of the years during which at least one of the break-through companies was in its first thirteen years as a public company.
4. Chico's Quarterly Company Update, January 24, 2006; Research Interview subject #57, Fort Myers, FL, transcript #C-1.
5. Paychex annual reports, 1983–2006; Research Interview subject #66, Rochester, NY, transcript #K-5.
6. Glenn R. Carroll and Michael T. Hannan, *The Demography of Corporations and Industries* (Princeton: Princeton University Press, 2000), 313–331.
7. Amar V. Bhide, *The Origin and Evolution of New Businesses* (New York: Oxford University Press, 2000), 13.
8. "Around and About," *Industrial Distribution,* May 31, 1998, 12; "Top 100 Distributors," *Industrial Distribution,* June 30, 1998, 68; "Industrial Distribution's Top 100 Industrial Distributors," *Supply Chain Management Review,* May 30, 2002, 86; "Target Market Reports; Fasteners," *Industrial Distribution,* August 1, 2002, F7; "Son Takes Over as Head of Brillion, Wis., Fastener Supply Company," *The Post-Crescent,*

February 4, 2004; "The Big 50," *Industrial Distribution,* June 1, 2004, 36; "Distribution 2005," *Purchasing,* May 5, 2005, 28; "Ferguson Purchases Endries," *Industrial Distribution,* May 23, 2005.

9. Research Interview subject #37, Rochester, NY, transcript #K-1.

10. Jeffrey L. Rodengen, Richard F. Hubbard, *The Legend of Polaris* (Fort Lauderdale: Write Stuff Enterprises, 2003), 80–85.

11. Research Interview subject #97, Medina, MN, transcript #M-1.

12. Research Interview subject #90, Huntsville, AL, transcript #A-1.

13. Research Interview subject #45, Winona, MN, transcript #G-4.

14. Express Personnel 2006 Annual Report; Research Interview subject #43, Oklahoma City, OK, transcript #E-1.

15. Research Interview subject #38, Cary, NC, transcript #O-5; Research Interview subject #14, Mountainview, CA, transcript #I-1; Research Interview subject #97, Medina, MN, transcript #M-1; Research Interview subject #37, Rochester, NY, transcript #K-1; Research Interview subject #25, Fort Myers, FL, transcript #C-2; Research Interview subject #31, Oklahoma City, OK, transcript #E-7.

16. Suzanne Taylor, Kathy Schroeder, *Inside Intuit* (Boston: Harvard Business School Publishing, 2003), 27, 209–210.

17. "Best Places to Work," *Fortune,* 2006; Intuit ranked no. 43.

18. "Best Places to Work," *Fortune,* 1998–2007.

19. Eric G. Flamholtz, *How to Make the Transition from an Entrepreneurship to a Professionally Managed Firm* (San Francisco, Jossey-Bass Publishing, 1986).

20. Walter Lippmann, *A Preface to Politics* (New York and London: Mitchell Kennerley, 1914), 196.

CHAPTER 3: CROWNING THE COMPANY

1. David Sutherland (producer), *George Washington: The Man Who Wouldn't Be King* (Boston: WGBH Boston).

2. Frank Deford, *The Heart of a Champion* (San Diego: Tehabi Books, 2002), 133–134; Research Interview subject #92, Addison, TX, transcript #Q-11.

3. Research Interview subject #92, Addison, TX, transcript #Q-11.

4. Ibid.

5. Research Interview subject #74, phone interview, transcript #Q-9.

6. Research Interview subject #74, phone interview, transcript #Q-9.

7. "Gordon Long to Staubach in Growth Bid," *Crain's New York Business,* December 14, 1992, 3; "Ex-Football Star Staubach Expands His Real Estate Presence in Philadelphia," *Philadelphia Inquirer,* September 20, 2004; "A Tenacious Broker Who Avoids the Pack," *The New York Times,* January 1, 2006; "Manhattan-Based Corporate Real Estate Firm Changes Hands," *Daily News,* December 17, 2002; "Boom-Time Beneficiaries: Brokers—Julien J. Studley Inc.," *Crain's New York Business,* January 15, 2001.

8. "New Executive: High Rise for Tenant Rep; Studley's Top Broker Becomes CEO After Leading Buyout, Takes Firm in New Direction," *Crain's New York Business*, March 17, 2003, 11; Research Interview subject #92, Addison, TX, transcript #Q-11.

9. Companies were classified based on interviews and observation of small group discussions.

10. David Sutherland (producer), *George Washington: The Man Who Wouldn't Be King* (Boston: WGBH Boston).

11. My friend Ichak Adizes first introduced me to the term "sovereign organization." For his ideas on the subject, see his *Managing Corporate Lifecycles*, Adizes Institute, Santa Barbara, 1999.

12. Research Interview subject #56, Winona, MN, transcript #G-6.

13. Ibid.

14. Ibid.

15. Fastenal Annual Reports 1987–2006.

16. "Fastenal's Oberton Is Morningstar's CEO of the Year," *Star Tribune* (Minneapolis, MN), January 5, 2007, 1D.

17. Additional information on the TAIS can be found at www.breakthrough company.com.

18. Research Interview subject #92, Addison, TX, transcript #Q-11.

19. "How Chico's Got Its Groove Back," *BusinessWeek*, June 6, 2001; "Return Engagement," *Chain Store Age*, July 1999; "Chico's FASt Track," *Chain Store Age*, January 2002; Research Interview subject #57, Fort Myers, FL, transcript #C-1.

20. Research Interview subject #57, Fort Myers, FL, transcript #C-1.

21. "Do Company Founders Make Better CEOs?" *Fortune* Magazine, April 18, 2006.

22. William Blair's Annual Growth Stock Performance: Fastenal Presentation.

23. Research Interview subject #94, Winona, MN, transcript #G-8.

24. Research Interview subject #97, Medina, MN, transcript #M-1.

25. Research Interview subject #57, Fort Meyers, FL, transcript #C-1.

26. Research Interview subject #14, Mountainview, CA, transcript #I-1.

27. Research Interview subject #57, Fort Myers, FL, transcript #C-1.

28. Research Interview subject #25, Fort Myers, FL, transcript #C-2.

29. Chico's Annual Reports 1993–2006.

30. Research Interview #47, phone interview, transcript #C-4.

31. "J. Jill Group Shareholders OK $517 Million Acquisition by Talbots," The Associated Press State & Local Wire, May 1, 2006; "In Surprise Move, Talbots to Buy J. Jill," *The Boston Globe*, February 7, 2006; "Talbots Said Nearing Deal with J. Jill," *The Boston Globe*, February 6, 2006; "Disappointed J. Jill Cuts Expectations," *The Boston Herald*, December 16, 2003, 40; "Retailer Chico's Offers Its Own Style to Customer," *The Miami Herald*, April 22, 2002; "Blunders Push J. Jill Group's Shares Out of Fashion," *The Boston Herald* December 6, 2002, 35; "J. Jill Earnings Stun Analysts," *The Boston Herald*, July 10, 2002, 31; "Shareholders Approve Name Change DM Management to Become The J. Jill Group, Inc.," *Business Wire*,

May 25, 1999; "DM to Try Retail On for Size," *The Boston Herald,* February 17, 1999, 31; "DM Management Company Commences Public Offering of 1,800,000 Shares of Common Stock," *Business Wire,* November 2, 1993.

32. Research Interview subject #25, Fort Myers, FL, transcript #C-2.

33. Ibid.

34. Research Interview subject #5, Charlotte, NC, transcript #Q-1.

35. Research Interview subject #4, Cary, NC, transcript #O-1; Research Interview subject #52, Addison, TX, transcript #Q-8.

36. Research Interview subject #92, Addison, TX, transcript #Q-11.

37. Research Interview subject #5, Charlotte, NC, transcript #Q-1.

38. Research Interview subject #45, Winona, MN, transcript #G-4.

39. Research Interview subject #25, Fort Myers, FL, transcript #C-2.

40. Sutherland, David (Producer), George Washington: *The Man Who Wouldn't Be King* (Boston: WGBH Boston).

41. Research Interview subject #56, Winona, MN, transcript #G-6.

42. Research Interview subject #102, phone interview, transcript #G-12.

43. The terms "commanding" and "coaching" appeared in a leadership repertoire in Daniel Goleman, Richard Boyatzis, and Annie McKee, *Primal Leadership* (Boston, Harvard Business School Press, 2002), 53–88.

44. Research Interview subject #25, Fort Myers, FL, transcript #C-2.

45. "Why Entrepreneurs Don't Scale," Hohn Hamm, *Harvard Business Review,* December 2002, 2–7.

46. Research Interview subject #73, Winona, MN, transcript #G-7.

47. Research Interview subject #52, Addison, TX, transcript #Q-8.

48. Robert A. Kierlin, *The Power of Fastenal People* (First Pacific Enterprise Publishing Company, 1997).

49. Research Interview subject #56, Winona, MN, transcript #G-6.

50. Ibid.

51. Research Interview subject #58, Medina, MN, transcript #M-4.

52. Research Interview subject #4, Cary, NC, transcript #O-1.

53. Barry K. Wilson, *Benedict Arnold: A Traitor in Our Midst* (Canada: McGill-Queen's University Press, 2001), 147–163.

CHAPTER 4: UPPING THE ANTE

1. Research Interview subject #14, Mountainview, CA, transcript #I-1.

2. Ibid.; Suzanne Taylor, Kathy Schroeder, *Inside Intuit* (Boston: Harvard Business School Publishing, 2003), 47.

3. Research Interview subject #14, Mountainview, CA, transcript #I-1.

4. Ibid.; Suzanne Taylor, Kathy Schroeder, *Inside Intuit* (Boston: Harvard Business School Publishing, 2003), 48–49.

5. Steve Shiendling, *Fumbles, Field Goals and the Myth of the Hail Mary* (Dallas:

Brown Books, 2006), 4. Here's what Roger Staubach told us happened: The term "Hail Mary" was coined by Roger in December 1975 while playing quarterback for the Cowboys. With 36 seconds left in a game against Minnesota and trailing 14–10, Roger fired the ball down the right sideline to Drew Pearson, who made his way across the goal line for the winning score. When asked by the media after the game how he pulled it off, Roger said, "I threw the ball to Drew and then closed my eyes and said a 'Hail Mary.' "

6. Research Interview subject #14, Mountainview, CA, transcript #I-1; Suzanne Taylor, Kathy Schroeder, *Inside Intuit* (Boston: Harvard Business School Publishing, 2003), 47.

7. Research Interview #I-1; Suzanne Taylor, Kathy Schroeder, *Inside Intuit* (Boston: Harvard Business School Publishing, 2003), 49–50.

8. Research Interview subject #14, Mountainview, CA, transcript #I-1.

9. Quote widely attributed, source unknown.

10. Daniel Kahneman, Amos Tversky, *Judgment under Uncertainty: Heuristics and Biases* (London: Cambridge University Press, 1982).

11. Research Interview subject #14, Mountainview, CA, transcript #I-1.

12. Ibid.

13. Research Interview subject #56, Winona, MN, transcript #G-6.

14. Research Interview subject #57, Fort Myers, FL, transcript #C-1.

15. "The Big Picture," *Inc.* Magazine, October 15, 2003, 87–94.

16. Amar V. Bhide, *The Origin and Evolution of New Businesses* (Oxford: Oxford University Press, 2000), 32.

17. Suzanne Taylor, Kathy Schroeder, *Inside Intuit* (Boston: Harvard Business School Publishing, 2003), 17.

18. Amar V. Bhide, *The Origin and Evolution of New Businesses* (Oxford: Oxford University Press, 2000), 41.

19. Research Interview subject #94, Winona, MN, transcript #G-8.

20. Suzanne Taylor, Kathy Schroeder, *Inside Intuit* (Boston: Harvard Business School Publishing, 2003), 93.

21. Research Interview subject #22, phone interview, transcript #I-2.

22. Suzanne Taylor, Kathy Schroeder, *Inside Intuit* (Boston: Harvard Business School Publishing, 2003), 102–107.

23. Ibid., 132.

24. Research Interview subject #14, Mountainview, CA, transcript #I-1.

25. Ibid.

26. Jeffrey L. Rodengen, Richard F. Hubbard, *The Legend of Polaris* (Fort Lauderdale: Write Stuff Enterprises, 2003), 80.

27. Ibid., 84.

28. Jeffrey L. Rodengen, Richard F. Hubbard, *The Legend of Polaris* (Fort Lauderdale: Write Stuff Enterprises, 2003), 98.

29. Ibid., 85.

30. U.S. Small Business Administration, 2005.

31. Amar V. Bhide, *The Origin and Evolution of New Businesses* (New York: Oxford University Press, 2000), 21.

32. Research Interview subject #64, Medina, MN, transcript #M-2; Research Interview subject #97, Medina, MN, transcript #M-1.

33. Jeffrey L. Rodengen, Richard F. Hubbard, *The Legend of Polaris* (Fort Lauderdale: Write Stuff Enterprises, 2003), 86–87.

34. Ibid., 87.

35. Research Interview subject #64, Medina, MN, transcript #M-2.

36. Jeffrey L. Rodengen, Richard F. Hubbard, *The Legend of Polaris* (Fort Lauderdale: Write Stuff Enterprises, 2003), 95–96.

37. Ibid., 97.

38. Market share information, confidential company reports.

39. Jeffrey L. Rodengen, Richard F. Hubbard, *The Legend of Polaris* (Fort Lauderdale: Write Stuff Enterprises, 2003), 115–116.

40. Research Interview subject #97, Medina, MN, transcript #M-1.

41. Intuit 2006 Annual Report.

42. Polaris Annual Reports 1983–2006.

43. "Chinese Motorcycle Makers Put U.S. Hubs in Dallas," *The Dallas Morning News,* February 18, 2007; Motorcycle Industry Council: www.mic.org.

44. Research Interview subject #14, Mountainview, CA, transcript #I-1.

45. Ibid.

46. Intuit 2006 Annual Report.

47. Research Interview subject #50, phone interview, transcript #I-4.

48. Suzanne Taylor, Kathy Schroeder, *Inside Intuit* (Boston: Harvard Business School Publishing, 2003), 32.

49. Research Interview subject #14, Mountainview, CA, transcript #I-1.

50. Research Interview subject #97, Medina, MN, transcript #M-1.

51. Research Interview subject #14, Mountainview, CA, transcript #I-1.

52. Suzanne Taylor, Kathy Schroeder, *Inside Intuit* (Boston: Harvard Business School Publishing, 2003), 185–192.

53. Research Interview subject #97, Medina, MN, transcript #M-1.

54. "Snowmobile Industry Gets Back on Track," *St. Louis Post-Dispatch,* November 24, 1989, 13C; "Chris Twomey's Got Arctco on Track," *Star Tribune* (Minneapolis MN), April 27, 1992, 1D; "Arctco Considering New Products," *Star Tribune,* June 17, 1993, 3D; "Arctco Stock Plummets Nearly 20% as Company Announces Rebates," *Star Tribune,* 1D, June 16, 1995; "Bombardier to Roll Out ATV," *Canadian Press Newswire,* February 13, 1998; "Polaris Revs Up for Motorcycles; Plymouth-based Polaris Industries Inc. Confirmed That It Will Build a Heavyweight Victory Bike Akin to the Choppers of Harley-Davidson," *Star Tribune,* February 20, 1997, 1D.

55. "Arctco Expanding into ATV Market," *Star Tribune,* August 5, 1994, 3D.

56. Suzanne Taylor, Kathy Schroeder, *Inside Intuit* (Boston: Harvard Business School Publishing, 2003), 185–197.

57. Research Interview subject #25, Fort Myers, FL, transcript #C-2.

58. Research Interview subject #64, Medina, MN, transcript #M-2; Research Interview subject #3, Medina, MN, transcript #M-3.

59. Research Interview subject #37, Rochester, NY, transcript #K-1.

60. Research Interview subject #97, Medina, MN, transcript #M-1.

61. Ibid.

62. JDPower.com, December 2006: http://www.jdpower.com/autos/ratings/motorcycles.

63. Polaris 2006 Annual Report.

64. Suzanne Taylor, Kathy Schroeder, *Inside Intuit* (Boston: Harvard Business School Publishing, 2003), 151–156.

65. Ibid., 156–160.

66. Research Interview subject #86, phone interview, transcript #I-3; Research Interview subject #50, phone interview, transcript #I-4.

67. Suzanne Taylor, Kathy Schroeder, *Inside Intuit* (Boston: Harvard Business School Publishing, 2003), 160.

68. "Noisemakers," *Forbes,* October 29, 1990, 104.

69. Jeffrey L. Rodengen, Richard F. Hubbard, *The Legend of Polaris* (Fort Lauderdale: Write Stuff Enterprises, 2003), 105; Polaris Industries Annual Reports 1983–2006.

70. Research Interview subject #97, Medina, MN, transcript #M-1.

71. Quote widely attributed, source unknown.

CHAPTER 5: BUILDING COMPANY CHARACTER

1. Research Interview subject #85, Rochester, NY, transcript #K-2.

2. Ibid.

3. Research Interview subject #37, Rochester, NY, transcript #K-1.

4. Research Interview subject #98, Rochester, NY, transcript #K-7.

5. Research Interview subject #53, Rochester, NY, transcript #K-4.

6. Paychex 2006 annual report.

7. Research Interview subject #66, Rochester, NY, transcript #K-5.

8. "InterPay, Inc. Celebrates 30 Years as a Payroll Leader!" *Business Wire,* April 26, 2001; "Wholesale Payments: Shawmut to Buy Payroll Servicer for $12M," *The American Banker,* July 12, 1995; "Staples Rolls Out Payroll Services for Small Business Customers," *Business Wire,* May 25, 1999; "Golisano's Paychex Acquiring a Fleet Unit," *The American Banker,* March 18, 2003; "Paychex, Inc. to Acquire InterPay, Inc.," *Business Wire,* March 17, 2003.

9. Research Interview subject #93, Salt Lake City, UT, transcript #E-8.

10. Research Interview subject #70, Medina, MN, transcript #M-5.

11. Research Interview subject #38, Cary, NC, transcript #O-5.

12. Ibid.

13. "Chief at World's Largest Private Software Firm Takes Long-Term Approach," *The Charlotte Observer,* March 18, 2003; "Cary, N.C.–Based SAS Sees Double-Digit Growth in Business Software Sales," *News & Observer* (Raleigh, NC), January 9,

2004; "SAS Sales Rise 12 Percent; Bigger Jump Predicted for '07," *News & Observer,* February 14, 2007.

14. "Software Firm Aims for Bigger Numbers; Capital Infusion to Aid SPSS Push," *Crain's Chicago Business,* January 7, 1991, 3; "SAS Institute Says Tech Support Sells," *Business Wire,* December 17, 1997; "For SPSS, So Much to Buy, So Little Cash: Weak Stock Price Could Crunch Firm's Acquisition Strategy," *Crain's Chicago Business,* November 30, 1998; "Cary, N.C.–Based Software Giant Aims to Raise Its Low Profile," *The Charlotte Observer,* March 7, 1999; "Longing to Be Listed; Many Companies Go all Out to Make Magazine's Ratings of Best Places to Work, But Is Effort Misguided?," *The Houston Chronicle,* February 4, 2001, 1; "At 35, Software Firm SPSS Is Older Than Digital Dirt," *Investor's Business Daily,* September 3, 2003.

15. Research Interview subject #38, Cary, NC, transcript #O-5.

16. Sarah F. Brosnan and Frans B. M. de Waal, "Monkeys Reject Unequal Pay," *Nature* 425 (2003): 297–299.

17. Research Interview subject #56, Winona, MN, transcript #G-6.

18. Research Interview subject #40, Winona, MN, transcript #G-3; Research Interview subject #93, Salt Lake City, UT, transcript #E-8.

19. Research Interview subject #37, Rochester, NY, transcript #K-1.

20. Ibid.

21. Research Interview subject #92, Addison, TX, transcript #Q-11.

22. Research Interview subject #14, Mountainview, CA, transcript #I-1.

23. Research Interview subject #38, Cary, NC, transcript #O-5.

24. Research Interview #O-6; Copy of e-mail addressed to Jim Goodnight from Oracle sales representative.

25. Ralph Waldo Emerson, *The Conduct of Life* (West Valley City, Utah: Waking Lion Press, 2006), 143–175.

26. Research Interview subject #56, Winona, MN, transcript #G-6.

27. Research Interview subject #45, Winona, MN, transcript #G-4.

28. Ibid.

29. Research Interview subject #85, Rochester, NY, transcript #K-2.

30. Research Interview subject #92, Addison, TX, transcript #Q-11.

31. "Economics Discovers Its Feelings." *The Economist,* December 23, 2006, 35.

32. Research Interview subject #5, Charlotte, NC, transcript #Q-1.

33. "The Cheapest CEO in America," *Inc.* Magazine, October 1997; "Hardware Distributor Sticks to Nuts-and-Bolts Strategy," *Wall Street Journal,* July 3, 2001, B2.

34. Research Interview subject #94, Winona, MN, transcript #G-8.

35. "How Indian Got Its Vroom Back," *CIO Magazine,* June 15, 2001; "Indian Motorcycle Firm May Be Sold, Liquidated in Mid-January," *The Milwaukee Journal Sentinel,* December 27, 2003; "The Last Indian," *Daily Deal/The Deal,* September 29, 2003; "A Motorcycle Maker Wants to Avoid the Fate of Its Predecessors," *Star Tribune,* February 16, 2004; "Victory Motorcycles Establishes Foothold against Harley-Davidson," *Chicago Tribune,* June 13, 2004.

36. Research Interview subject #4, Cary, NC, transcript #O-1.

37. *Training Magazine:* www.Trainingmag.com.

38. Research Interview subject #85, Rochester, NY, transcript #K-2.

39. Research Interview subject #40, Winona, MN, transcript #G-3.

40. Research Interview subject #58, Medina, MN, transcript #M-4.

41. Research Interview subject #97, Medina, MN, transcript #M-1.

42. Research Interview subject #37, Rochester, NY, transcript #K-1.

43. Research Interview subject #92, Addison, TX, transcript #Q-11.

44. Research Interview subject #14, Mountainview, CA, transcript #I-1.

45. Max Weber, *The Theory of Social and Economic Organization,* Translated by A. M. Henderson & Talcott Parsons. (New York: The Free Press, 1947), 328–362.

46. Research Interview subject #40, Winona, MN, transcript #G-3.

47. Research Interview subject #47, Salt Lake City, UT, transcript #E-9.

48. Ibid.; Research Interview subject #40, Winona, MN, transcript #G-3.

49. "Western Temp May Let Public Share in Firm," *San Francisco Business Times,* September 6, 1991, 17; "Founder of California-Based Westaff Anticipates Strong Growth Past 2000," *Knight-Ridder/Tribune Business News,* October 27, 1998; "Western Staff Services of Walnut Creek, Calif., Picks New Name," *Contra Costa Times,* September 25, 1998; "Temporary Sanity: W. Robert Stover Is Too Private to Ever Go Public. Yet His Walnut Creek Temporary Agency—First of Its Kind in the West, Now 10th-Largest in the Country—Is About to Do Just That," *Diablo Business,* January 1993; "Western Staff Services Acquires MERBCO, Inc.," *Business Wire,* October 23, 1995; "Walnut Creek, Calif.–Based Temporary Hire Firm Hopes Stock Rebounds," *Contra Costa Times,* April 11, 1999; "Westaff Appoints Its First Vice-President, Franchising," *Business Wire,* February 13, 2007.

50. Research Interview subject #97, Medina, MN, transcript #M-1.

51. Research Interview subject #82, Plymouth, MN, transcript #G-10.

52. Research Interview subject #46, Plymouth, MN, transcript #G-11.

53. Research Interview subject #82, Plymouth, MN, transcript #G-10.

CHAPTER 6: NAVIGATING THE BUSINESS BERMUDA TRIANGLE

1. Our idea of sustaining advantage is different from the concept of *sustainable advantage* that was introduced by Michael Porter in *Competitive Strategy* (New York: The Free Press, 1980) and *Competitive Advantage* (New York: The Free Press, 1985). Porter posited that there are three fundamental "generic strategies" through which a firm can create a sustainable competitive advantage: low cost leadership, differentiation, or focus. From our vantage point in 2007, the idea that a firm can deploy a particular strategy that ensures them long-term competitive advantage seems unlikely. As advances in technology and globalization create powerful disruptive forces that make the very boundaries of most industries unclear, sources of advantage today seem to us to be far more transitory. We think

it is a mistake for a firm today to believe it has "cracked the code" in achieving a sustainable competitive advantage. Better to look to the development of *sustaining* advantages, leaving open the likelihood that new sources of advantages will need to be added or integrated in the future.

2. Research Interview subject #90, Huntsville, AL, transcript #A-1.
3. ADTRAN company reports.
4. Research Interview subject #90, Huntsville, AL, transcript #A-1.
5. Ibid.
6. Research Interview subject #11, Huntsville, AL, transcript #A-5.
7. Research Interview subject #90, Huntsville, AL, transcript #A-1.
8. "Why Size Matters," *Inc.* Magazine, October 2004.
9. Research Interview subject #11, Huntsville, AL, transcript #A-5.
10. Research Interview subject #65, Huntsville, AL, transcript #A-2.
11. Research Interview subject #90, Huntsville, AL, transcript #A-1.
12. ADTRAN Annual Reports 1989–2006.
13. Research Interview subject #90, Huntsville, AL, transcript #A-1.
14. Ibid.
15. Ibid.
16. Research Interview subject #11, Huntsville, AL, transcript #A-5.
17. Research Interview subject #90, Huntsville, AL, transcript #A-1.
18. Ibid.
19. "Minnetonka, Minn.–Based Internet Firm Hopes Acquisition Boosts DSL Effort," *Saint Paul Pioneer Press,* February 24, 2000; "ADC Completes Acquisition of Pair-Gain Technologies," *Business Wire,* June 28, 2000; "ADC and PairGain Announce that the Hart-Scott-Rodino Waiting Period Has Expired on Proposed Merger," *Business Wire,* May 8, 2000; "Earnings Lag for Tustin, Calif.–Based Communications Technology Firm," *The Orange County Register,* September 11, 1999; "Profits Tumble at Tustin, Calif.–Based Data Transmission Firm," *The Orange County Register,* July 14, 1999; "PairGain Employee Pleads Guilty in Securities Case," *USA Today,* June 22, 1999.
20. Research Interview subject #11, Huntsville, AL, transcript #A-5.
21. Research Interview subject #90, Huntsville, AL, transcript #A-1.
22. Research Interview subject #91, Huntsville, AL, transcript #A-3.
23. Research Interview subject #11, Huntsville, AL, transcript #A-5.
24. Research Interview subject #91, Huntsville, AL, transcript #A-3.
25. Ibid.
26. Research Interview subject #21, Winona, MN, transcript #G-2.
27. Research Interview subject #37, Rochester, NY, transcript #K-1.
28. Research Interview subject #97, Medina, MN, transcript #M-1.
29. Research Interview subject #14, Mountainview, CA, transcript #I-1.
30. Research Interview subject #25, Fort Myers, FL, transcript #C-2.
31. Research Interview subject #40, Winona, MN, transcript #G-3.

32. Research Interview subject #91, Huntsville, AL, transcript #A-3.

33. Gian Quasar, *Into the Bermuda Triangle* (New York: The McGraw-Hill Companies, 2004); Bermuda-Triangle.Org, www.bermuda-triangle.org.

CHAPTER 7: ERECTING SCAFFOLDING

1. Research Interview subject #92, Addison, TX, transcript #Q-11.

2. Ibid.

3. Ibid.

4. Research Interview subject #39, Cary, NC, transcript #O-8.

5. Research Interview subject #97, Medina, MN, transcript #M-1.

6. Research Interview subject #14, Mountainview, CA, transcript #I-1.

7. Suzanne Taylor, Kathy Schroeder, *Inside Intuit* (Boston: Harvard Business School Publishing, 2003), 142–144.

8. Research Interview subject #80, phone interview, transcript #I-5.

9. Research Interview subject #14, Mountainview, CA, transcript #I-1.

10. Research Interview subject #25, Fort Myers, FL, transcript #C-2.

11. Ibid.

12. Ibid.

13. Stoyan Sgorev and Ezra Zuckerman, "Improving Capabilities through Industry Peer Networks," *Sloan Management Review,* Winter 2006, 33–38.

14. Research Interview subject #92, Addison, TX, transcript #Q-11.

15. Research Interview subject #90, Huntsville, AL, transcript #A-1.

16. I was a member of YPO myself for a number of years and have served as a speaking resource for WPO and Vistage.

17. Research Interview subject #5, Charlotte, NC, transcript #Q-1.

18. Research Interview subject #97, Medina, MN, transcript #M-1.

19. Research Interview subject #25, Fort Myers, FL, transcript #C-2.

20. Research Interview subject #53, Rochester, NY, transcript #K-4.

21. Ibid.

22. Research Interview subject #25, Fort Myers, FL, transcript #C-2.

23. Research Interview subject #14, Mountainview, CA, transcript #I-1.

24. Research Interview subject #15, phone interview, transcript #C-5.

25. Research Interview subject #91, Huntsville, AL, transcript #A-3.

26. Research Interview subject #64, Medina, MN, transcript #M-2.

27. Research Interview subject #38, Cary, NC, transcript #H-5; Research Interview subject #90, Huntsville, AL, transcript #A-1.

28. Research Interview subject #56, Winona, MN, transcript #G-6.

29. Research Interview subject #15, phone interview, transcript #C-5; Research Interview subject #53, Rochester, NY, transcript #K-4.

30. Research Interview subject #92, Addison, TX, transcript #Q-11.

CHAPTER 8: ENLISTING INSULTANTS

1. "Improving Capabilities Through Industry Peer Networks," *Sloan Management Review,* Winter 2006, 33.
2. For more on Ichak's view of insultants, see Ichak Adizes, *Managing Corporate Life Cycles* (Adizes Institute: Santa Barbara, 1999).
3. Research Interview subject #70, Medina, MN, transcript #M-5.
4. Research Interview subject #3, Medina, MN, transcript #M-3.
5. Survey results ad reported in Scott Cook's keynote presentation to the 2006 *Inc.* 500 Conference.
6. E. P. Torrance, "Some Consequences of Power Differences on Decisions in B-26 crews," *United States Air Force Personnel and Training Research Center Research Bulletin* 54-128 (1954); Torrance, "Some Consequences of Power Differences in Permanent and Temporary Three-Man Groups," in *Small Groups,* edited by A. P. Hare et al. (New York: Knopf, 1955). For more on these and several other interesting research studies referenced in this chapter, see James Surowiecki, *The Wisdom of Crowds* (New York: Random House, 2004).
7. Research Interview subject #97, Medina, MN, transcript #M-1.
8. David Romer, "It's Fourth Down and What Does the Bellman Equation Say? A Dynamic-Programming Analysis of Football Strategy," *National Bureau of Economic Research,* June 2002.
9. "Reward Outgains the Risk of Fourth-and-Short," *The New York Times,* December 19, 2004, 11; "Sabermetrics for Football," *The New York Times,* December 12, 2004, 91; "Football; Kicking Around New Math," *The Boston Herald,* September 13, 2002, 112.
10. Research Interview subject #65, Huntsville, AL, transcript #A-2; Research Interview subject #90, Huntsville, AL, transcript #A-1.
11. Research Interview subject #98, Rochester, NY, transcript #K-7.
12. Research Interview subject #37, Rochester, NY, transcript #K-1.
13. Research Interview subject #98, Rochester, NY, transcript #K-7.
14. Ibid.; company reports.
15. Research Interview subject #37, Rochester, NY, transcript #K-1; Research Interview subject #66, Rochester, NY, transcript #K-5.
16. Research Interview subject #14, Mountainview, CA, transcript #I-1 / Scott Cook's keynote presentation at the 2006 *Inc.* 500 Conference, Savannah, Georgia.
17. Research Interview subject #40, Winona, MN, transcript #G-3.
18. Research Interview subject #25, Fort Myers, FL, transcript #C-2.
19. Research Interview subject #40, Winona, MN, transcript #G-3.
20. Research Interview subject #57, Fort Myers, FL, transcript #C-1.
21. Daniel Goleman, *Primal Leadership: Realizing the Power of Emotional Intelligence* (Boston: Harvard Business School Press, 2002), 10–11, 33–35.
22. Research Interview subject #37, Rochester, NY, transcript #K-1.

CHAPTER 9: GRADUATING FROM TOUGH TIMES U

1. Research Interview subject #90, Huntsville, AL, transcript #A-1.
2. "Reprogramming the Company," *Inc.* Magazine, Summer 1995, 36.
3. Research Interview subject #90, Huntsville, AL, transcript #A-1.
4. Research Interview subject #25, Fort Myers, FL, transcript #C-2.
5. Research Interview subject #97, Medina, MN, transcript #M-1.
6. Research Interview subject #40, Winona, MN, transcript #G-3.
7. Ibid.; Research Interview #E-3.
8. Research Interview subject #90, Huntsville, AL, transcript #A-1.
9. Research Interview subject #14, Mountainview, CA, transcript #I-1.

CHAPTER 10: BULDING BREAKTHROUGH CAPABILITIES

1. Herbert A. Simon, *Administrative Behavior* (New York: The Free Press, 1945).

AFTERWORD

1. Research Interview subject #14, Mountainview, CA, transcript #I-1.

INDEX

ABOUT THE AUTHOR

At the age of twenty-six, Keith McFarland was named associate dean of a major U.S. business school. He went on to serve as CEO of two leading technology companies before founding McFarland Strategy Partners, a strategic advisory firm. He writes a regular online column for *BusinessWeek*. Keith and his family live just down the hill from the chairlifts at Snowbird, Utah.